HERITAGE OF FIRE

HERITAGE OF FIRE

The Story of Richard Wagner's Granddaughter

BY

FRIEDELIND WAGNER

AND

PAGE COOPER

ILLUSTRATED

GREENWOOD PRESS, PUBLISHERS
WESTPORT, CONNECTICUT

Library of Congress Cataloging in Publication Data

Wagner, Friedelind, 1918-
    Heritage of fire.

    Reprint of the ed. published by Harper, New York.
    1. Wagner, Friedelind, 1918-   2. Germany--
Politics and government--1933-1945. 3. Musicians--Cor-
respondence, reminiscences, etc. I. Cooper, Page,
1891-1958, joint author. II. Title.
DD247.W3A3 1974   914.3'03'860924 [B]   74-6781
ISBN 0-8371-7573-9

Originally published in 1945 by Harper & Brothers Publishers,
New York

Reprinted with the permission of Harper & Row, Publishers, Inc.

Reprinted in 1974 by Greenwood Press,
a division of Williamhouse-Regency Inc.

Library of Congress Catalog Card Number 74-6781

ISBN 0-8371-7573-9

Printed in the United States of America

To my two fathers

Siegfried Wagner
and
Arturo Toscanini

CONTENTS

LIST OF ILLUSTRATIONS

*These illustrations, grouped in a separate section, will
be found facing page 110*

INTRODUCTION

The Germany in which I was born in 1918 was a chaotic, devastated land but Bayreuth, my own particular corner of it which I have tried to recapture in these pages had suffered in especial ways. The Festspielhaus was closed. Singers and visitors alike had vanished. My first memories of Wahnfried are not of the big building, Wahnfried proper, but of my father's little bachelor house right next to it, into which my family had moved when they could no longer afford to heat the big house. We moved back only in 1922. During all those years the lawns and gardens were used to grow cabbages and potatoes but by the time the visitors returned in 1924, lawns and gardens were once more in order.

After father revived the festivals in 1924, which he did by dint of every sort of self and family denial and with the aid of music lovers and friends, great singers and great conductors once more interpreted Wagner's music dramas in the theater that he had built for them on the hill above the little city. Music lovers from the farthest reaches of the world filled the summer air with their score reading and fascinating polyglot chatter as they sipped tea or Bavarian beer during the intermissions. Daimlers, Mercedes, and Rolls Royces crowded the streets. Kings, queens, princes, princesses, grand dukes and duchesses, none the less picturesque because some of them had lost their crowns, supped with the artists and visitors after the performances, showering them with *Bravi* as they came down the wide staircase to the lower restaurant floor. Wahnfried was open house to distinguished visitors just as it had been before the war, when Cosima had received like a queen.

I had been old enough to understand and share father's dreams when he reopened the Festspielhaus after it had been closed for ten years, so it was with this for background that I later watched the blight that Hitler and his National Socialism cast upon Bayreuth and all of Germany.

The rebirth of Bayreuth after the last war as a world center of music is an eternal monument to my father who lived only a short time after, although long enough to see success crown his efforts. But he was too tired and overworked to endure the arduous tasks which mounted day by day. He collapsed after the general rehearsal of Götterdämmerung in 1930, symbolically enough just after the playing of the music of Siegfried's "Funeral March." My mother carried on heroically. What followed is described in these pages.

But the Bayreuth of my father, of Cosima and my grandfather is no longer. I feel very strongly about the frequently heard statement, totally untrue, that my grandfather was a Nazi in spirit and that his music exemplifies the Nazi ideology. He never could have endorsed such a pattern of thinking. His whole life, his writing and his music all deny such a possibility. If only people would read what he wrote instead of listening to Nazi propaganda.

Wagner foresaw with prophetic clarity the drama and tragedy of our time. If Hitler had read the Ring of the Nibelung with understanding he could have foreseen his own doom. Symbolically, in the Ring, he who uses the gold for his own aggrandizement comes to destruction. So long as the gold represented beauty it was a safe and lovely thing but when Alberich forswore love and took the gold and fashioned the ring he gathered unto himself power and enslaved others and set in motion the whole selfish pattern which we see repeated today. If Hitler and those who repeat his misstatements about Wagner could or would look at the parallel they would understand Wagner.

They would then understand the eternal theme which runs through all his works, that of redemption through love and redemption through pity. It is always love and supreme sacrifice which bring redemption in Wagner's dramas.

Grandfather once wrote: "I would give up and destroy everything I have ever created, with joy, if I knew that it would further the cause of justice and liberty in this world."

Toscanini put the quotation at the head of a letter to me long after I had become a voluntary exile in the same cause.

So I follow in the steps of my grandfather who was intolerant only of intolerance, always a rebel against injustice. As a child and young girl I saw the stage being set for the present world drama. In the early twenties my mother met an unknown young fanatic and became an ardent follower of his, believing that he was indeed the "savior of the world." Her enthusiasm can be understood only by those who knew the postwar Germany of that era, when everyone was ardently looking for someone to lead the German people out of the mess. It seems to me that the fact that Adolf Hitler was the only leader to emerge will be an everlasting monument to German stupidity.

Hitler became a frequent visitor in our home, so I knew him as only a few people ever knew him, informally, without "stage make-up," as it were. My father laughed about my mother's strange messiah. He, in common with many others, felt that the new self-elected savior didn't have one chance in a million to succeed. It was this one factor that helped Hitler most in his amazing rise to power. No one of importance took him seriously. The guardians of the Versailles Treaty were as successfully lulled to sleep as were the German people. Nobody bothered to stop him because everyone thought that he would presently vanish from the scene.

Of course I saw at first hand what happened to the

cultural and artistic life of Germany. It is hideously evident to everyone today. The world in which I grew up seems almost like a fairy tale, as though it couldn't have been quite true even then. I am happily grateful that I got a solid basis of beauty, love and kindness, music and the arts before I had to become aware that life can be awfully tough and not a bit pretty. I managed to steer through the hatred and deceit and brutality without getting caught in it, thanks to that unique background and thanks to the determination to uphold the things my father had taught me to love—and to fight for them. After I saw the horrid spectacle of a people changing, always for the worse, under that dictatorship, my whole life became a constant rebellion against everything and everybody.

My final link with Germany ended in Switzerland in the spring of 1940 when I bade my mother good-by for the last time. After that farewell on the station platform at Zürich on a raw spring afternoon, I began another life, it would perhaps be more accurate to say that I took another step forward; actually I had long been without a country.

With the assistance of the British government which had accepted my services as being of "unique propaganda value," I returned to England where I spent months doing whatever I could and writing for newspapers until the collapse of Belgium and Holland made it seem necessary for the English to intern all enemy aliens. I then spent some months in an internment camp on the Isle of Man. In September, just in time for the blitz, as it happened, I was moved to London.

During all this time Toscanini had been trying to effect my release. In the summer of 1940 he arranged passage for me to Argentina but it was not until the spring of 1941 that I reached there.

In June Toscanini arrived for his concert season in Buenos Aires and six weeks later with Maestro and Mrs. Toscanini I flew to New York. We arrived at La Guardia Field at six o'clock on a late summer afternoon. At nine o'clock the next morning I made application for my first American citizenship papers. Again I will belong. How good it is to have a country in which one can work and breathe and live in amity with his neighbors, only those can know who have experienced the other kind of life.

Friedelind Wagner
New York, N.Y.
1945

HERITAGE OF FIRE

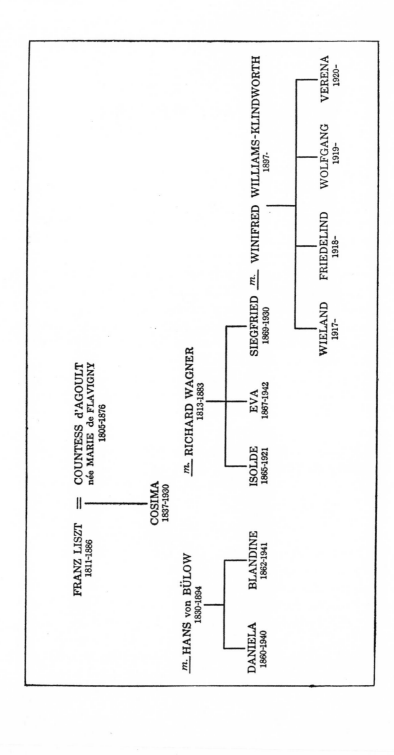

FRANZ LISZT
1811-1886

= COUNTESS d'AGOULT
née MARIE de FLAVIGNY
1805-1876

COSIMA
1837-1930

m. HANS von BÜLOW
1830-1894

m. RICHARD WAGNER
1813-1883

DANIELA
1860-1940

BLANDINE
1862-1941

ISOLDE
1865-1921

EVA
1867-1942

SIEGFRIED
1869-1930

m. WINIFRED WILLIAMS-KLINDWORTH
1897-

WIELAND
1917-

FRIEDELIND
1918-

WOLFGANG
1919-

VERENA
1920-

CHAPTER I

VISIT FROM A SAVIOR

COSIMA lay on the couch in the upstairs drawing room with her blind eyes turned away from the light and let us play "doctor." Wieland was taking her temperature with a pencil, I felt her pulse, Wolfgang tried to balance a level teaspoon of water over a glass, and baby Verena, who was only two and a half, played with the cushions on the floor. We liked Cosima's room with its deep chintz-covered chairs and the bust of Wagner on the mantel. It was next door to our nursery and less formal than the rooms downstairs. Best of all, we liked the balcony that looked down on the back garden, the fountain with the rose beds around it and Wagner's tomb, a slab of unmarked gray marble with ivy around the base. Grandmother never spoke of Wagner nor did anyone in her presence—when his birthday or the anniversary of his death approached, they told her the wrong date until it had passed, but they said she called his name in her sleep.

Everybody except the grandchildren who knew no awe of anyone, tiptoed about this tall dominant old lady with the aquiline face that must always have been interesting rather than beautiful. Now she was nearly ninety but I liked to imagine her when she sat for the portrait over the mantel, or those in the library downstairs, the two by Lembach, one in a black dress, another in white, and the one Youkowsky did of her in the oriental gown. Those were the turbulent days when Great-Grandfather Liszt was alive, when scandal buzzed around Cosima's consecrated head and the Berliners booed the overture to *Tannhäuser.*

1

Cosima and the aunts—her daughters Daniela and Eva —the portraits and the pianos, the garden and the tomb were all a part of the Wagner tradition that lived on in Wahnfried, this house that Grandfather had built some fifty years earlier in Bayreuth, the charming little Bavarian city in which he had elected to erect the perfect Festspielhaus for his music dramas. He designed Wahnfried on spacious lines to be a hospitable center for musicians and artists, just as the theater was for the dramas, and did finally achieve in it the peace which he had always craved.

For the Wagner grandchildren born into this beautiful and confusing world of ancestors and traditions, Wahnfried had the old and mellow quality of a legend. During the thirty years since Wagner died in Venice on the little sofa that Cosima brought home to Wahnfried and kept in her bedroom—we were not allowed to touch it—Grandmother had ruled with dictatorial power. In all that time not a thing had been changed. In the huge library lined with books, beautifully bound after Wagner's own design, the odd and precious presents that his worshipers had sent from all parts of the world remained in the exact spots that they had occupied when he lived. His spectacles lay in a drawer of the glass-topped desk where he had left them. The pianos in almost every room had never been moved an inch. We were not allowed to touch them.

"This one belonged to Liszt," we were told. "Wagner traveled with the French Erard that he called his swan and on the black Steck he composed *Parsifal*. The ebony one with the inscription inside was presented to your grandfather by Steinway. On the Bechstein your father composes. You may practice on your own upstairs." Above all there was the fascinating chair that Liszt had designed to hold him when he leaned over backward to play. To be truthful there had been two but we broke one, tipping back in it to "play the way Liszt did."

Now I understand what a disturbance we four latecomers must have made in this world consecrated to a

2

tradition. Father was forty-six and our beautiful young English mother, eighteen, when he brought her as a bride to Wahnfried. The arrival of Wagner's first grandson in 1917 was an occasion for great rejoicing; on the day of his birth Cosima for the first time since Wagner's death sat down at the Steinway and played a few bars of the "Siegfried Idyll." I followed on Good Friday, fifteen months later, but was not so honored; neither were Wolfgang and Verena who soon joined us: Cosima never touched the piano again. We climbed about on the sacred chairs, played with the Master's souvenirs, even put on his spectacles, to the delight of my father and the shocked disapproval of his sisters who were divided between horror at the desecration wrought by our baby fingers and pride in the vigor of the new Wagners.

But we romped happily through our uninhibited days, attracted but never overawed by our breath-taking ancestors. On this bright May morning of 1923 when we were playing doctor in Cosima's room we were particularly delighted because Wieland had been kept at home from school. Mother was expecting a guest and later we were to go downstairs to meet him, but we were accustomed to guests and didn't let them bother us. Even when we were babies we had crawled about on our knees, playing among the feet of distinguished musicians, writers, artists, crowned heads, the continual flow of distinguished visitors to Wahnfried.

Cosima was too frail to see many of them, only the most faithful of the old friends, but we always told her about them.

"Who is coming this morning?" she asked.

"Another one of Winnie's enthusiasms," answered Daniela who was in attendance at the time. "That young Adolf Hitler whom she met in Munich. She thinks he is going to be the savior of Germany."

Cosima's daughters divided the days between them. In the morning Daniela sat with her mother; in the after-

3

noon, Eva. Or sometimes Eva came in the morning and Daniela in the afternoon. They met and parted with restraint for Eva's husband, Houston Stewart Chamberlain, was one of the objects of Daniela's hatred and the feud had created a coolness between gentle Eva and her sister. Daniela was always hating or loving somebody with violence and never could endure to see anyone happy. If she had lived in another world or another age she would have made a career in one of the professions for she had a brilliant mind and a driving energy, but, cramped by Cosima into the narrow confines of German Society (she was a von Bülow and was presented at court in spite of Cosima's divorce) she was continually exploding, wrecking everything about her, continually repenting and flagellating herself for her outbursts.

Daniela's chief fascination for us was her eyes, one blue, the other brown. According to the legend, when Cosima looked at her first baby and saw the eyes she shuddered, afraid the baby would develop a double personality. She dreaded that the child might inherit the unstable temperament which had made her own life with von Bülow hell.

Daniela loved the grandchildren and was indulgent to us, but her voice was sharp as vinegar when she spoke of Mother. She had not approved of Father's marriage to a girl young enough to be his daughter. Furthermore, although she was the adopted daughter of Karl Klindworth, the famous pianist-conductor, Winifred Williams was English and an orphan. The two had disliked each other from the time they first met when Cosima had sent Daniela to Berlin to select the trousseau for Siegfried's bride. Daniela in her fierce conservatism had insisted upon dresses in which no self-respecting bride would be seen; they were more appropriate for a grandmother. The shoes had such pointed toes that Mother took them all to a cobbler to have them rounded off. When she arrived in Wahnfried she gave away the trousseau and wore her schoolgirl dresses.

4

Since the unhappy outcome of her own marriage which had ended in a divorce shortly before the war, Daniela had centered her interest upon Father. After his marriage she had served as a nurse at the front. When she returned to Bayreuth several years later, Father naturally offered her a home in Wahnfried but her hatred of Mother so poisoned the atmosphere that there was no living in the house with her. Soon Daniela moved into rooms not far away. Now there was a truce of sorts between her and Mother.

We always hung breathlessly on Mother's stories about those first days in Wahnfried. Cosima treated her as if she were barely out of the nursery, required her to write daily French exercises and dust the library for a half hour every morning. Mother hated it all but endured it because Scheuernbrandt, the aged butler, was an appreciative audience. He, Chamberlain and father managed to keep her bright spirit from being crushed by the overpowering ghosts of Wahnfried.

"Winnie's enthusiasms." Daniela had managed to put a volume of contempt into her tone. We paid little attention for we were much more interested in persuading Cosima to go out on the balcony than we were in the prospective guest.

"Grandmother," asked Wieland, "may I take you in the wheel chair?" He was the only one of us large enough to manage it and he wasn't permitted to touch it except with the help of one of the aunts.

Cosima stood up from the couch. She looked so tall and thin, so wax-white and fragile, that I was afraid she would break in two. Her white hair, parted in the middle and pulled back in a Grecian knot, was still thick and beautiful.

In a little procession we went out onto the balcony. Wolfgang dragged a blanket to put over Cosima's knees and Daniela wrapped her in a shawl. Outside it smelled of spring. The leaves on the elms were beginning to uncurl,

5

a pale faint yellow against the firs, and the grass between the flower beds was new green. Putzi, our Skye terrier, stopped chasing a fly and barked at us furiously.

"It's Putzi," explained Wolfgang (Wolfi we called him). "She wants to come up."

Cosima laid her transparent old hand on his head. She had never seen any of us, but she always knew which one was near her and she was glad that we were all blond as ripe wheat.

"Children, children." Emma was in the door of the drawing room, calling us. "Time to come down."

Reluctantly we kissed Cosima on each cheek and followed Emma. We adored this handsome tall nurse of ours. She helped Wieland with his lessons, listened to our complaints, straightened out our troubles, but would stand for none of our nonsense. Every night she threatened to leave because we had been naughty, and we never failed to believe her and plead with her to stay.

In no time we were washed and brushed, baby Verena in a white embroidered frock and I with a blue ribbon in my hair. Emma sent us down to the music room where Father and Mother were waiting. I ran over and put my hand in Father's. Every moment that I was with him I was completely happy. Mother, with her eyes bright and her cheeks flushed, sat at Wagner's piano and dusted her fingers over the keys.

This room was the scene of most of the important occasions of our lives. It was the heart of the house, a great two-story salon with solid walls for proper acoustics and a glass roof for light. High up under the balcony that ran completely around the room Cosima had put King Ludwig's gift of oil paintings illustrating the Ring cycle, having them paneled against the wall like a frieze. They were so many that she couldn't think what else to do with them. The six marble statues on their pedestals were also Ludwig's gift; Lohengrin, Siegfried, Tannhäuser, Tristan, Walter von Stolzing, Parsifal. They made good pegs for

6

Christmas wreaths. Here among the busts and the heroes we celebrated birthdays and Christmas, and when Father and Mother gave parties we crept onto the balcony to peep down at the guests.

For a long time we waited. Mother was talking to Father eagerly, telling him how wonderful the young man was. Presently Wolfgang and I grew impatient and went to the front door to watch for a car coming up the drive between the borders of the chestnut trees. At last one turned in from Richard Wagner Street. We called Father and Mother and all of us went to greet the visitor at the front door. A young man jumped out of the car and came toward us. He looked rather common in Bavarian leather breeches, short thick woolen socks, a red and blue checked shirt and a short blue jacket that bagged about his unpadded skeleton. His sharp cheekbones stuck out over hollow pasty cheeks and above them were a pair of unnaturally bright blue eyes. There was a half-starved look about him but something else too, a sort of fanatical glow.

The young man shook hands with my mother who introduced him to Father. He followed them shyly, awkwardly into the music room and library, tiptoeing among the souvenirs as though he were viewing relics in a cathedral. He looked with reverence at the crystal opium pipe that someone had given Cosima and the lovely little shrine of Buddha, paused before the collection of butterflies that Wagner had bought from a man on the street in Naples, and stood for a long time before the plate of Wagner's last photograph hung so that it could be seen against the light. Ever since he had heard *Lohengrin* when he was twelve years old he had looked upon Wagner as "the greatest German who ever lived."

The two rather hideous blue vases decorated with Lohengrin and the swan—also gifts of Ludwig—Hitler passed without a second glance but he read the inscriptions on the medals and picked up one of the silver laurel wreaths that Mother would have put out of sight if it hadn't

7

been for the aunts—holding it carefully in his thin, delicate hands.

Later we trooped after our parents and the stooping, hesitant man into the garden where he seemed less crushed by the Wagnerian atmosphere. There he told Father and Mother about the coup which his party was planning later in the year, a move which, if it succeeded, would mean immediate power. As he talked of his plans his voice took on tone and color and grew deeper and deeper until we sat like a circle of little charmed birds listening to the music although we didn't pay attention to a word he said.

Presently the young man left and we returned to our games. At luncheon Mother was still talking about Hitler, telling Father how Frau Bechstein had fed and clothed him, taught him rudimentary manners, taken him to the opera, provided him with money and given dinner parties at which she introduced him to influential people. Herr Edwin Bechstein, the famous piano manufacturer, was Mother's guardian and she had caught the fever while visiting in his Munich home.

"Don't you feel that he is destined to be the savior of Germany?" she insisted.

Father laughed at her indulgently. He was not impressed with the cadaverous young man.

CHAPTER II

CINDERELLA CHILD

WHEN Father was at home it was always a holiday. During the fall and winter he and Mother went away on concert tours and we were left with Emma and the servants, Cosima and the aunts, a full enough world for any five-year-old girl, but there was always the secret fear at the bottom of my heart that Father might not come home.

Most of the summer of 1923 he was at Wahnfried. Usually he worked until teatime, after which we took a long walk before gathering at six in Cosima's room. Sometimes the whole family went, sometimes—rare and precious occasions—I accompanied Father alone. We walked in the park that was separated from our garden by an iron gate. Father liked crowds and stopped to chat with the bench sitters. When he went to the station to catch a train, he started a couple of hours early to watch the people, many of whom turned up later in his operas.

Occasionally we crossed the meadow paths or climbed the gentle wooded hills around the city. When we were alone he taught me English and French. He had spent most of his childhood abroad and spoke both languages without a trace of accent. In Italian he could imitate almost every dialect and liked to pretend for me that he was a Lombardy farmer or a Neapolitan fisherman. Indeed he was such a good mimic that he could imitate people to their faces without their knowing it.

He examined me in opera motives or we produced operas together in our imaginations. We also made lovely plans for the time when I would be old enough to accompany him on his tours and assist in producing the festivals. The one driving purpose of his life was to reopen the Festspielhaus which had been closed since the beginning of the war. To that end he went on concert tours and dashed about from one corner of Europe to the other, conducting at concerts or at performances of his own operas. Next year, he thought, in 1924, he would surely be able to hold a festival.

He wanted Cosima to hear one more cycle before she died. Father idolized her. Nobody knew better than he what strength of character it had taken for her to turn over the management of the festivals to him. She had

9

carried them to a glorious success, selected and trained the artists, managed the technical staging, the financial end, everything. At first Father conducted, later he became Cosima's assistant and when finally she believed him prepared, she withdrew completely.

"She'll never be able to keep her hands off," people said, but she did. From that moment the festivals were Father's whole life. My childish heart nearly burst with pride when he spoke of me as his successor.

"One day you will be able to carry on," he often said. I had never seen a festival and didn't understand exactly what he meant but I replied quite seriously, "Of course I will."

When he was absent-minded on our walks I knew that "papa is composing" and ran along beside him careful not to make a sound. It was fun trying to keep step because he changed speed according to the tempo of the theme he was fashioning. At these times he forgot all about his daughter until he reached the gate of Wahnfried. Then he laughed and told me I would be a wonderful wife for a composer.

"Of course," I agreed. "Don't you want to marry me?" He had a difficult time explaining why a little girl cannot marry her father.

On rainy summer afternoons Father sometimes paid us a visit in the nursery. Wieland was usually sketching. He drew with his left hand and, as his teacher scolded him in school, trying to make him use the proper hand, he drew at home in protest and was always teasing us to sit for him. Father sympathized with Wieland because he himself had conducted with his left hand until his musicians complained that he was too difficult to follow. Wolfi stopped dismembering his fire engine and we gathered around Father when he told us stories of his boyhood or how he courted Mother.

His Winnie was a Cinderella child. Both her mother, a young actress, and her father, an engineer, a bridge builder

10

who wrote novels and music criticism at odd moments, died before Winnie was two years old. Her Danish grandfather who was having a difficult time in London, was so appalled at the prospect of bringing up a child that he was tempted to kill the baby and commit suicide. Winnie escaped to a miserable childhood in an English orphanage. When she was ten years old she was sent to Germany to the wife of Karl Klindworth who was a distant relative. When the Klindworths went to the station in Hanover to meet the pale, beautiful little girl with the tag around her neck, they fell in love with her at once. The vacation for which she had come was extended indefinitely and after a few years the pianist-conductor adopted her.

Mrs. Klindworth who was English and spoke very bad German, sent Winifred to a German school but also took her to the services of the Church of England on Sunday, and all of the English tea parties in town. The conductor taught her piano and let her accompany him to the best concerts in Berlin. When she was fifteen Winnie heard my father conduct, fell in love with him and spent her school days penciling his profile in her textbooks which we still had in Wahnfried. All of her pocket money she spent for librettos of his operas.

Two summers later, in 1914, Klindworth took Winifred to the Bayreuth festival, the general rehearsals of which were by invitation and much more fashionable than the public performances. The pianist was an old friend of Wagner and Liszt and an intimate at Wahnfried, so he presented Winnie to Cosima and the family who were enchanted with the beautiful girl. Certainly Siegfried was enchanted for at every intermission he invited her to the Wagner table for tea. Mother had a weakness for preserves and he was so infatuated that he urged her to eat them right out of the pot. Thus the seventeen-year-old girl with jam on her pretty fingers, captured one of the handsomest, wealthiest and most distinguished bachelors in Germany.

11

There was mourning, I understand, among the dowagers with marriageable daughters.

But the wooing was not without its hardships. As soon as Father settled the affairs of the festival which in 1914 was stopped in mid-season by the war, he went to Berlin and made the long pilgrimage to Lichterfelde, the home of Klindworth. He even endured a vegetarian luncheon at the Klindworths' but when he left bought a huge order of ham at the first restaurant in Potsdam.

When Father proposed in the spring of the following year, Klindworth approved.

"Do you want Winnie to finish school," he asked, "or do you want to marry at once?"

"At once," said Father, but there remained one obstacle in the way. Winnie was an enemy alien and had to report to the police twice a day. After unending red tape and three months of waiting, Father succeeded in getting her naturalized. For one day she was a citizen of Prussia; on the next day she married Father in Bayreuth and became a citizen of Bavaria.

From the moment that she entered Wahnfried, Mother was the very breath of life to Father. She became his secretary and in a few years was tending to all of the business affairs of his concert tours, accompanying him everywhere, lifting his spirits with her gaiety and charm. He enjoyed her foibles and poked gentle fun at them. Her enthusiasm for Hitler he regarded as just another hobby. She was young and bubbling with life and vitality, why shouldn't she run about to rallies and wave a swastika on street corners or in beer halls—if she must go to beer halls. Her ardor would cool in time.

Father was disillusioned with postwar Germany. In his heart he was still a monarchist as were the majority of Germans; he could never understand or forgive the Kaiser's flight and had no sympathy with the Weimar Republic which failed although it meant well. He was a liberal but also a conservative and the sight of Germany

12

torn by revolution and bloodshed, spawning one sinister "messiah" after another, distressed him. Germany was a pigsty, he said, and he meant it. But Father had too international a background to be agitated about party politics. He had spent much of his life abroad; each year he traveled all over Europe, and when he was at home Wahnfried, with its guests from everywhere, was decidedly international. So he teased Mother about her rallies and refused to look upon Hitler as a saint.

The summer of 1923 passed and my heart took a little dip of terror when the concert season began; this time there was talk of going to America. Early that momentous November, the ninth to be exact, Father went with Mother to Munich where he was to conduct a concert. After his arrival, he discovered that the concert had been canceled on account of the *Putsch* on the eighth. The rooms in the hotel overlooked the Feldherrenhalle. Hearing a commotion in the street he and Mother looked out the window to see Hitler and General Ludendorff marching down the middle of the avenue at the head of a company of storm troopers in ordinary khaki waterproof jackets. Nearer and nearer they came, keeping step with the general whose commanding figure made Hitler look woefully unmilitary. Suddenly as the procession drew opposite the Feldherrenhalle it was stopped by a spattering of machine-gun fire. The storm troopers scattered. In the confusion Mother couldn't see what had happened to Hitler and Ludendorff. The general was safe, they said, but Hitler had been wounded in the arm and nobody knew where he was hiding.

Father was horrified to think that the Bavarian government would fire on General Ludendorff, the idol of all Germany. While he was in this sympathetic mood, Mother induced him to go to Innsbruck where Göring who had fled across the mountain passes, lay in a hospital severely wounded. Father, who was always moved by distress, found Göring being cared for by his beautiful Swedish wife who

13

was very ill herself and penniless. He paid their bills and arranged for them to go to Venice where they lived for a year in a hotel whose proprietor, a friend of Father's, never charged them a cent.

This was my father's only contribution to the cause. He forgot about the matter and came home for Christmas which was one of the biggest festivals of the year at Wahnfried. For weeks we children had been scurrying around, hiding presents for the aunts and Cosima and Emma. We had dressed the bust of Wagner in the music room with one of my berets and Wolfi's scarf, and tied Father's brightest tie about the neck of Liszt. The big tree was lying on the floor. When it was trimmed and lifted upright it was so tall that we could touch the star on the topmost branch by leaning over the balcony.

When the bell rang at six o'clock on Christmas Eve, we all filed in and stood about the tree lighted with real candles. Father played, Mother read the Christmas Gospel, we sang a carol. At last the presents! The cook who had become an intellectual snob at our house, wanted books about Wagner. Emma was loaded with presents from the guests as well as the family; everyone who came to Wahnfried loved Emma. Then we moved about the little tables ranged around the tree, the family, the guests, the servants, the children, admiring our Christmas presents.

Soon after the wonderful day the trunks were brought upstairs and the beds in Mother's room were covered with dresses. Father and Mother were going to America. Father had been looking forward to this tour but in one way it was a disappointment. When he arrived in New York, he noted a certain cautious reserve, even among his closest friends. Later he learned that one of his ill-wishers had cabled to New York the story that Father had contributed to the Hitler *Putsch* all the money for the reopening of the festivals, some of which had been contributed by Wagner enthusiasts throughout the world, although he raised the greater part of it by his concerts. My mother's open devotion to the movement had been represented as that of my father and as the attitude of Bayreuth as well.

We children did not know about Father's worries for we were occupied with a tragedy of our own—this was the spring that Putzi died. One of the maids ran in from the garden while we were at luncheon and told us our pet had drowned in the fountain. After we had wept over Putzi we buried her in the garden by the back fence, near the graves of her predecessors, the parrots and the young blackbird that I had found dead in the grass and interred in an old shoe box. At the head of each grave was a tombstone, even larger than that of Russ, Wagner's Newfoundland who grieved himself to death when his master died and was buried at the foot of Wagner's tomb. His stone was of granite and bore the inscription, *Hier Ruht und Wacht Wagners Russ*. The others in the little graveyard by the fence were inscribed simply with the names of the dogs and parrots buried there.

I have always regretted that I came too late to know the parrots, that raucous pair who screamed Brünnhilde's battle cry, "Hojotoho" at startled guests. They were alive when Mother came to Wahnfried. She used to tell us that one of them, perhaps it was Gockel, was worse than human. He had taken a dislike to Eva and cackled maliciously when he found the opportunity to sneak into that aunt's room and tear at the papers on her desk. Once Gockel heard Eva burp and afterward, whenever Eva entered the room, the bird gave a loud derisive imitation.

But Gockel loved Cosima; he slept next to Grandmother's bedroom and when his mistress was restless in the night, called "Dora come, Dora come!" until the nurse appeared. One night when burglars broke in downstairs, Gockel made himself a hero by wakening the household with his "Dora come." Gockel's grave was old but we tended it with the same care that we spent on the dogs we remembered.

Now we carried Putzi to the graveyard and laid her on

15

the grass. She should be buried next the blackbird I decreed, and marked out the spot with a stick.

"May I dig, Mausi?" Wolfi asked. As Wieland was in school I was next in command and superintended the arrangements. Wolfi went to the garden house for a shovel and came back with old Hoffmann, the gardener, who wanted to see that we didn't do too much damage to the lawn. He thought more of his rose garden and his grass than anything else in the world. Once when the old man received news that his son had been decorated with the Iron Cross in the war, Cosima came out into the garden to congratulate him.

"Thank you very much, Gnädige Frau," he said, "and I'd like a new pair of pruning shears."

We planned to carry flowers to Putzi's grave every day but forgot about it in the excitement of getting ready for the festival. Contractors were hurrying back and forth from the Festspielhaus to Wahnfried, telegraph boys dashed continually up and down the chestnut drive, spattering the gravel with their bicycles. Mother was busy too, answering letters, seeing to a thousand things, but she found time to learn that Hitler and his companions were imprisoned in the fortress of Landsberg-am-Lech. The party seemed to have disappeared, and only a few of the most fanatical Nazis were carrying on underground. Hitler's loyal admirers felt so sorry for the poor man that they sent him mountainous parcels of food, especially sweets, candy and cakes for which he had a passion. It was at the fortress that he lost forever his half-starved look.

As Landsberg was seven and a half hours by local train from Bayreuth, Mother didn't attempt to see Hitler but she immediately set to work collecting money, clothes and food for the families of convicted Nazis. The chief of police summoned her to his office and gave her a paternal warning to stop this nonsense or one of these days she would land in jail, but nothing influenced her. Since she knew that many others were sending sweets to Germany's convicted "savior," she tried to think of something else that he might need. At the stationer's on Bayreuth's main street she bought quantities of paper; typewriting paper, carbon paper, pencils, pens, ink, erasers. We helped her tie them up and they looked as gay as a collection of Christmas packages. She didn't know that Hitler had literary aspirations but it was on her paper and with her ink and pencils that he wrote the first volume of *Mein Kampf*. As long as he was in prison she sent him supplies of everything a presumed genius might need.

These activities worried Father for they were building up an unfortunate atmosphere for the opening of the festival. It wasn't funny any more. He felt that he simply must stop Mother but he didn't know how to be stern with her. A comment that he made then was the only bitter phrase I ever knew him to say: "Winnie destroys everything that I try so desperately to rebuild."

CHAPTER III

FESTIVAL

WITH the reopening of the Festspielhaus in 1924 we children began to live in a fairy tale come true. No longer did we want to be doctors, engineers, train conductors, we were captured by Wagner's music and the goings-on at the theater and had no further doubts as to our chosen profession. Every day we told Father a new and wonderful plan about the way we were going to produce when we took over.

At first there was the excitement of watching the Festspielhaus repainted and furnished after it had been closed for ten years. During May Wolfi and Verena drove across

17

Bayreuth with Father every morning to see how the work was progressing while Wieland and I, the unlucky ones who were still in school, waited until Father sent the car to fetch us when our lessons were over.

No one ever told us to go or to stay, but Father seemed to think it natural that we wanted to tag along, so there we were in the car whenever we had the chance. Down Richard Wagner Street we drove, turned in the square around the traffic policeman who always called "good morning" and past the bronze horseman above the fountain commemorating some famous regiment, then on across a bridge of the Main, such a tiny stream in the summer that it was almost lost between its high banks, and up the hill to the Festspielhaus. The engine raced as we climbed the drive through the park that stretched up the hillside to the theater. After the war the city fathers employed the inmates of the local jail to landscape it with footpaths, fountains and little pools stuck in corners under clumps of willows.

We liked the simple red brick building among the firs. It was built from Wagner's design, hollow inside like a cello; the open cavernous spaces underneath the stage gave resonance, and the ceiling was so thin that the sound went up to the roof. It was said to have the best acoustics in the world.

Inside the theater there was a great stir: carpenters pounding, painters moving about their ladders and spotted canvases, scrub women slopping along the corridors with mops and buckets. Everywhere were the fascinating odors of paint and turpentine and naphthalene. Kranich, the technical director, had already arrived. His two children played with us, climbing up to the platforms among the ropes under the roof, scurrying among the massive props deep below stage.

Daniela who was in charge of the wardrobe, had the sewing woman make miniature costumes for us, exact copies of the originals. When we weren't at the Festspiel-

18

haus we paraded in the garden dressed as Wotan, Fricka, Froh, Freia, or Siegfried and Brünnhilde, rushing madly about, brandishing spears, uttering inhuman battle cries. To our performance of the Ring we charged an entrance fee of twenty cents and gathered an audience from the strangers who wandered about the front garden as though they were visiting a shrine. Mother later kept the back gate into the park closed and reserved the lawn behind the house for the family, but at that time tourists were still free to walk in the entire garden and there they were every day, talking to the dogs in English, Dutch, Scandinavian, every tongue except German, stopping to read the inscription over the door or look at the bust of King Ludwig that stood fenced off in a little clump of yews in front of the entrance.

On the first of June the rehearsals began, the painters and carpenters moved out and the performers moved in: the coaches and musicians, the needlewomen and tailors and stagehands. Never from that time to the day I left Bayreuth did I miss a rehearsal. Hour after hour I followed Father around on the stage, playing "assistant" until my legs ached from standing on the floor which slanted toward the footlights. He had angelic patience and never seemed to feel that I was in the way. Between rehearsals we ran in and out of the dressing rooms, watched the fittings upstairs, women on one side of the building being pinned and basted into costumes, men on the other trying on shields or winged helmets. At one end of the wardrobe room a shoemaker hammered on sandals for the gods and goddesses.

To find us was a foot-wearing odyssey; we were playing hide and seek among the rocks or up among the ropes or hiding in the stomach of Fafner. No one bothered until Kranich's son chased a workman through a window instead of a door and fell two stories. The boy hit the only soft spot of the Rheingold rock and broke no bones but

19

suffered from a concussion that lasted several days. From then on the most dangerous spots were out of bounds.

The apparatus that pulled around the Rhinedaughters in *Rheingold*, swinging them up and down, east and west, around the rock with the gold on top, something like one of the rides at Coney Island, was a special thrill for a six-year-old. We watched popeyed while two stagehands handled the wires and a couple of others the ropes.

"*Weia! Waga! Woge, Du Welle, Walle zur Wiege! Wagalaweia! Wallala, weiala, weia!*" sang Woglinde, praying she wouldn't be seasick, while three assistants to the musical director ran about with scores in their hands giving the workmen the cues. The Rhinedaughters dreaded this ride in the wave machine which must be taken every day of the season until they were sea-proof but we envied them and were always daring each other to go up in it.

"Bet you're afraid to be a Rhinedaughter."

"Bet I'm not."

Sometimes we persuaded the workmen to let us climb in before a rehearsal and ride until one of us lost his lunch.

It was fun down in the orchestra too when the musicians were tuning up. The orchestra was invisible from the audience. The conductor was hidden by a shell that curved toward the stage, and the musicians were ranged on steps reaching so deep under the stage that the drummers and trumpeters couldn't hear the singers. The singers on the stage could see only the conductor and the violins. Wagner had worked out a new arrangement of seating the instruments; the first violins didn't all sit on the left and the bass viols on the right but were interspersed to blend the tone more perfectly. Some of the vainer conductors regretted not being seen by the audience but on hot midsummer days they liked to shed their coats and ties. Sometimes they were a sight for the gods.

Father had selected a hundred and thirty musicians chosen from sixty different orchestras, chiefly those in the larger German cities. But never either soloists or musicians from Munich. The old feud between the cities still flourished. In Cosima's time Munich built a big rival opera house in the style of the Festspielhaus and put on festivals at the same time as ours in Bayreuth, but unfortunately their building didn't have good acoustics. I am the only Wagner who has ever stepped inside the building.

Father's way of selecting his singers seemed casual but he thought it far better than formal auditions. He insisted that auditions were unfair to an artist who always gets the jitters and is never at his best. Then too, how were judges to know whether the singers were able to sing anything else except the aria on which they might have worked for years? He preferred to slip in at the performance and listen to the artist in whom he was interested; when he liked a singer he went backstage after the performance and made an offer; when he didn't he went quietly away and no one was the wiser, no feelings were hurt.

Finding a personality with a voice was a talent upon which Father prided himself. One time at a bar in Dresden he saw a man who looked the perfect Beckmesser.

"Sir," said Father. "You must sing Beckmesser in Bayreuth."

"I never sang in my life," said the astonished stranger.

"That doesn't matter; you are going to," answered Father. And so the man did. He was one of our best Beckmessers and sang the role in 1924 and 1925 when we did *Die Meistersinger*.

But Father's system of intuition didn't work with his friend Peter Passmann, the handsome lumber merchant who never missed a performance of his operas.

"You are a perfect Siegfried. You should have a voice," lamented Father. But they both knew that Peter couldn't sing a note and never would.

With the beginning of the second week in July the Valkyries leaped expertly over the rocks and the Rhinemaidens had become accustomed to their bouncing waves. During the week of the general rehearsals Bayreuth had a

21

festival air. We liked this week better than the actual performances because during the rehearsals the audience was composed of musicians and friends of father's and the Bayreuth neighbors; no outsiders to interfere. We were all one big informal family.

After the festival opened, of course, sleek Rolls Royces and Daimlers honked through the streets, the hotels were bursting with guests and every family of any importance boasted a celebrity to tea. The city was so full of foreigners that one seldom saw a German face. At Wahnfried Mother kept open house from eleven to twelve on each performance day. Eva entertained her sister, Blandine, the most beautiful of Cosima's daughters, who had married Count Biaggio Gravina at nineteen and lived a gay social life in Florence. At first she returned for long visits, but as the years passed the visits grew shorter and farther apart until finally she came only for the festivals and hurried away immediately afterward to escape the raw Bayreuth climate.

Daniela and Eva looked upon Blandine as something of a stranger. Daniela had submitted to Cosima's dictatorship, body and soul, and Eva had been her willing drudge until at forty-one she snatched what she hoped would be "really beautiful freedom" by marrying Chamberlain, but Blandine had very early developed a wearing-down technique that got her what she wanted. She and Daniela didn't get along too well but Blandine of them all, never bothered Father or later, Mother, by making constant objections to every improvement that was made in the Festspielhaus.

We children approved of Blandine because she never corrected our manners and we were fond of all her children whom we called "Uncle" and "Aunt" because they were older than Mother. Beautiful Maria and her husband stayed with us and so did Manfredi with his wife, our favorite of them all, Maria-Sofia, with a dark Roman profile and an understanding of children.

These were carefree days because everybody was too busy to correct our manners and look to see if our hands were clean. Usually Daniela, and to a lesser degree, Eva,

22

tried to make us conform to the standards of deportment that Cosima had imposed on them. We paid as little attention as possible but occasionally we rebelled, especially Wieland. To one of Daniela's lectures on manners befitting a Wagner, he is quoted as replying that his family wasn't so refined after all, "Papa whistles at the table, Mama reads the paper and Mausi sings."

Wieland with his blond page boy haircut and engaging lisp, Verena with her high innocent little-girl voice, Wolfi with his bland indifference, managed to get away with an amazing lot of things, but I, unlucky child, had no guile. My bounding energy and unrestrained candor were always landing me in trouble.

One of these episodes happened during the general rehearsal of *Siegfried*. What put the idea into my head I haven't the faintest notion; it popped out of nowhere into my mind and to act on it was but the matter of the few seconds it took to wiggle between the curtains. I was always intrigued by the queer titles which Father chose for some of his operas. For instance: *An Allem ist Hütchen Schuld*, which roughly translates as "It's all the Fault of the Mischievous Elf"; *Bruder Lustig*, which becomes "The Jolly Brother"; *Schwarz-schwanenreich* ("The Realm of the Black Swans"); and *Bärenhäuter* ("The Bearskinned"). Perhaps I was trying to go him one better. Anyway, all I was conscious of was that I had a grandiose scheme.

The stage was already dark for the second act. Alberich was lying in front of the Neidhöhle ready to brood gloomily at the first note of the orchestra. Slipping between the curtains I stood in the faint glow of the orchestra pit and looked up at the shadowy faces that rose in tiers like a ghost audience in an amphitheater. Taking a long breath I shouted at the top of my lungs, "My father's next opera will be called, *Der Kuhwedel* ("The Cow's Tail"). After a moment of astonished silence the dim cloud of white suits and pale summer dresses quivered with amusement as the audience howled with laughter. A hand grabbed me by the neck, I was dragged back through the curtain

23

just as the orchestra burst into Alberich's lament, and hustled into the wings. The stage manager who was holding me by the collar, dumped me by Wieland standing in the wings with the Wanderer waiting for his cue.

"Go out front, you two." The stage manager was choking with laughter as he shoved us out of the way.

"Ja, ja," taunted Wieland, "you must have pulled an awful boner. What did you say?"

"Nothing, nothing at all," I answered haughtily. "You know people laugh at anything. Besides, you can't talk. Remember how everybody howled when Verena was a new baby and King Ferdinand of Bulgaria asked you about her. You told him that Emma said, 'When the fifth one comes, I go.'"

Quarreling amicably we went out front into the parquet. At the rehearsals we were allowed to sit wherever we wanted to, but during the performances we were herded into the family box. The aunts found us a great nuisance, in fact the matter of the Wagner box grew more urgent as the festival progressed. Daniela and Eva said we made such a disturbance that we should not be allowed to sit in it, but Father held firmly to his determination that we should have the very front seats. He finally settled the matter by building another box for his family. As for me, it was an academic matter because to this day I never really enjoy a performance unless I am backstage.

Father's dream that Cosima would be able to see another performance of the Ring materialized. Frail as she was, Grandmother made the journey across town to the Festspielhaus several times and was rolled up to the box in her wheel chair. Every day Dora dressed her with special care for the reception of exceptionally honored guests whom one of the aunts took upstairs to pay their respects.

We children liked best the parties in the restaurant after the performances. Artists and friends drifted from table to table, chatting, laughing, flirting. Romances flourished. Every day had a holiday air. When there were no performances the artists and the visitors made excursions to the Eremitage, the beautiful baroque palace, or to pleasant inns which served special trout dinners—to dozens of beautiful spots in Franconia.

The first season drew to a brilliant and successful close during a spell of broiling weather. Father who always conducted the last cycle of the Ring, stripped to shorts, and so did the members of the orchestra. The Valkyries vowed they would faint under their armor, but we children throve on the heat. We consumed unbelievable numbers of ices at intermission time and looked contemptuously at the fashionable ladies mopping their brows and surreptitiously powdering their noses.

The morning after the last performance there was a great exodus from Bayreuth. All day the big cars flashed past on their way to Marienbad, Carlsbad or the Bavarian Alps and by evening the little city was dead as a bewitched town in a fairy tale. For almost two blessed weeks we had Wahnfried to ourselves. No tourists in the garden to pat our heads and tell us how much we looked like our grandfather, no artists in the guest rooms taking Father's attention. He loafed in the garden with us, listened to our grandiose schemes for next year's festival and played with the dogs, as carefree as we were. Then it was time for school.

CHAPTER IV

COSIMA REMEMBERS

THE first year at school was a new experience, tame after the Festival but pleasant enough. The teacher who was interested in local history, told us marvelous tales about Bayreuth in the days when it was a residency and the sister of Frederick the Great was building the big palace that her brother called the "goat shed." We enjoyed too the fifteen-minute morning intermission during which we gathered in the big dining room for *Quakerspeise*, rice pudding, cocoa or some other nourishing food. None of us knew what the word meant and not until years afterward did I learn that the food was sent by American Quakers for underfed German children.

Wieland and I were lucky in that we had several unofficial holidays; we were taken along to the performances of Papa's operas in other German cities. These excursions were not too well liked by the school authorities—one of our masters exclaimed, "Praise heaven we have no other children whose fathers are composers"—but Wieland and I loved them. We were permitted to stay up late at the performances and collected many a chocolate drop from the orchestras.

The only scholastic achievement of the year was my earning a bicycle. During the summer I had learned to ride one and wanted a wheel of my own with such intensity that it was almost an obsession. But Mother didn't intend me to get it too easily; she believed that I should earn it by good marks at school. According to my lights this was blackmail but as it was the only way to acquire the bicycle, there was nothing else to do.

Earning good marks was not too difficult; at Easter I produced a perfect report except for needlework which was one of my lesser accomplishments, and Mother weakened. Perhaps Father softened her, I never knew; he never interfered with her discipline. He wanted only the companionship and love of his children.

The whole winter of effort had not been particularly discouraging but what did depress me was the discovery that Mother looked upon the wheel as a means of forcing my good conduct. When all of the other punishments failed, my precious bicycle would disappear and remain lost until I mended my ways.

Perhaps I was unfair to Mother who certainly had her

difficulties with me, but I was always the one who suffered most from her enthusiasms. That year, too, she discovered a miracle-working doctor at Kassel who was going to make over our lives with his vegetarian diet. Emma was dispatched with the four of us to Kassel for the cure which consisted of a fare of nothing but vegetables and, after lunch, an hour of compulsory relaxation on the bare, hard boards of the balcony floor. That was bad enough but when we returned we were kept on the hateful diet and compelled to eat our supper nude. Later on we were permitted to eat a little meat once or twice a week after downing a punishing amount of vegetables.

Peas and beans I simply could not swallow. After many reproaches at the table, Mother would lose her patience and send me out of the room to finish them on the stairs. Later, when she found them still untouched, she spanked me, then forced them down my throat. I promptly vomited; Mother spanked again and gave me another forced dose which I disposed of as easily. Another spanking, another dose. It was open war but Mother was the loser because she spanked me with her bare hand. In addition to the ache in her fingers she was outraged by my laughter. I had discovered that a laugh is just as effective a release from pain as a scream, so the harder she beat, the louder I laughed.

After a year of this warfare between us, Mother gave up physical punishment. She could never "beat the stubbornness out of me." Next, she tried keeping me in bed on bread and water, a dreary punishment for an active child, and now the bicycle.

Most bitter of all, after Wieland, Wolfi and even baby Verena had learned to ride on mine, they wheedled bicycles out of Mother without having to do a stroke of work for them. That was always the way. She never handled them roughly and they got whatever they wanted without the slightest difficulty while I had to make all kinds of effort for every little thing upon which I set my heart. My

27

unduly sharpened sense of justice was often my undoing. Injustice either to me or to others threw me into fits of rage and rebellion that were not in character with my usually even disposition.

Sometimes I guessed that Father suffered for me, but at such times the best he could do was to show me afterward how much he loved me by paying grave respect to my opinions. For the same reason the aunts ranged themselves on my side, which hurt my mother and stiffened her efforts to master me.

When Father was at home nothing could blight me for very long, and as he made no long tours it was a happy winter. At the end of October the books for the first festival season were closed, showing that the deficit had not been large enough to discourage plans for the season of 1925. Father intended to continue the traditional system of repeating the festival for a second year with the same dramas, then skip a season to prepare a new series. Always we gave the Ring and *Parsifal* and varied the sixth drama.

During the winter famous tenors and sopranos, bassos and contraltos came to Wahnfried to coach for their parts. The rehearsals were held in the music room with the chairs and couches pushed here and there to represent props on the stage. Father took the other parts and gave the singer his cues while I sat solemnly and watched, pretending to be the prompter. By the end of the season I knew practically all of the Ring by heart.

That winter Father let Wieland start his piano lessons; he thought it nonsense for a child to begin earlier because his hands were not strong enough; if the child waited until he was eight or nine he would learn in a few weeks what he would have absorbed earlier in two or three years. Once Wieland had started, I made a nuisance of myself, pleading and teasing until my parents let me begin lessons a few months later, but I never made the sensational debut that Wieland quite unintentionally achieved.

Before Christmas our teacher gave her annual recital

28

for the fond parents and friends of her pupils. To Wieland who had been studying for only ten days she taught Luther's lovely Christmas carol, "*Vom Himmel Hoch*," in the simplest possible arrangement, single notes, alike in both hands, something in the manner of "chopsticks" that American children play except that he used the prescribed number of fingers. To give the arrangement a little volume and dignity, she played a two-hand bass. In reporting the recital the local paper mentioned that Wieland made his debut as a pianist playing "*Vom Himmel Hoch*." The Berlin newspapers picked up the item and enlarged on it to the effect that Wieland made his debut as a pianist, giving the impression that the recital was his. The French, English and Italian press indulged in flights of improvisation about the sensational debut of Wagner's grandson, but the American papers outdid them all; they printed long feature articles displaying Wieland's picture and describing emotional scenes at the debut of the nine-year-old prodigy who rivaled his great-grandfather, Liszt. When my parents saw the clippings they read the accounts to us children and we all thought it a wonderful joke.

Another incident of that same year had its humorous aspect but as I was the victim I was in no position to appreciate it. Wieland and I brought home lice from school and before anyone knew it, Wolfi and Verena caught them too. The blame fell on me just as it always did for bringing home measles, whooping cough, mumps, all the children's diseases. Usually all four of us had them at the same time and after our nursery had been a hospital for weeks, Mother came down with the same disease which she had escaped when she was young. Emma, worn to the edge of her patience, swore that if we caught another plague she would surely leave. In the case of the lice, Emma was particularly stern with me because she and Mother were sure I had caught them through my too democratic choice of friends. Whether or not it was my fault, I suffered most because I had the longest hair, and the daily

29

treatment, the dousing with some sort of vermin killer and the eternal digging with a fine-toothed comb, were torture. The final humiliation was Father's birthday party at which we usually wore our prettiest clothes and wreaths of flowers in our hair. On this day we were allowed to attend the party in the garden. It was June, the roses were in bud, everything was blossoming but there were no wreaths in our hair. We stood over near the hothouse with hangdog heads while the guests, who tried not to laugh at us, kept at a safe distance.

It was a busy season for Father. Every morning after breakfast he and Mother tackled the day's business, correspondence, interviews, a mountain of details, with sometimes a few hours to play with the dogs and us in the garden. One success accomplished and another in prospect, he ceased to worry about Mother's pro-Nazi activities. Now that Hitler was out of jail she no longer dashed about town making collections for the party.

Everybody talked politics at Wahnfried but we paid little attention to them; it was not until later that Mother tried to indoctrinate us with Nazism and an appreciation of Hitler's "supreme personality." Although she didn't want to hurt Father by her cause, her ardor was just as strong as it had been when she first joined the party in 1920 or 1921. She was not one of the original seven but she was well among the first few hundred. In those early days when it was Hitler's job to fill out the membership cards in the party's dark little hole of an office behind a Munich pub, the cards bore no numbers. When the party was reorganized after Hitler's release from prison, Mother joined again and her number was in the eighty thousands. This time the Nazis had money for a fine new respectable office, and before many days, a mouthpiece, the *Völkische Beobachter* which Hitler bought and printed on his own press.

Mother went to Munich for the reopening of the party in February, 1925, shortly after Hitler's release from the

30

fortress. After the meeting she drove back to Wahnfried with Hitler and his aides and kept them concealed there overnight. Nobody knew the secret except Wieland and he kept it so well that I didn't worm it out of him for thirteen years.

In those days Hitler was in constant fear of his life so we met him in all sorts of out-of-the-way places. Mother took us along to rendezvous in little restaurants outside of Bayreuth or meetings beside the road. Sometimes Hitler's car crept up the drive after midnight and he would steal secretly into the house. Late as it was, he never failed to come into the nursery and tell us gruesome tales of his adventures. We all sat up among the pillows in the half-light and listened while he made our flesh creep, showing us his pistol which, of course, he carried illegally—a small one that he could hide in his palm, but it held twenty bullets.

Hitler had put on weight. The sweets that he ate in prison had filled out his hollow cheeks so well that he looked positively pudgy. The bags under his eyes—he told us they were caused by poison gas—were larger than ever and emphasized his lashless eyelids that had a peculiarly naked look.

In spite of skirmishes with Mother and periods of grieving for the lost bicycle, it was a glorious spring. Wieland and his playmates admitted me to their games and at seven years my ambition was to outdo them all. Once, for the reward of a frankfurter, I dived from a nine foot diving board; and at a swimming test I stayed in the water so long that they took me home with a heart attack.

When the aunts saw me bouncing around in the garden, laughing and shouting, they would smile and say to one another, "Just like Isolde." But never in the hearing of Cosima. In Grandmother's presence no one dared mention the name of her favorite daughter. The legends about Isolde had always fascinated me, the scraps I pieced together from the comments of the aunts. She was the oldest child of Wagner and Cosima, an irrepressible girl, bubbling

31

with high spirits. While Daniela and Eva worshiped, almost feared their mother and strove to be little patterns of correct behavior, Isolde danced through Cosima's reserve and treated her with casual affection.

"Now, Mama, this is all nonsense you are talking," she often commented, and her mother would give a delighted chuckle.

But in the end Cosima won; she managed to prevent Isolde from marrying the man she loved. For seven years the girl tried to forget, then made her escape by marrying a young conductor, Beidler. It was an unfortunate marriage and was soon followed by a quarrel that resulted in a break with the whole family. To Cosima, Isolde was dead although she did not actually die until many years later. Eva and Daniela visited her secretly when she was desperately ill of tuberculosis but never spoke her name to their mother. Poor brilliant tempestuous Isolde, with such a capacity for joy. Every time the aunts said lovingly, "How like Isolde," I was determined that I would never let anyone crush my life.

Often when I saw Cosima surrounded by the reverent Daniela and Father and the guests who acted as if they were standing before a shrine, I wondered about her. Nobody ever told me her story but there it was all around me in fragments that fitted together like the bits of a mosaic. In almost every room was a reminder of Great-Grandfather Liszt—we knew very well what he looked like, what his temperament was and, above all, how he interpreted this passage or that. Up high on the library wall hung the portrait of Cosima's mother, the Countess d'Agoult—we children pronounced her name "ragout" because the D didn't sound familiar to our ears. Often I stared at the romantic Frenchwoman who believed that Liszt would be content to live and compose in blissful solitude nurtured by her love. She was disillusioned when she realized that as a composer he was not a genius. When Liszt, starved for the appreciation that is the breath of life to a musician, shattered the idyll and returned to the adulation of the world, Madame d'Agoult established a salon in Paris where she became a brilliant but embittered writer.

Cosima spent a forlorn and constricted childhood. She was fifteen when she first met Wagner in Paris and heard him read his poem, "Siegfried's Death," later *Götterdämmerung*, to a circle of Liszt's friends. After a few years she and her sister Blandine were sent to Berlin to Madame von Bülow, the mother of Liszt's pupil and Wagner's best friend Hans, a brilliant pianist and later the most celebrated conductor of his day.

Hans gave Cosima lessons and was so stirred by her talent that he tried to gain Liszt's consent for her appearance in public, but her father would have none of it. All about her waged the controversy over Wagner; the concert halls were battlegrounds on which critics and audience literally resorted to physical violence. Von Bülow was Wagner's most ardent champion and his concerts were riots. On the night Hans conducted the première of the overture of *Tannhäuser*, the booing, whistling and stamping so harassed the young conductor, who was always a bundle of nerves, that he collapsed on the podium. Liszt, who was in the audience, walked Hans through the streets for hours. At home Madame von Bülow and Blandine finally went to bed, but Cosima waited until almost dawn in the cold drawing room, haunted with inexpressible fears.

At last, as the night was graying outside the windows, Liszt brought home the spent and tortured conductor. He turned to Cosima for solace and she, moved by pity and generosity, promised to marry him, believing she could comfort and protect him. The following year Cosima and Hans were married, but not the wisest love could bring harmony to his erratic, unhappy temperament. Long after, Cosima confessed to Daniela that during the first year of their marriage she often thought of suicide.

At that time Cosima and von Bülow spent their summer vacations in Zürich to be near Wagner. Hans made the piano arrangements of Wagner's music dramas and was of great help to the man whom he considered master. Later on, when Wagner was called to Munich by King Ludwig II of Bavaria, he arranged that von Bülow be offered the position of conductor at the opera. Von Bülow, eager to work with his friend, dispatched Cosima to Munich with the two children, Daniela and Blandine, and followed later.

When the cabal against Wagner forced him to leave Munich, Cosima realized that she loved him above everything. He and his work became her supreme effort, her mission in life. She followed him to Lucerne. In Tribschen, the rambling villa on the lake that was immortalized by their idyll, she lived with him and her young daughters. For five years she entertained his guests, bore his children and held herself proudly above scandal until von Bülow gave her the divorce that freed her to marry Wagner in 1870.

Cosima was magnificent, but as I sat by Grandmother upstairs and looked at that proud, blind face behind which dwelt so many secrets, I wondered how she felt toward Hans von Bülow who had loved and needed her and tried so hard to be less difficult. That she did carry this burden on her conscience for more than sixty years, I know, for on her deathbed she addressed to von Bülow her last word, "forgive."

CHAPTER V

PROCESSIONAL

FESTIVALS, operas, concerts, trips to Nuremberg, Dresden, Stuttgart, Emma marshaling Wieland and me, trying to keep our faces clean and our excitement within bounds; it was a magical childhood. The highest moment of them all, the episode that charged my eight-year-old heart with an almost unbearable load of embarrassed pride, happened in Weimar in 1926, the summer between the festival seasons at Bayreuth. Alexander Spring, the stage director of the Weimar opera, was an old friend and pupil of Father's. He had come to Bayreuth from Stuttgart after he was discharged from the Army and became assistant stage director. We often saw him at Wahnfried, very tall and thin and military, a monocle clamped firmly in his eye even when he wasn't entirely sober. This summer Spring organized a Siegfried Wagner festival at Weimar.

Mother and Father went early and stayed at the hotel where the Wagner devotees gathered. We were taken later by Emma and permitted to stay in a pension around the corner. It was like the happy times before the war, Father said—the holiday air about the hotel; the gathering of Peter and Margarete Passmann, Dr. Vering, Stassen and the others; the company of music lovers who in the spacious days before 1914 traveled with Father from city to city for his concerts or the premières of his operas, meeting at luncheon, tea, gay dinners after the performances, taking excursions together, making Father's tours a light-hearted musical processional.

The group had never abandoned this custom but its members were older now, and poorer. Some of them scraped up the pennies to make the trips, but these weeks at Weimar they seemed to have recaptured the old enchantment. Through their eyes I caught a glimpse of the gracious Germany in which they had lived before the war.

Peter Passmann was my favorite, the one who looked like Siegfried and couldn't sing a note. In the old days he was wealthy; he owned the Eden Hotel in Berlin as well as large lumber interests. He still had a careless air of magnificence, a fresh and cheeky good humor that nothing could dampen. In contrast, his wife, Margarete, was tiny, exquisite and very feminine. She viewed Peter's escapades with tolerance for, whatever his adventures, he always came back. She was continually doing pleasant things for Wieland and me, inviting us to tea, giving us treats in the sweetshops on the square. So was her sister, a gay little old lady even smaller than Margarete.

We also looked upon Dr. Vering as a likely prospect for treats although we weren't on quite such an intimate footing with this bald, courtly, very precise old bachelor who blushed behind his pince-nez at the very mention of a, woman. Dr. Vering translated Plato and gave delightful parties; otherwise he was something of a mystery. Nobody knew what his business was until Mother and Father called upon him in Hamburg one day and saw his study desk covered with maps of real estate developments.

Franz Stassen, who before the war had been one of the most successful painters and illustrators in Germany, was Father's best friend and practically a member of the family. He knew Wagner and Göthe and Schopenhauer by heart and also an inexhaustible supply of jokes. Franz was my godfather and I loved the big fellow with the immense nose and the heavy features topped by a gray mane that made him look like a lion. He was poor in those days but happy, and somehow he always managed to follow Father on all of these expeditions.

Then there were Father's three devotees—Margarete Strauss, Rosa Eidam and Marianne Lange. Wherever he went women clustered around him, attracted by the warmhearted simplicity and charm that made him the most widely loved person I have ever known. Men and women alike were drawn to him, became his devoted companions and friends. Margarete Strauss came from Magdeburg. Tall, charming, still beautiful, she looked a queen of society as, indeed, she was. For many years she had been president of the Richard Wagner clubs of Germany which financed student tickets for the festivals at Bayreuth. Wieland and I looked upon Marianne Lange with more curiosity than warmth, wondering why her husband, a very proper Prussian judge, had once, in the absence of any justification, challenged Father to a duel over this fat reddish blonde, who to our critical eyes was far from beautiful. Rosa Eidam we considered an oddity. We enjoyed the legend that she wanted to marry Father and laughed at the idea of such a mother. This withered, red-nosed, threadbare old woman who wrote poetry and looked like a shrunken mushroom, had followed Father for years, staying at cheap little pensions, living on biscuits and coffee. In the old days when the parties after the performances were both glittering and costly, it had been Father's task to persuade her gently that she needed a long night's rest. Now he quietly managed to see that she had the means to make the pilgrimages. Later Mother inherited Rosa and found a place for her in a good old ladies' home in Bayreuth.

These friends, Spring and the numberless others who gathered for the festival, the musicians, the singers, the visiting conductors, collected in little parties for luncheon, dinners and excursions. Wieland and I, feeling very grown-up, stayed for the parties after the performances. And we didn't miss an excursion. We visited the houses of Göthe, Great-Grandfather Liszt, and Wieland the poet; we rode up the Wartburg on donkeys; we stuffed ourselves with cakes and bonbons and tea. In the mornings we collected in the museum, a convenient meeting place, sometimes Peter and Stassen, whoever was about before luncheon, often only Father and Mother meeting Emma with us in hand.

My contribution to the gaiety of the Weimar party was quite unintentional. Like Wieland who had been Hitler's darling ever since the Führer's first visit to Wahnfried, I wrote occasional letters to Wolf (the name by which Hitler was known to his intimates). What my idea of a newsy letter was, I cannot imagine, but when I overheard Mother reading one of my dispatches to a crowd of friends at tea and saw them convulsed with laughter, I decided that Wieland could have the exclusive privilege of the correspondence.

The experience that was one of the most exciting moments of my childhood happened at a particularly good performance of *Das Sternengebot*. At the last curtain a crowd of students who were in the audience, mobbed my father in his box, lifted him on their shoulders and carried him through the foyer into the street. Poor Father was crimson with embarrassment. I followed, glorying in their cheers, fairly bursting with pride but trying to mask my emotions behind a face which, I hoped, looked grown-up, and, above all, blasé.

Second to the festival which we remembered none the less happily because Father and his friends had to pay the deficit, was the excitement of watching the new additions to the Festspielhaus.

Father was building a four-story addition at the sides and back of the Festspielhaus, space for the office which had been in the city, a large ballet rehearsing room, new spacious dressing rooms and more space for the wardrobes and fitting rooms. We played about the new high closets, watched the painters label them with the names of the dramas and sniffed the naphthalene on the costumes that were moved in. The stage, which was already as deep as the parquet, was further enlarged. Father designed it to be used in three sections—the real stage, the center stage for greater depth, and for the last act of *Die Meistersinger* the entire stage on which he could use a chorus of several hundred.

When there was nothing that needed his attention at the Festspielhaus, Father worked on his new opera. He had already completed the libretto and every morning after breakfast he went over to his bachelor house to get on with the score. Here it was understood he was never to be disturbed, but when the maid took a glass of milk to him at ten o'clock I often slipped in behind her and hid under one of the pianos. Of the three in his study the hardest to reach and perhaps for that very reason my favorite, was the one that had belonged to Liszt. It stood in the back of the long room that was built on two levels with the far end several steps higher than the front, and from under it I could watch Father at work.

This building, especially this room, was Father's retreat from the family, the children, business, everything. In it were the pieces of comfortable furniture he •liked, his desk, the couch on which he took a nap after luncheon, and about him were the things he loved, the odds and ends he had collected, his books, his scores. The walls were covered with oils, pencil drawings, etchings—he was very fond of etchings. In one corner were framed programs of the premières of his operas. Many of the etchings were views of Roman streets, sketches of temples, ruins, details of ancient buildings. When he was a boy Father had intended to be an architect and drew sketchbooks full of plans for a dream city that he called "Wankel." Later he actually studied architecture for several terms at the universities of Berlin and Karlsruhe. Sitting cross-legged under Liszt's piano I used to listen to him working out a theme and wonder what made him change his mind, and what had made him suddenly, when he was touring the Orient, cable Cosima that he had decided to give up architecture and study music.

If Father had been an architect instead of coming home to study composition with Humperdinck in Frankfurt, I wondered what he would have built. It was fun to speculate. •Young as I was, I somehow knew that he was hampered by the greatness of his father. He was too modest, too deeply devoted to Wagner's works to achieve fame for himself as a composer, yet he was great in his own right. He had a gift entirely unlike that of his father. His was not expressed in broad dramas, but as a poet, a lyricist, and he had a voice that was outstandingly pure and fine.

Now I know that he was the greatest stage director of his time. Only those who came to Bayreuth year after year realized what he achieved in training several generations of Wagnerian singers who attained world renown. From the moment in 1906 when he took over the management of the Festivals from Cosima who had carried them for twenty-two years of superhuman effort, he subordinated himself to the works of his father. Who can say whether he was happier? Certainly not the little girl who sat under the piano waiting for him to come to luncheon.

The stems and pods of the roses in the garden began to turn red. Old Hoffmann puttered about with his wheelbarrow, carrying mulch and picking up fallen leaves; it was time for school. This year my teacher, the same pleasant man who had an interest in history, thought of an innovation which seemed innocent enough but completely wrecked the harmony of his class. Believing that his children should know something about Wagner who gave the little city its chief claim to immortality, he invited Daniela to give us a series of lectures, one on each of the music dramas. My aunt liked the idea and took pains to adapt the stories to her young audience, giving them a fairy-tale-like quality that delighted the children. After the story period our teacher asked us to illustrate the dramas. These drawings which were given to Daniela brought roars of laughter from many a famous artist and conductor.

Unhappily for Daniela, I knew the dramas practically by heart. When she returned to the original saga or expurgated the Wagnerian version for the ears of her young audience, I, too young to realize her purpose, protested violently. My spellbound classmates were further entertained by hot arguments between us. Daniela appealed to Father to keep me quiet during the lectures, but he was delighted with my stand and refused to support her. Thus encouraged, I stuck to my point and fought over every deviation from the Wagner script. Soon I had a camp of eager followers who absorbed my corrections and stuck to my version when we were asked to retell the stories at the beginning of the following session. Daniela

40

scowled while I sat by and listened with a triumphant grin on my face.

As Daniela grew more and more irritated she took it out on me at home. She even went so far as to take back her Christmas present which, this year, was a dozen handkerchiefs. Every time I argued with her in class she took away a handkerchief. Had I been dependent upon her gift for this polite accessory, I would have been doomed to a season of unladylike sniffles.

Except for my skirmishes with Daniela my affairs went smoothly that winter, no serious clashes with Mother, no mishaps. Every bright day I played football with the boys and when it stormed played theater in our nursery upstairs. Among our toys was a large model theater as wide as a good-sized table top, with complete stage settings for the Wagner dramas and little painted wooden characters. The dolls weren't puppets and didn't move their arms and legs, but they were attached to a wire with a loop for the finger and could be moved about to fit the action. Many an afternoon we gave a performance of *Rheingold* or *Götterdämmerung* and gathered all of our playmates for an audience.

Then there were the afternoons in Cosima's room. Although Grandmother was not visibly growing frailer she rested for longer periods on the enormous couch, and the aunts were very careful that we shouldn't tire her. Everybody was watchful to avoid the mention of anniversaries or subjects that were painful to her. One day as I was sitting by her on the couch, telling her about my affairs at school, I felt that her attention had wandered. Presently she interrupted me to call Daniela.

My aunt who was reading by the window, dropped her book and came over to the couch.

"Daniela," asked Grandmother when she felt her daughter's hand on her shoulder, "how old am I?"

Daniela hesitated, looking anxiously at the old lady, but

41

there was no help for it; her mother was waiting for an answer.

"Ninety years old, Mama."

We both held our breath, wondering how Grandmother would take the news. Age was a subject that hadn't been mentioned for years and years.

Cosima lifted her blind eyes toward us and laughed.

"Am I, really!" she said.

The winter after Houston Stewart Chamberlain's death, Daniela started to visit Eva and finally took her meals with her sister. The aging writer had been paralyzed for a long time prior to his death. He left behind him a claim to immortality as the "prophet of the Third Reich." Hitler when he was a very young man read a copy of *Grundlagen des 19. Jahrhunderts* and was so impressed with Chamberlain's use of the word "Aryan" in a restricted racial sense that he built upon it his preposterous concept of racial purity. On the day he paid us his first visit in the garden at Wahnfried, Hitler had made a pilgrimage to the house across the street. I often wish I had seen that meeting between the young, awkward, hesitant but demon-driven master of the Third Reich and the sick old prophet who couldn't have dreamed what his words had spawned.

Another season and again it was time for the 1927 festival. On the hill we children dashed about, shooing people whom we disliked from the benches at the side of the Festspielhaus that were marked FOR PERFORMERS ONLY. We visited Hugo Rüdel, the chorus director, in the apartment behind the chorus rehearsing room, "Rüdelheim" it was called. He could step directly from his living room into the hall for the morning rehearsal. Rüdel was a kindly old owl; he was the most famous choral director in Germany, an institution both at the Berlin state opera and Bayreuth.

After the week of the general rehearsal Bayreuth came to life again; the streets, the churches, the palaces and our front garden were crowded with foreigners on a holiday.

42

From the open windows up and down the street floated the leitmotif of the drama that was to be performed in the afternoon. Music lovers were reading their scores—every piano in Bayreuth was rented for the season.

Guests and parties, a pageant of famous visitors patting us on the head, commenting upon our resemblance to this one and that—we loved the excitement. But to the older members of the family and the servants this was also a time of stress, frayed nerves and short tempers. We kept out of Emma's way as much as possible and also avoided the aunts. Usually Daniela and Eva celebrated the middle of the festival with an emotional explosion, quarrels and recriminations against Mother and Father for one thing or another. This year, I remember, the tempest burst early, at the end of July. The thunder rumbled about Father's unprotected head but nothing could ruffle his good humor.

"My dears," he protested mildly, "you're out of season. It isn't August yet."

Another member of the family who didn't like the hubbub was Straubele, our new Schnauzer which Mother had given to Father for his birthday. The dog was devoted to us; we could maul him or chase him, but he didn't like strangers, and we had to keep a careful watch on him while Wahnfried was full of guests.

The only stranger Straubele ever admitted to his immediate friendship was Hitler. The first time Wolf visited us after Straubele came, the dog trotted up to him immediately and nuzzled his hand. He never left Hitler's side while the Führer remained. In this respect the dog was like all the others that followed him, big wild fellows who never went near anyone but the family. Immediately they made friends with Hitler and so did children. He drew them all quite effortlessly with his hypnotic power.

In those days Hitler had replaced the Bavarian outfit with a dark cheap-looking blue suit, the famous trench coat, and always a different hat to change his appearance and keep him from being recognized on his journeys. He

43

never wore gloves but carried a dog whip in his hand. The whip, trench coat and his Mercedes—these were his trademarks in the interval between the *Putsch* and 1933. He told us that the whip was the only weapon he carried, but we children had not forgotten the tiny pistol. Actually the whip with which he was always photographed was meant to melt the hearts of the sentimental German people who were touched by the dauntless little man, facing certain death at the hands of heavily armed Communists, armed with nothing but a dog whip.

Straubele, Wieland, Wolfi, Verena, I, we all liked Wolf because we loved to listen to the stories of his adventures while touring Germany, especially the one about the pitch-black night on which Maurice drove his car into a dangerous ditch, and the ensuing trouble in getting the car out of it. His life was fascinating to us, because it was so completely unlike ours—it all had a story-book quality, his dropping in on us late at night, his being constantly threatened by someone.

CHAPTER VI

FATHER NEEDS ME

THE first three years of school were the pleasant years, guided by a sympathetic teacher, enlivened by the tilts with Daniela; but in the fourth grade my luck changed. There I encountered a class master who was a sadist in a cautious way. He was considerate enough of the children from well-to-do families, those whose parents were "somebody," but indulged himself by torturing the poorest and most defenseless pupils who were perhaps below the average in intelligence but trying desperately to keep up. Day after day I watched him goading these poor children and punishing them when they could not answer his tricky questions. When I could endure it no longer I challenged him.

"It's outrageous to take your spite out on these children who can't defend themselves. It's a disgrace and an injustice. Why don't you ever take it out on me? You know you wouldn't dare touch a Wagner."

My outburst modified the man's behavior but made life difficult for me. Twisted by repetition, my words became the phrase, "One doesn't beat a Wagner," and were quoted to me whenever any member of the family wanted to be particularly disagreeable and remind me of my hopeless arrogance.

To make matters worse I learned when I was well along in the fourth grade that I should have skipped it and entered the upper school immediately. The instructors were sure that I could have passed the entrance examinations with no trouble, but they neglected to tell my parents until it was too late by several months. Perhaps they wanted to spare Wieland's pride by keeping his younger sister from joining his class, or again they may have simply forgotten. In any case the omission had a disastrous effect on my grades. Until then they had been the pride of the family—I had stood highest in my class—but for the rest of the year, smarting with injustice both to myself and to my luckless playmates, I devoted less time to my studies and more to annoying the master.

Life at home became proportionately difficult. The school authorities talked to Mother, and Mother, bewildered by my attitude, punished me at home. She tried everything—sending me to bed with a supper of bread and water, depriving me of my treasures, but all she achieved was a state of sullen hostility between us.

By the time I entered the upper school in the spring of 1928, I was ten years old and Mother's problem child. The aunts who automatically opposed Mother and championed me, the cousins, the family friends who belonged to the old guard and considered Mother an outsider, took a lively and sympathetic interest in my affairs, which, in turn, wounded Mother who resented their lack of interest in her other children. It would have been less than human of me to ignore the advantages the situation offered. In no time I was an uncontrollable rowdy. I played football with the boys, climbed trees, dashed about with Verena (Nickel, we called her) on the handlebars and Wolfi on the back wheel of the bicycle, paying attention to everything except my homework.

Poor Father, he must have suffered from these warring personalities around him. Although he singled me out as his companion, kept me under his wing as much as possible, he never once entered the battle or lost his sunny good humor. On the surface the family life flowed along smoothly because one could not live in disharmony with Father. The family celebrations, Christmas, birthdays followed each other with the traditional fun, the presents, the ceremonies, the pleasant little surprises.

For Christmas and her birthday Father always prepared elaborate jokes for Mother, usually exploring the ridiculous aspects of the Nazi party which furnished the happiest sort of material for such nonsense. Sometimes it was a poem or a painting or a whole stage setting worked out with meticulous detail. One Christmas Father built a medicine chest and filled it with bottles labeled with the queer names of the Nazi party members in Bayreuth (as it happened, most of them did have strange and amusing names). Accompanying the chest was a poem telling what ills each bottle was supposed to cure. This joke was intended to tease Daniela as well as Mother; my aunt was a fanatical homeopath and was always carrying about a box filled with at least a hundred different bottles of pills.

Another time Father built a cave with a wolf and a badger in it. "The wolf in the badger's cave," he named it. This was to represent Hitler and his landlady in Munich

46

who was named Mrs. Dachs, meaning badger. It would have been even funnier a little later, for Mrs. Dachs became mentally unbalanced and behaved in a fantastic manner. For a long time Hitler was the only one who could soothe her. In his presence she was still somewhat normal until one day she attacked him with an ax. Wolf ran for his life and hastily changed his living quarters.

Nothing that would amuse or entertain us was too much trouble for Father. He wanted to give us a bulwark of happy memories and he succeeded. For his own birthday we schemed and planned weeks in advance. He sometimes celebrated it too by surprises for us. On his sixtieth birthday in the spring of 1929 we and the guests at the birthday dinner found at our plates the printed librettos of his new opera, *Das Flüchlein das Jeder Mitbekam* ("The little curse that everybody bears"). Shooting through my pride and delight was the suspicion that I might be his little curse. Filled with good resolutions, I flung my arms around Father's neck and gave him a mighty hug. He straightened my hair and smiled, and I knew he understood.

But for all my good resolutions the second year of the upper school was worse than the first. The doctrine of revenge was hammered into us day after day with Teutonic fervor. By every teacher, whatever his subject, we were bombarded with the "truth" about Versailles, the enormity of the "war-guilt lie," the "fact" that Germany never was defeated. These were dinned into us as incontrovertible facts, no questions, no explanations. Clemenceau was presented to us as the great criminal, the blackest villain the world had ever known.

Perhaps I might have been more easily convinced if my teachers had known how to pronounce "Clemenceau," but, contrary as I was, it occurred to me that if they were wrong in their pronunciation they might be in error as to their facts. So I found a new cause. Trying to inform myself on both sides of the war-guilt matter I asked question after obstinate question. All I achieved was the satisfaction of annoying my teachers who answered me with such impatient remarks as "You must believe it," or "You must not doubt our word," which, indeed, I did and said so.

Again I was in open rebellion. My sessions at school became one long battle. The tension grew.

As always in Germany I was tormented by the feeling that I was being choked by a rope which was being tightened at both ends. The teachers complained; Mother was at the end of her wits. She took me out of the school and for punishment that summer sent me to a camp where I was so unhappy that I persuaded her and Father to let me come home.

She and Father took me with them on a tour of the Bavarian and Tyrolean Alps, just the three of us; the other children were with friends at Lake Constance. Perhaps this was Father's idea, I never knew, but it was one of the happiest intervals of my eleven years. Mother did not try to discipline me, and I spent long, blissful days tramping along mountain trails beside Father, an alpine stick in my hand. Father never tried to make record climbs—he ambled along, stopping to admire a patch of moss or a cluster of alpine flowers, talking to everyone he met along the way. In the afternoon we returned to our hotel or reached some mountain inn for tea on a veranda overhanging a gorge or looking across a high alpine valley to distant layers of mountains. I sat there beside Father blissfully eating bread and jam, listening to the buzz of conversation—wherever he was people gathered —and wishing this summer would go on forever.

But it ended; soon I was back in school fighting the same old skirmishes. This year I had a new cross—Latin. When we were assigned two or three pages of irregular verbs to learn by heart each day, I went on strike and devoted myself entirely to thinking up schemes to annoy my teachers. Soon all the pupils were taking sides, the boys supporting me, the girls betraying me. The school authorities threatened me with expulsion. Mother was compelled to act; she decided to take me out of the Latin School and send me to the girls' *lycée*, but since in this school English was required instead of Latin she, or was it my father, suggested that I go to school in England for a term to catch up with my class.

The English school was a thrilling idea; what girl wouldn't have been eager to go, but secretly I began to be homesick in advance for Father. I clung to him as though I were his shadow. In the evening when Mother read aloud (Father had inherited Cosima's eyes that were painfully affected by light, and never read or worked by electricity) I sat quietly near him, content to watch his face. Sometimes he let me stay in the bachelor house while he worked or wrote letters. One morning he translated for me the postscript on a letter that he was writing to Toscanini. "Excuse my Italian; I learned it from cooks and housemaids." Toscanini was an old friend of Father's and was coming to Bayreuth to conduct at next summer's festival.

"I must teach you a greeting for him," Father said. "Repeat after me, *Caro Maestro, siamo felici di salutarla a Bayreuth.*"

"*Caro Maestro, siamo felici di salutarla,*" I repeated several times to get the accent exactly right. Father was proud of my ear. Neither Mother nor Wieland would try to speak Italian. Mother read it but she limited herself to an amusing collection of swear words.

Suddenly my voice choked. "I'm going to miss you terribly," I mumbled.

"You'll be coming back for the festival. You know I couldn't get along without you."

Christmas came and went. My brothers and Nickel regarded me as something of a personage and included me in their most secret enterprises. Wolfi let me help him with the new electrical contraptions he was building in his basement shop. It was not unusual in those days for all the lights to go off suddenly because Wolfi had blown a fuse. Nickel tagged around after me and I promised her my toy printing press.

At the end of January we finally set out. I went upstairs to Cosima's room to kiss Grandmother good-by. She passed her fingers over my face lightly as though she wanted to be sure to remember me, and I knew suddenly that this was good-by for the last time—I would never see her again.

Eva who was with her turned her face away and her eyes filled with tears. But Cosima was not sad; she smiled at me and the smile lit up the parchment-thin whiteness of her face as though it were a lantern.

For three days Father, Mother and I stayed in a fairy-tale suite in the Mayfair Hotel in London where we were guests of the Columbia Phonograph Company for which Father had begun to record some of the Bayreuth performances several years earlier. Of a morning Father showed me London which he knew as well as he knew Bayreuth—the interesting buildings, the walks in the parks and the mellow old squares with a history. Mother let me attend the luncheons, the tea parties and dinners, all the social affairs which didn't interfere with Father's business. My head was in a whirl with so much excitement, so much happiness.

Then it was time for Father to fulfill his concert engagements in the south. At noon on a day early in February I kissed him good-by in front of the Mayfair Hotel. The taxi started; I waved, he waved. We were both laughing, but my heart constricted with that old childish foreboding which seized me every time he left for a concert tour. Maybe he would never come back. This time the dread was so strong that it was almost a physical pain.

Mother and I set out for Brighouse in Yorkshire where I was to enter a girls' school conducted by an old friend of mother's who had been her English teacher in a girls' school near Berlin. Miss Scott—she was Irish,. not much older than Mother and must have been a very attractive girl when she began her friendship with mother by slap-

50

ping her naughty face—was very kind to me. She took
me into her house which was a minute's walk from the
school and made me feel wanted. In no time I was speaking English. I liked the teachers and the girls. They liked
me; there were no problems; I was suddenly a normal,
happy child. The only cloud in my sky was an occasional
anxious dream, a foreboding that some disaster would
call me home.

In April Cosima died. Her death did not make me too
unhappy for she belonged to me in such a permanent sort
of way, she was so much a part of the indestructible
memories of my childhood that she slipped naturally
from the present into the vivid and enduring past. But
her death increased the dread that something terrible
would make me return to Germany.

I was so happy at Brighouse, so fearful lest it wouldn't
last that I bombarded my parents with letters begging
them to let me stay there and finish school instead of
forcing me into another German institution. In reply I
received a long letter which was typed by Mother but
dictated by Father; I could tell by the wording and the
corrections which were in his handwriting. In it Father
said that he was nearly sixty-one and missed me terribly;
no one knew how long we would belong to each other.
Then, too, there were my brothers and sisters—I should
not risk an estrangement from them. Above all my father
wanted me at home for I would soon be able to assist him
in Bayreuth and accompany him on his tours. So there was
no alternative—I must return home. Again Father said
how miserably lonely he was for me.

This letter which should have filled me with loving
pride only increased my anxiety. No date was set for my
return but every day I lived in fear. Spring lengthened into
summer without diminishing my forebodings. Finally, on
an evening in late July a telegram came for Miss Scott who
was at a teachers' meeting in the school. I took it over to

51

her, knowing that it was my fate I carried in the little yellow envelope.

That evening Miss Scott said nothing but was particularly kind to me. In the morning, a Saturday, she told me that my father was very ill. The next day she took me up to London and handed me over to Auntie Edie, a distant relation of Mother's, a dim little spinster whom I remembered from her two earlier visits to Bayreuth for the festivals.

We arrived in Bayreuth at noon. Mother did not meet me at the station but I found Maria-Sofia, the wife of my Italian cousin Manfredi. She took my hand and said quietly that mother was at the hospital. Kind Maria-Sofia, I had always loved her. Wahnfried was a pandemonium, full of the family, and guests assembled for the festival. One of the maids took me upstairs to Cosima's room which had been done over for Nickel and me. The boys had been moved into the nursery and Mother and Father had taken over our enormous old dormitory. I asked the maid where Wieland and Wolfi and Nickel and Emma were. She kept saying, "I can't understand you. For heaven's sake, speak German," but I managed to learn that they had not been recalled from their vacation.

Everything was strange. Frightened and confused, I went downstairs to the music room where my French cousin, Blandine, was chatting with a group of friends. We went in to luncheon. It was a little difficult; Auntie Edie spoke nothing but English; my Italian cousins and Blandine, who were at home in all four languages, kept changing from one to the other; several friends who spoke nothing but German were annoyed; and Manfredi, who was slightly deaf, had difficulty in keeping up with it all.

I did my best as hostess but my heart kept thumping so loudly that I thought everyone must have heard it. After luncheon I tore to the hospital. Mother threw her arms around me.

"I'm so glad you've come, Mausi." She leaned on my

52

shoulder and burst into tears. Never had we been so close to each other. When she was a little quieter she told me what had happened. Father had an embolism of the heart. The festival had been trying—an unusual amount of bickering between the principals and one of the conductors. After the general rehearsal of *Götterdämmerung* he had collapsed. She had sent for me, wanting me there if he asked for me. Piteously she was staking her last hope on the idea that a sudden shock of joy on seeing me might give him a turn for the better.

But the doctors were adamant; they insisted that a sudden shock might make his condition worse. Day after day I tiptoed past his room, waiting, hoping that he might rally and ask for me, hoping that they might let me see him anyway. But they never did. They knew that he was beyond aid yet never told him that I had come home, never gave him the happiness of knowing that I was by his side. Neither Mother nor I ever forgave them.

The days seemed endless, hanging in space, separated by short, uneasy blobs of darkness. I dressed, ate, went to the hospital, to the performances, waited, always waited, each hour as weary as the last and filled with that terrible anticipation. Mother I saw only at the hospital where she stayed day and night with Father. Finally it happened and I wasn't there. On August the fourth when I returned to Wahnfried at about six o'clock, the maid opened the front door and I saw that the place was deserted. Her lids were red and the corner of her apron was damp and crumpled from dabbing her eyes.

"Your father is dead," she told me, "and you are to go over to your Aunt Eva's."

I closed the door softly and started down the drive. Straubele and his new playmate, Stritzi, came from the back garden gloomily, with their tails between their legs, and rubbed against my side.

"Go back," I told them, and watched them sidle toward the gardener's house, looking for comfort.

For a moment I waited to get command of myself, then crossed the street and entered Eva's drawing room. She was there alone so I went over and slipped my arm through hers. A moment later the door opened; a slight man with deep, gentle eyes and fine sensitive face took Eva in his arms, then me, the child whom he did not know.

This was my first meeting with the man who thereafter came nearer than any other to taking my father's place. Toscanini!

CHAPTER VII

WAR ON THE PODIUM

BY EIGHT o'clock on the morning after Father's death Mother was at his office in the Festspielhaus, taking over the work at his desk. Her other duties, and they were none the less duties because they were of a lighter social nature, had to be ignored or, when it was possible, turned over to one of us. Now there was no time for cosseting Karl Muck who had been Mother's special charge ever since she had come to Wahnfried. Muck was a tradition at the Festspielhaus; he went back to the time of Cosima who had engaged him in 1900, and for thirty years he had been one of the most famous of the conductors at the festivals. But he was not particularly loved—everybody feared his acid tongue, his witty, vinegary remarks, so quotable that they were repeated everywhere.

Dr. Muck didn't like Father who left him to Mother's gentle devices. During the festival season she drove Father to his office every morning at eight o'clock and then went over to the Küffner villa to entertain Muck at breakfast. During the performances at which he conducted she never

54

dared to be absent during the intermission at which he consumed a pound of caviar—Mother's caviar at seventy marks a pound.

During the general rehearsal Muck had made himself particularly difficult, puffing continually at his special cigarettes that were as strong as cigars, drinking vast quantities of black mocha, working himself into a vile mood because Toscanini was to conduct *Tristan* and *Tannhäuser*. All those years he had managed to prevent Father from engaging Toscanini. Mother told me that the discord undoubtedly aggravated the condition of Father's heart.

Mother's appearance in Father's office at the Festspielhaus, which no doubt seemed to her the natural and inevitable thing to do, was actually a declaration of war against the faction of old devotees who had been patrons of the festival for many years, some of them as far back as Cosima's time. Led by Daniela and, to a lesser degree, Eva, they organized almost overnight to control the festivals and "preserve the Wagner tradition." Before Father was buried the mayor of Bayreuth and the city fathers urged Mother to turn over Wahnfried to the city for a Wagner museum. They had even gone so far as to find a house for her. Overnight Mother found herself transformed from Siegfried Wagner's petted, courted young wife to an outsider, resented by the old guard who felt that they alone knew the true spirit of the festivals.

Then for the first time Mother felt a kinship to Cosima and understood what she had endured when she undertook to carry on the festivals after Wagner's death. Then Cosima was the foreigner, "that Frenchwoman who never engaged German singers." now it was Mother, "that Englishwoman who would never know how to carry on the Wagnerian tradition."

The city was supposed to take charge of Father's funeral. Like all the Wagners he was an *Ehrenbürger*, an honorary citizen—a distinction which was attested by a handsome parchment scroll and entitled the holder to a funeral at

55

the city's expense. However, in this instance (were the city fathers annoyed because Mother refused to let them have Wahnfried?) the bills all came to Mother and she paid them without comment.

We did not go to the cemetery. Wieland, Wolfi and Verena who had returned the evening before, Mother and I, came directly home to Wahnfried from the funeral service at the church. We found the house locked. All the servants had gone to the burial, so we waited in the little portico of the bachelor house. Stritzi and Straubele bounded toward us, looking for Father, but sensed our unhappiness and lay down quietly at our feet. Absently I pulled Stritzi's ear. In the grief that encased us all like an invisible wall, I was apart, miserably lonely, shut off from the others. From the time the other children returned Mother gathered them around her for comfort and I no longer mattered. I had no more reality for her than the air about us. That moment in which she had depended on me, loved me and felt me supporting her against the doctors, against everyone who would deny Father a last moment of happiness, was gone as though it had never been.

In spite of the storms and intrigues beneath the surface, the festival proceeded in a particularly exalted mood. Herbert Janssen whom Father had engaged to sing at Bayreuth for the first time, more than fulfilled his expectations. Janssen was such a perfect artist that neither Father nor Toscanini needed to coach him. Toscanini ran through the score with him once and said, "I won't need to see you again until we're on the stage." When Janssen substituted on short notice for our ailing Amfortas, Muck called from the orchestra, "That's the first Amfortas I've heard since Reichmann."

Muck himself was chastened by Father's death and made no difficulties; young Karl Elmendorff, one of Father's protégés, gave a good performance; Toscanini conducted magnificently. Both from an artistic and a box office standpoint it was the most successful of all the

56

festivals since the war, and the *Tannhäuser* which Toscanini conducted was considered the most brilliant production of Father's career.

I saw Toscanini often that summer at luncheon and
dinner and in the restaurant during intermissions. Without many words the Maestro managed to encourage me and
make me feel that he was upholding me with his sympathy.

When I wasn't at the Festspielhaus I was busy at Wahnfried looking after the guests. They came and went in
such a procession, so many famous names, so many na-
tionalities, that I rarely sorted them out until I looked
over the list of visitors which the butler compiled from
the cards that he had gathered at the door. He was a special
butler on duty for the festival. Every day until the performance started he stood at the door with his silver card
tray and ushered in the guests; and later in the afternoon
he rode about town on his bicycle dropping Mother's
cards. Venizelos I remember as a pleasant old gentleman
who liked to walk in the garden, and later I identified
Madame André Maurois as one of Blandine's friends who
was in the music room when I came home.

At last the festival was over and Bayreuth settled back
into a coma. But not Wahnfried. Now the committee of
the old guard came out into the open and accused Mother
of falsifying Father's will which left the Festspielhaus
and Wahnfried to his children equally, with Mother in
complete control until we were of age. They were wrong,
but in one respect Mother did try to alter it. She had
always centered most of her affection on Wieland and
wanted him to be sole heir. The relationship with the
aunts became more strained than ever. Daniela, who had
taken her meals with Eva since Chamberlain's death,
dominated her entirely and kept her away from Wahnfried as much as possible—they would have stayed away
altogether but they wanted to know what was going on.
They even stopped inviting us children to the weekly

57

luncheons which had been a custom ever since the death of Chamberlain.

In the autumn Mother entered me in the girls' *lycée*. She was restless and spent much of the time away from home, making trips to Zürich to her bank every week or so and to Berlin, engaging singers and musicians for the coming season. Every time she came home Stritzi and Straubele rushed upstairs to Father's dressing room where they had always found him cleaning up after a trip, and every time they came sadly back again down the stairs. It was several months before they stopped looking for him.

That autumn the dogs were the closest friends I had, especially Stritzi who was intelligent beyond most of her kind. She loved to sit on the chairs—both of them did— and chose unfailingly the best ones in the drawing room on which to lie in uneasy triumph, with their paws hanging over, until they heard Emma's step. Before she reached the door they were lying on the rug as innocent as a couple of whiskered cherubs. Stritzi liked especially to be with us at luncheon when she sat on a chair against the wall and followed the conversation with a knowing air.

During our November holiday Mother took us to Lake Constance where she had just bought a delightful house at Nussdorf on the Baden side. It sat at the point of a little peninsula that made a harbor almost at our door. For several years she and Father had been looking for a summer home. Father knew Italy and Switzerland much better than he did rural Germany until Mother began to drive him about the beautiful German countryside. During the last few summers in which he and Mother had explored, Mother had become so familiar with every house on the lake that she knew how many bedrooms and baths it had.

The one which she finally bought had belonged to a Jewish collector of Chinese art who was selling all of his German possessions and leaving the country. The walls were painted in Chinese colors or papered with oriental prints, so Mother occupied some of her restless energy remodeling and redecorating the place.

One day of that week end we went to Lucerne where for the first time I saw Tribschen, the house in which my father had been born. The city of Lucerne had bought the house to save it from demolition by a manufacturing company and planned to restore it as nearly as possible as it was in Wagner's day. The second floor was to be reserved for the Wagner family so the city officials had invited Mother to consult with them in the matter of the furnishings. It was an idyllic place, this big rambling old-fashioned Swiss villa looking out over the lake through a grove of poplars. There was an air of peace about it, and I understood Cosima's deep and silent affection. Mother appreciated the gracious gesture of the city but we never lived at Tribschen; early the next spring Daniela and Eva moved in and spent the rest of their summers there. We didn't mind. We had our own place on Lake Constance.

The holiday at the lake was the last tranquil period we were to know that season. Scarcely had we returned from our Christmas holiday in Switzerland, to which we had been sent with Emma for the skiing, when Lieselotte Schmidt dropped into our lives. Lieselotte was the daughter of two devout Wagnerians who had owned a wholesale tobacco business in Stuttgart. She came for a short visit in January to be with us while Mother was away on one of her trips, and stayed the rest of her life. At first we didn't actually dislike Lieselotte; she was a small, dark, attractive girl and an excellent pianist. It was pleasant enough to have her about to help with the homework or sit with us while we practiced.

Then, too, Lieselotte took our side in the matter of the tutors. Not long after Christmas Mother began to feel that we needed the influence of a stronghanded man so she looked about for one. The likeliest possibilities were

59

impoverished Prussian noblemen who were unfitted for any sort of work whatever. The first applicant came to tea and decided the position was not for him. The second stayed for one long, miserable month. He was tall, fortyish, affected riding boots and was rather good-looking in an arrogant sort of way, but as a tutor he was a complete loss. He knew less about our lessons than we did. At first Mother tried to strengthen his authority by insisting that he was right when he was wrong; consequently there was open war between us.

After the Prussians left we sighed with relief, but Lieselotte was beginning to be a more subtle problem for us. True, she intrigued against the tutors but only because she wanted the perquisites herself. By that time she had learned to type after a fashion and called herself Mother's secretary. She was an insinuating little creature, worming her way into Mother's life, trying to alienate her from her children. When Mother was away Lieselotte assumed her place, tried to sit in her chair at the table until I ousted her, and worked at Mother's desk. Furthermore, when Mother telephoned, Lieselotte always leaped to answer.

"Your mother called," was all she would ever say, believing she was keeping us in our place by refusing to tell us what Mother wanted.

One of the duties which Lieselotte assumed in Mother's absence was the making of the menus, but she never seemed to be able to think of more than seven menus, and we refused to have the same thing every Saturday or Sunday or Monday. Emma was momentarily appeased when we rebelled and took over ourselves; she hated Lieselotte as did all the servants, and was constantly threatening to leave. There were terrible rows between them. Several times I worked Mother up to the point of saying, "In that case Lieselotte must return home," but always at the crucial moment my brothers and sister deserted me because she was good about helping them with their lessons.

60

So the winter hitched along with quarrels and intrigues and lonesome stretches when Mother was away. Before there had always been Cosima upstairs in her sunny drawing room, ready to love us and listen to our childish affairs —she and the aunts who now came to Wahnfried very seldom.

When she was at home Mother didn't talk much about her difficulties, but we knew that she had a battle on her hands. Dr. Muck had deserted her; he refused to conduct at the 1931 festival because Toscanini had been engaged to return. Mother was looking for another conductor of prominence, but Muck was doing everything he could to make things unpleasant for her.

On one of her returns from Berlin Mother told us that she had engaged a new conductor, but she wouldn't tell us his name. He remained the mysterious Mr. X even when he came to Wahnfried and spent a night in the bachelor house. We children were permitted to meet him after dinner and speculated about him; but did not learn until shortly before the opening of the new festival that this tall, emaciated, middle-aged man with a long head perched on a longer pipestem neck was Wilhelm Furtwängler, today Germany's most famous conductor. Women swooned when he conducted and threw themselves into his arms with a fervor that made gossip wherever he went.

To me, however, the most momentous event of the spring was the birth of Stritzi's puppies, eight of them, her first litter. Wieland, Wolfi, Nickel and I each chose one for his own. On the advice of our elders they selected the strongest, healthiest looking ones, but I fell in love with the tiniest and determined to bring it up. I also assumed the care of Stritzi and on the advice of the vet, bottle-fed three of the pups with a real formula on which they flourished. But in spite of all my care, my tiny one never caught up with the others and several months later died of distemper. Her death filled me with despair which was all the more bitter because the cynics said "I told you so."

Well, I could meet cynicism with cynicism. After that I kept my feelings to myself.

Early in June the performers arrived for the rehearsals. Toscanini, who was without his family this season, was a guest in the bachelor house. Every morning he took his breakfast on the little glass-enclosed balcony which got the full sun and was so hot that Wieland named it "Toscanini's Turkish bath." But the Maestro loved the sun. He was one of the most pleasant guests we ever entertained, the maids adored him because he liked his meals and gave them no trouble. He kept his own car and chauffeur and never upset the household routine with demands for service.

Toscanini was amused by my candid remarks.

"You are so fonnee," he used to tell me between chuckles. On days when there were no rehearsals or performances we sometimes drove to inns up in the mountains for tea, visited the beauty spots of Franconia or just drove about in the pleasant summer afternoons.

Furtwängler was one of Mother's chief problems. She had contracted to furnish him with a saddle horse, a stable, a stableboy, a car and chauffeur, and she was a bit nervous about his relations with Toscanini. Then, too, she didn't know how the other artists would feel about Dr. Geissmar, Furtwängler's famous secretary who devoted herself to his publicity. It was true that Dr. Geissmar had made him the first artist in Germany to hold weekly press conferences and used her undoubted talent to build up his fame; but when I heard him conduct I knew that Furtwängler was a great artist and would have had an ardent following, press receptions or no press receptions. However, Geissmar was invaluable to him and there wasn't a conductor in Europe who didn't wish he had a secretary like her.

Actually this graying Jewish woman was not employed by Furtwängler, but was engaged by the Berlin Philharmonic Orchestra and during the sixteen years that she was associated with Furtwängler never received a cent from him; furthermore, she was well-to-do herself.

All these artists strengthened the vague purpose that was struggling inside me, trying to get to the surface, and quickened my consciousness of my responsibility not only then but for the future. It was one of my unspoken grievances against Mother that she did not try to make my brothers and sister conscious of their responsibility, and as soon as Nickel was old enough I determined to make her understand.

Furtwängler and Toscanini couldn't abide each other, and their dislike was fanned by the third personality that made the season of 1931 completely mad. Soon after the rehearsals began Heinz Tietjen whom Mother had engaged as artistic director for the next season, 1933, arrived at Bayreuth to look things over.

This small, dark little man with the thick spectacles was one of the most sinister and astonishing of all the creatures who scrambled to hold their power in the early, confused days of the Third Reich. He never appeared in public. Indeed if he had he was so insignificant looking that he wouldn't have been noticed. His fellow artists paraphrased the title of a book then popular in Germany, *Did Christ Ever Live?* and asked each other "Did Tietjen ever live?" In my opinion, his business abilities far outstripped his conductorship. At that time he was both artistic and business director of all the Prussian state theaters which included the all-important Kroll and Staatsoper in Berlin where he had his offices, and was the great power in those theaters.

Tietjen was half British and half German. He was born in Tangier and grew up in Constantinople, England, Africa, India and South America. In the first World War he was one of the thirty-five German intelligence officers sent to Turkey. Certainly he was a born diplomat and practiced his talent by surviving every change of government that threatened his position.

63

In no time at all Tietjen had Mother in his pocket and the entire staff of the festival by the ears. Furtwängler was his easy prey because the conductor was weak and indecisive; he listened to the advice of everybody, distrusted everybody including himself and fell a prey to every intrigue. Temperamentally he was an irritant to Mother who was a forthright person and couldn't understand people with devious personalities.

"He's like a sponge," she once said. "Whenever you try to get a firm hold of him, he can squeeze himself in a dozen different directions."

Tietjen fanned this dislike into guerrilla warfare by telling Mother Furtwängler's remarks about her and carrying Mother's comments to Furtwängler. Each had perfect confidence in Tietjen and considered him a true friend and adviser. Furtwängler who was always sulking, hesitant and difficult, became suspicious of Mother and convinced that she disliked him violently. As a consequence there was anything but a happy atmosphere about them.

In like manner Tietjen husbanded the dislike between Toscanini and Furtwängler, but in this instance he did not have so much luck because Toscanini thoroughly disliked him. However, in the long run the result was just the same because the relations among the three were worse than strained.

CHAPTER VIII

ANNIVERSARY

WITH a tempest threatening to break at any moment the general rehearsal progressed, the opening of the festival passed smoothly enough and we approached the fourth of August, 1931, the anniversary of Father's death.

64

Two memorial concerts were planned; one in the Festspiel-haus given by the artists and orchestra of the festival, another, a small morning affair, in a concert hall in the city. At the large concert in the evening each conductor was to take part.

Toscanini, who had chosen the Faust overture, was half mad with the pain of neuritis in his right arm, and had been conducting by supporting the arm with his other hand until he finally abandoned the right and used his left arm altogether. He demanded that there be no audi-ence at the morning rehearsal.

I was unable to be at the Festspielhaus that morning as I was to play a two-piano arrangement of the "Siegfried Idyll" at the morning concert with Karl Kittel, one of the coaches at the Festspielhaus. As I drove to the hall with Gilberto, another of my Italian cousins who was to play Father's flute concerto, the sultry heat sat like a load on our shoulders. It was an unpleasant day, full of forebod-ings, and I wished it were over.

Before we set out I had met our business manager, Albert Knittel, on the way to a conference with Mother and we had exchanged frozen "good mornings." There was something about the man's heavy pink face and oily man-ners that had made me distrust him from the minute Father brought him to the Festspielhaus four years earlier. He was wealthy, the owner of the Karlsruher *Tageblatt* and a large art printing house in the same city, but he found time to see a great deal of the family and was always entertaining us elaborately, especially in his summer home on Lake Constance.

With the approach of Father's sixtieth birthday Knittel was frequently at Wahnfried for he was a member of the executive committee that managed the *Tannhäuser Spende*, the fund which Mother and some of Father's friends had collected for a new *Tannhäuser* production as a present for Father's birthday. During the following years Knittel administered the fund singlehanded and refused to give an accounting to the other two members of the committee. He told Mother that he had speculated with the original sum of a hundred and twenty thousand marks and had increased it to seven hundred thousand. She was so impressed with his financial genius that after Father's death she made him her business manager. Everybody was touched when he would take no salary, saying that it was a great honor to contribute his services to Bayreuth.

While Father lived Knittel was pleasant enough to me but afterward discarded all pretense of liking me. Indeed, he was very pointed about it; on Christmas and birthdays when he sent my family lavish gifts he didn't send me so much as a good wish. So we were open enemies and I was proud of it. The only ray of comfort I got from the summer's turmoil was the knowledge that Knittel feared and distrusted Tietjen who was already trying to undermine his influence with Mother.

Knittel was only one of the gloomy subjects of my thoughts as we drove languidly to the concert hall. The auditorium was crowded with visitors to the festival, and the program went off smoothly enough. Gilberto played first. He stood too near the piano, so when I sat down to play my duet with Kittel I found the keys of the upper register swimming with saliva. Overwhelmed with thirteen-year-old embarrassment, I skittered around over the wet keys, not daring to swab them with my handkerchief.

When we returned I ran to the bachelor house to see if Toscanini had come home from the rehearsal at the Festspielhaus. Wahnfried was crowded with guests who had overflowed into the garden, but I made my way through them, thinking that Mother and Toscanini might be in Father's study. There they were and also Tietjen. The Maestro sat with his face to the wall and refused to utter a word. Mother was pleading with him, Tietjen was pleading, but he didn't even bother to shake his head. I gathered that the rehearsal had not been without an audience and he had walked out, refusing to conduct. The Maestro's heavy brows were drawn together and his eyes were smoldering. Tietjen circled around him, crooning in his soft voice, peering hopefully through his thick spectacles, but every word the little man said further enraged Toscanini. Finally Mother and Tietjen came wearily away leaving the Maestro staring at the wall. Mother said Alexander Spring would have to announce that Toscanini was ill and let the audience think what it would.

In spite of the absence of Toscanini the concert was memorable. Furtwängler outdid himself and the women in the audience fairly swooned with ecstasy; even Daniela was swept away by the warmth and color of his conducting and fought her way to the podium to congratulate him. Later, at supper, when he came down the stairs from the balcony, his head on top of the long neck darting this way and that, one could hear a sigh sweep over the place and a rustling as the women gathered about him, thick as bees at a honeycomb.

For me, however, the most vivid episode of that turbulent day happened in the morning. After breakfast Mother asked us children to wait in her study and as we dawdled along the hall, speculating about what she wanted, I had an unhappy feeling that she was going to spring something unpleasant on us.

My eyes ran about the gracious, feminine little room, lingered on the cherry desk with ebony inlay, Mother's armchair and her delicate sewing table, the etchings of the Colosseum and the Via Appia and the clocks, half a dozen of them—a friend had left us part of her collection. They were all familiar, reassuring. Wolfi's clock with its silly, round, Bavarian peasant face ticked away as it always had, its eyes turning right, turning left with the swing of the pendulum. Wolfi was looking at it as he sat in the window that opened on the rose beds, his yellow curls making a halo against the light. It was all as it had been yesterday and the day and the year before; there was no reason to

67

feel apprehensive, yet there it was, that uncomfortable and persistent feeling.

Presently Mother came; we heard her talking to one of the guests in the hall. She sat in the armchair by the sewing table as though she had but a moment to spare, and told us briefly that she had decided to make Tietjen our legal guardian in case of her death. We looked at her wordless; we didn't know what to say. I was shocked and resentful; why should he be our guardian; he meant nothing to any of us. Then I found my voice and objected, but the other three, unwilling to displease Mother, outvoted me. Again I had opposed her, raised an issue between us, marked myself as an unmanageable child. Just one more skirmish in the weary battle of wills between us.

At last the festival was over. On the very day it closed Emma had us all packed and ready to get away to Lake Constance. As she was an excellent cook and liked to humor us with our favorite dishes, we enjoyed the freedom from the other servants. Mother was away most of the time so we had a blissful, unhampered two weeks of swimming, boating, going native on the beach.

School again—I returned to the *lycée* for an uneventful month or two. The only episode that broke the monotony was the debut of Verena and me as singers in Liszt's oratorio, *Die Heilige Elisabeth*, which was produced by the choral society of Bayreuth. Nickel sang baby Elisabeth's one-line part with complete *sang-froid*, but I didn't do so well with young Ludwig's equally brief role, I hiccupped in the middle of it and the orchestra had to wait for me.

Not long after the October holiday Mother took me out of school and sent me to Professor Ibrahim, the famous child specialist of Jena, with the hope that he might be able to do something about my overweight which she suspected was glandular. I spent three days in Professor Ibrahim's clinic, but as he did not have a machine for measuring metabolism he sent me to Professor Veil who was the head of the *Medicinische Klinik* at the University Clinic, a city of hospitals and medical buildings in the heart of Jena.

The minute I set eyes on Dr. Veil I took a strong dislike to him. There was something about the fat, short, stocky creature with a shock of red hair and green eyes which flickered when you looked straight at them, that reminded me of a character out of Dante's *Inferno.* He disliked me heartily also, but he did me a good turn for he sent me to Wigger's Sanitarium in Garmisch-Partenkirchen where I spent the most delightful two months one can imagine.

No one was seriously ill at Wigger's; everyone was taking the baths as if the whole idea were a particularly carefree holiday. I was on my own, the only child in the place, and I was riotously happy, stuffing every hour with enjoyment. Of a morning I faithfully took the cure, salt baths, massage, a very strict diet supervised by a handsome young doctor who had all the pretty female patients in the place. In the afternoon there were skiing, mountain climbing, trips up Wank or Kreuzeck by the cable cars, races on Lake Eibsee at the foot of the Zugspitze. Once a year planes and motorcars raced each other on the lake. Udet who was there doing stunt flying, varied his sensational trick of picking up a handkerchief with a wing of his plane—impossible on the ice—by swooping down on the lake and scraping it with his wing. Rudolf Hess was there too, doing stunts in a little sports plane marked with a swastika. There was always a circus of one kind or another to ripple my spine with thrills.

The other patients were kind to me, including me in sleighing parties to little inns on the mountainsides where we had tea on overhanging balconies and watched ski competitions. They told me their love affairs; perhaps because I was young and didn't understand what they were talking about most of the time, they confided in me their passions for the Bavarian mountaineers, dashing, handsome fellows

69

in their musical comedy costumes, famous for *Fensterln*. They boasted that no window was too high for their conquests. Even strangers confided in me. One attractive American girl whom I met on the way to Garmisch walked along with me and unburdened her heart about her fear that her gallant mountaineer was exhibiting his prowess at somebody else's window.

This enchanted interlude ended and I returned to Wahnfried. In the autumn Mother had told me that she wanted me to be confirmed in March with Wieland. I didn't want to be confirmed. The dogma of the church had no meaning for me, and I had too much respect for religion to want to go through the ceremony as a hollow and hypocritical gesture to please Mother. But she was firm and required me to go to the confirmation class with Wieland. When I went to Partenkirchen our pastor gave me a letter to the pastor in the Alpine village, but I didn't attend more than one or two of the classes. The only preparation I made was to sketch a confirmation dress which Zum Tobel, Bayreuth's smartest dress shop, undertook to make from my design.

Back in Wahnfried there was no escape. The pastor refused to confirm me because I had not taken the course, and so did the pastor at Partenkirchen. In neither place had I taken the examination. But Mother put on the pressure; she overrode both me and the pastor. On the morning of the confirmation, the thirteenth of March, I remember because it was Election Day, I stood with Wieland and the rest of the class but refused to make the responses.

Mother and the grownups went directly from the church to the election booths to vote for Hitler who for the first time was running for President. Feeling in Germany was high—for weeks Mother had been getting threatening letters from the opposition. The anti-Nazi paper in Bayreuth, noting the flowers that were delivered to Wahnfried for Wieland and me, announced that they were for

70

Mother's wedding to Hitler. This was the basis of the rumor that the opposition papers repeated at every opportunity. It both amused and plagued us for several years. The affair of the confirmation had stirred in me such frustration and bitterness that I couldn't face the thought of remaining at home and demanded to be sent away to school. Mother, however, paid no attention to me; she was rarely at home and when she did spend a few days at Wahnfried she was occupied with her own affairs; the difficulty she was having in persuading Toscanini to return in 1933; the bitter press campaign that Furtwängler, abetted by Dr. Muck, was waging in the Left-wing papers, accusing her of the mismanagement of Bayreuth.

Tietjen appeared every so often, fanning all these animosities in his quiet way. It was his tales about Daniela's intriguing with Furtwängler that finally brought the tension between Mother and the aunts to the breaking point. Among other things, Tietjen had said that Daniela, carried away by Furtwängler's performance at the memorial concert, had rushed to the podium and kissed him.

The clash came one Sunday in early April after luncheon at Wahnfried. Mother was flying to Paris that afternoon to see Toscanini who was still grumbling. After luncheon, Mother, Daniela and Eva retired to the music room. We children were not permitted to follow, but as it was a warm spring day and the doors were open, we heard it all.

At first we paid little attention to the rumbling of angry voices—just another row between Mother and the aunts— but when we heard Daniela scream, "I didn't kiss him! It's a lie! I didn't kiss him!" we drew a little nearer in the hall and stretched our ears.

"Yes, you did kiss him," shouted Mother. Accusations, recriminations, denials flew back and forth. From the question of the mythical kiss, Daniela and Mother proceeded to air all of their pent-up grievances against each other. After that day Daniela never entered Wahnfried.

Somehow it was fantastic and ironical that the break

71

which would have come anyway—it was inevitable—should have been precipitated by the question of a kiss. Poor flustered, indignant, strait-laced, seventy-one-year-old Daniela about whom the legend clung that she had been married for twenty-eight years and was still unkissed!

My own affairs came to a head on the day before we departed for Lake Constance. Tietjen had come from Berlin on some business about the next festival, and evidently he and Mother found time to consider the case of Friedelind. That evening they called me into the drawing room and gave me a lecture on my delinquencies. Ignoring the fact that I had been pleading with Mother to send me away to school, they told me as if they were meting out a punishment that they had decided to send me to the strictest one in Germany. By this time I had learned how to infuriate Tietjen. Thanking them cheerfully I bade them good night, picked up my accordion in the hall and went upstairs playing the gayest tune I could think of.

We heard no more about the matter at Lake Constance until toward the middle of the summer when Mother and Albert Knittel drove away on a trip to look over a school that he and his friends had persuaded her would be just the place for me. Since Knittel had a hand in it, I guessed that it would be selected with a view to crushing my spirit. He was always advising Mother how to manage me and had invented a particularly disagreeable method of discussing me with Mother, in my presence, as if I were a piece of furniture. Of course I never let him see that I was hurt.

When they returned from the trip Mother said nothing at all about the school except that it was so charming to see the girls eating on tin plates. Wieland gave me the only real information about this Spartan penitentiary—details gathered surreptitiously from a prospectus he found on Mother's desk. Pupils were to wear black stockings and blue petticoats, never for any occasion silk underclothes. Navy-blue coats, woolen cardigans, in the winter navy-blue woolen pants! Oh well, I told myself, I couldn't be unhappier there than I was at home, so I made the most of the holiday.

We swam, we boated, we hiked about the lake, we drove to one of Hitler's rallies at Radolfszell down the lake. He was campaigning for the Reichstag elections, making four or five speeches a day, flying from one rally to another. This was one of the few times I heard him speak in public. We were ushered to the platform where we tried to keep awake during the efforts of a noble but harassed local party leader who was filling in the time until the arrival of the Führer's plane which was two and a half hours late. Finally we heard the drone of the motor. A few minutes afterward Hitler dashed up to the platform, red in the face, and began his address. He was hoarse from much speaking and his rasping voice, charged with emotion, swept over the audience like a high wind that takes the breath away and leaves one dazed but excited. When he had taken the last sip of water from the pitcher on the table and made another sprint for the plane, the crowd stirred.

"It's wonderful," they gasped, although they didn't comment on a word he said. In my fourteen-year-old opinion there was nothing remarkable about the speech.

With many secret consultations, Mother and Emma fitted me out for school, ordered my outfit in Berlin, but never once consulted me. Not until I unpacked my trunk at Heiligengrabe—the name of the penitentiary—did I see a single piece of my winter wardrobe or realize that I was to be no longer Friedelind Wagner but Number 27. Toward the last of August as *Der Tag* approached, I kept waking at night from a horrible nightmare to find my stomach in a knot and my heart pounding furiously, but I was much too proud to tell anyone about my discomfort.

By chance I learned that our letters would all be censored by the headmistress. A school friend of mine met this situation by consulting her father who was a chemist;

he took us into his laboratory and concocted a bottle of invisible ink for me to use whenever it was necessary. When I wrote between the lines with it, I was to underscore the date in the top left-hand corner of the letter. This was a great comfort. The kind chemist suggested also that I keep some money at hand in case the school was too awful to be endured. A girdle, we thought, was a safe hiding place, so I sewed a fifty-mark bill in one of them and left it there for at least six months until I realized that running away to England, as I had always planned, wouldn't help matters. I was under age and even if I reached my friends there, they would be obliged to turn me over to Mother.

On the last day of August Mother, Tietjen and I started north by car. That night we spent in Berlin and on the next day lunched at Kempinski's on the Kurfürstendamm where Mother met several friends and had an amusing time telling them about the school to which she was taking me. Everybody was gay, making little jokes about me and Heiligengrabe. I sat there with my eyes on my plate, forcing myself to eat a huge luncheon to show Mother I didn't care.

Afterward the two of us drove out the highway to Hamburg and soon turned into a Brandenburg side road, a dismal flat stretch of sand, little lakes and scrawny pines. After teatime we turned into a driveway that followed the walls of an ancient old red brick convent. This was Heiligengrabe. The Frau Äbtissin—she kept the old title although this was a Protestant school—came out to greet us. Here I made my first and greatest *faux pas*, I neither curtsied nor kissed her hand. Even worse, I addressed her normally in the second person instead of the royal third: "Will Frau Äbtissin please do this or that?"

We proceeded to Frau Äbtissin's drawing room through corridors so dark and narrow that they made my flesh creep. Mother looked out of the window facing the cloisters and murmured how romantic it must be to live in

74

a genuine thirteenth century convent. She glanced at the shapeless navy-blue pupils sitting at long green tables in the cloister yard.

"Aren't they charming?" she said.

To me, the world had come to an end but I didn't let her see me shudder.

CHAPTER IX

ROYALTY AND RASPBERRY SYRUP

UPSTAIRS in the attic which had been divided into a series of dormitories for the younger girls and tiny cubicles for the older ones, I found that I was specially privileged to share a room with one of the upperclassmen who was a school captain with all sorts of privileges. "Lilliput" we called our cell because it was just large enough for a couple of iron beds, two primitive washstands, a chest of drawers between us and a tiny table squeezed under the window sill.

In the matter of uniforms I had good luck. They belonged to the school and were handed down from one pupil to another until they wouldn't hold together any longer. Most of them were patched and as the color and pattern of the material that was reordered from the manufacturer often varied from the original, the effect was well calculated to kill whatever vanity we had. Because of my size and plumpness I was given a new one, a minor comfort. On top of these blue sacks we wore black aprons except at luncheon and supper. If we were caught without them for a single instant we earned a black mark. However, we liked to wear them because we could tie them tight around our waists and give ourselves a semblance of a human form. On Sundays we wore very wide blue skirts held around us by elastic bands, and above these, hideous black-and-white striped blouses, so wide that two of us could inhabit them at a time without the slightest discomfort.

That very first night I learned that the pupils and most of the teachers belonged to the Prussian nobility; in fact I was one of the very few pupils who lacked the proper percentage of blue blood. Heiligengrabe's proudest boast at that time was the Kaiser's granddaughter, the child of Crown Prince Wilhelm and Crown Princess Cecilie. To her and the other little princesses who had led an unspeakably dull life, shut in some dreary country palace with private tutors and an assortment of royal relatives, the opportunity to play with other girls seemed little short of paradise.

The daily procedure at Heiligengrabe, I soon discovered, was modeled as nearly as possible on old court etiquette. The Äbtissin had been the governess of the Kaiser's daughter, Viktoria Luise, and a lady-in-waiting for twenty-five years, so she conducted Heiligengrabe with the belief that the curtsy is a properly brought-up young girl's most important accomplishment. All day we curtsied. After breakfast at five minutes before seven (a piece of dark brown bread washed down with malt coffee) we ran back to our rooms or dormitories and formed in line for inspection. The dormitory mistress appeared, we curtsied, turned a hundred and eighty degrees in front of her, showed her that we wore warm pants and that our shoes were clean, then rushed to do our beds, empty our water pails and tidy our rooms before school started at seven forty-five. Then we ran downstairs, through the dining room, down a circular staircase in the Kaiser tower, through the cloisters, across the garden, past the Blood Chapel which was high Gothic in contrast with the earlier Gothic of the convent, and so to our classes. At recess we were served sandwiches and cocoa in the cloister. At the beginning of the term each pupil subscribed for the number of pieces of bread she expected to eat and was served her ration accordingly. There were three kinds of sandwiches—one with sausage, one with butter, another with lard or grease, so we quickly learned to barter.

After a fifth class we returned to our domitories, changed our morning horrors for our afternon horrors and were ready for luncheon. One of the seniors was accorded the honor of announcing luncheon to Frau Äbtissin. When we were assembled at our seats, the senior designated for the day, knocked at the Äbtissin's door. At the invitation to enter, she stopped at the line of the carpet to curtsy deeply and say "Frau Äbtissin, luncheon is served." Whereupon Frau Äbtissin handed the girl a packet of letters to be distributed after luncheon and entered the dining room with her messenger three paces to the rear. One of the pupils who held open the door curtsied as she passed, then we all who stood facing her as she entered, curtsied deeply. The Äbtissin reached her place at the top of the center table and sat in her special chair, an impressive one with arms and needle-point upholstery.

At dinner and breakfast we were not allowed to speak, but at luncheon we could talk to our immediate neighbors in a low voice unless the Äbtissin rang her little bell for silence. The senior at the head of each table ladled out the portions on the tin plates, and we were supposed to eat everything. It took adept sleight of hand to get some bits of particularly distasteful food out of the way without being caught.

Every day of every week we had potatoes. On Wednesday we had potato soup and yellow pudding; on Saturdays, vegetable soup and white pudding; on Sundays, if the supervisor of the woods was lucky in his hunting, we were served a smallish piece of deer, never eggs or milk or fruit. Mother supplemented my diet by leaving a standing order in Berlin for a nine-pound box of fruit each week. It probably saved me from some horrible dietary disease and

77

certainly gave me the means for barter. With the fruit that I didn't eat and boxes of chocolates sent faithfully by a sweet old friend, I managed to get one of my classmates to turn my mattress on Sundays, change my sheets and tidy the closet. Even my inspection mistress shared in the spoils so when she reproached me with the condition of my closet, I could say with impunity, "Didn't Ehrengard tidy up?"

But to return to the curtsies, the day was yet full of them. After luncheon the pupils formed a long line according to their ages and one by one curtsied to the Äbtissin, holding their skirts out at full width, sinking as gracefully as possible, then backing away to make place for the next in line. When the youngest child had curtsied, the letters were distributed. Frau Äbtissin called out the names of the recipients who came forward and curtsied at the moment the letters touched their fingers, then backed away again. We were not permitted to read them until Frau Äbtissin and the teachers had disappeared to the drawing room for their very bad coffee.

After luncheon we walked with one teacher at the end of the queue, then "tea," a malt coffee brew with one roll, no butter, and brown bread with prune preserve on it, the amount varying again according to the pupil's subscription at the beginning of the term. Next, our study period, two hours, the last part of which was also bath period. Each pupil was allowed one bath a week. Dinner, prayers, several hymns—by nine o'clock our day ended with, thank heaven, no final curtsy.

I disliked the place violently but surprised Mother by making good grades, a fairly easy accomplishment since we had an exchange system by which a high grade in one subject canceled a low mark in another. The young teachers were most of them poor instructors and a bit hazy about their subjects—easy to torment—but the older ones, the "Stifts ladies," members of the organization of Prussian noblewomen, had character and a certain unbending integrity. Two of them I visited in the evenings, each established in her own house and garden. They were genuinely fond of me and I of them even though it was treason to admire Napoleon, and I insisted that he should be looked upon with historical detachment. Of course I should have known that a detached point of view never did and probably never will exist in Prussia.

At the Christmas holidays I was eager to leave Heiligengrabe but dreaded to go home. When Emma saw me she threw up her hands.

"What has happened to your hair? You have hardly any left." It was true. My long thick pigtails had become very thin and wispy. The inadequate diet had affected my teeth as well, and the dentist almost spoiled my vacation by filling holes in them.

Otherwise nothing was changed—the same tree, the same wreaths, the presents. Wieland played from one of Father's scores; we sang carols; Mother read the Scriptures—all just as it had always been yet almost unbearably different because Father wasn't there.

After Christmas Lieselotte went to bed with a heart attack. I went to her room, newly furnished in accordance with her taste, in some remarkably ugly modern furniture, and tried to cheer her, but she shut her eyes and turned to the wall.

"Don't worry about her," advised Wieland, "She'll get up quickly enough if Frank calls from Munich."

So Lieselotte was in love with Frank! I remembered how fluttery she was when Schemm, the Nazi Gauleiter of Bayreuth brought him to call the summer before when he was speaking at a local rally. Frank "Zwei" he was called in the party to distinguish him from another Frank, also a lawyer. Later "Zwei" distinguished himself as the butcher of Poland.

They had stayed to luncheon; as it was nearly luncheon time I, who was hostess in Mother's absence, felt that I was obliged to ask them. If Lieselotte had lost her heart to Schemm I could have understood; he was at least hand-

79

some, but Frank—he was not attractive and he was a married man with a house full of children.

Lieselotte did recover, cured by a letter, not a telephone call, and before I left was cheerful as ever. Mother came with me to Berlin and promised to let me stay over a day to see a performance of *Der Fliegende Holländer* which had not been produced in Bayreuth since the re-opening of the festivals. At the Eden Hotel we found a letter from Hitler thanking Mother for her Christmas present. It was six pages, the longest one of his I had ever seen, written in pencil all over the sheet in a mixture of Latin and German letters.

The agitation in the handwriting reflected the miserable state of Hitler's mind when he wrote it.

> I have given up all hope [we deciphered]. Nothing will ever come of my dreams. Piled on so many bitter years of endless struggle there are now only greater disappointments. Until now I have never lost courage. I was able to save and reconstruct everything, even after 1923, but I have no hope left. My opponents are too powerful. As soon as I am sure that everything is lost you know what I'll do. I was always determined to do it. I cannot accept defeat. I will stick to my word and end my life with a bullet. This time it will be serious because I simply cannot see my way out.

Mother did not seem particularly disturbed by the letter, so I thought no more about it. Two weeks later Hitler "arrived." I learned about it in the afternoon when I returned from ice skating and found the female *Junkers* buzzing with excitement because Hugenberg and Seldte, two good Prussians belonging to the German National movement and the Steel Helmets, had been chosen to join the Cabinet.

The Äbtissin called me into her office.

"This certainly is a great day for your mother, my child. I know she is a stanch follower of Hitler."

I was so surprised that I forgot myself and began to think aloud.

"It's all pretty exciting, but I wonder how these people are suddenly going to be statesmen. Reconstructing a rundown country is more difficult than brawling in a beer garden."

"One always starves himself to freedom, my child," the Äbtissin answered dramatically.

"Freedom?" I questioned. The Äbtissin had never been dramatic but now she had forgotten that she was the headmistress of a girls' school; she was speaking as a Prussian, the granddaughter of General Gneisenau.

"Yes, freedom. But only with sacrifice can we fight for it."

I said no more. No doubt we would starve but I couldn't see how freedom would result from it. This January thirtieth marked the day of my mental coming of age. From then on I began to make my own observations about politics and think independently. In the meanwhile I tried to study *Mein Kampf* which some one had given me for Christmas.

The winter passed pleasantly enough. Although I was too fat for glamour I got the best parts in the school plays because of my good diction and resonant voice. The stage designing, scene painting and stage directing naturally fell to me; it was fun to order costumes from the Staatsoper in Berlin or from Bayreuth, and to disguise my playmates with real grease paint from a huge box of stage make-up. Our school chorus, which I conducted later, sometimes performed in church on holy days or at funerals. As the old ladies of the Stift were dying at a rapid rate, we were well trained for funerals. Then, too, I was permitted to play the organ in the big convent church, and many a winter afternoon I slipped into the empty church to practice away the blues.

The most dramatic event of the winter was Heiligengrabe's effort to put on style. On Sundays and holidays the dining tables blossomed out with china, tablecloths and real glasses. Through our grapevine news system we

81

learned that the old convent was dressing up for an invasion of royalty. Now that the Kaiser's granddaughter was a pupil, the faculty expected another one as well, and two princesses of the House of Mecklenburg. With royal pupils there would, of course, be royal visitors.

The first of them was the Crown Princess who came for Cecilchen's birthday. She sat in Frau Äbtissin's chair at luncheon, looking down on us and the china plates and the precious glasses. In the glasses of the grownups was red wine but ours were filled with a pink raspberry syrup. We stood at attention while the Crown Princess made a long and fervent speech about the return of her house to its rightful place. She spoke as though the Hohenzollerns were still the rulers of Germany and the Kaiser only on a visit in Holland. Finally she held out her glass and asked us all to toast the return of the Hohenzollerns. Everybody lifted the raspberry syrup except me. Not for worlds would I have drunk to such a toast.

After luncheon we all curtsied to the Princess instead of the Äbtissin, each with an exaggerated dip. At my turn Cecile gave me a smile of recognition, shook my hand and inquired after my mother, whereupon I had to kiss her hand and do an extra curtsy.

Shut away in Heiligengrabe I got only a faint and distorted picture of what was going on in Germany. The only clear impression was that something terrible was about to happen to the Jews. When I met Mother in Berlin for the Easter holidays I asked her what about the performers for the 1933 festival. The contracts were usually sent out and signed early in November, so this had all been done before Hitler came to power.

Mother told me that she called upon him in February and laid on his desk a list of the Jewish members, forty or fifty of them, telling him that the contracts were signed and she was not willing to break them. Since we were a private institution and there was as yet no law prohibiting the engagement of Jews, she hoped Hitler would see her point.

To her amazement, he did, indeed he insisted that no change be made, but added that these contracts should not be renewed unless Mother could find no substitutes for 1934. This allayed my uneasiness because after only a few hours in Berlin I had learned of numberless misfortunes that were already overtaking my Jewish friends.

Mother was genuinely trying to make my vacation happy. On my fifteenth birthday she gave a small dinner party in our living room at the Eden, but, as usual, she couldn't count upon her unpredictable daughter. I had just finished reading *Mein Kampf* and was eager to discuss it with somebody. Hitler's social and political theories made no impression on me, but several of his words inflamed my curiosity. While we were enjoying the roast I burst out in my resonant voice, "Will someone please tell me what 'prostitution' means?"

Dead silence. Everyone stared at me, knives and forks poised in mid-air. Tietjen was the first to recover.

"Where did you read the word?"

"In *Mein Kampf*. I just finished it."

"You must have made a mistake. There isn't any such word," he assured me.

"Why, of course, there is," I exclaimed, pitying the shocking ignorance of these grownups. Evidently not one of them had read the book. "Why, in *Mein Kampf* there are at least ten pages on the subject."

"You've just got it mixed with some other word." Tietjen again. Everybody suggested words with a like ending. It got to be quite a game, but I was not satisfied. Running to my room I brought the volume and after a long search, found the page.

"There it is, you see!"

But everybody laughed at me.

"You seem to be cleverer than the rest of us; we never heard of such a word."

This was supposed to close the subject, but I was not satisfied and finally had recourse to an encyclopedia. The word was there but after reading the article on it I was no wiser than I was before. After I returned to Heiligengrabe I tried to discuss another of my finds, "syphilis," with one of the mistresses. She blushed painfully and looked at me with shocked disapproval.

"When I was as old as you I certainly did not know anything about syphilis."

"That's just it. I don't know. I read about it in *Mein Kampf* and just want to find out what's wrong with it. If you don't tell me now, perhaps I won't know even when I'm your age."

But she did not enlighten me and neither did the encyclopedia, although I read the article several times. This was the end of my studious efforts to understand Hitler's book.

CHAPTER X

BERLIN HOLIDAY

DURING this same Easter holiday Mother and I were invited to luncheon at the Chancellery. It happened to be on the first of April, the very day of the Jewish boycott which everybody had been expecting in a vague way although no one knew exactly what the measure would be. Hitler was not then living in the Chancellor's palace but in the so-called New Chancellery, an enormous apartment which had usually been inhabited by a Secretary of State. The tables in the broad entrance hall looked like a ladies' church bazaar, covered with the embroidered offerings of Hitler's female admirers, cloths adorned with swastikas in every imaginable arrangement.

In the drawing room Mrs. Hess received us, a plump, inelegant blonde with a deep voice and evidently with a scorn of powder and make-up. She was taking her turn with the other wives of the leading party men, she told us, acting as hostess at the Chancellery. She offered us a plate of Hitler's favorite candies with which Hamann, a Berlin candy store, kept him supplied in large quantities; sometimes he ate as many as two pounds of them a day.

When we had almost exhausted the virtues and disadvantages of the different brands of candy, Hühnlein, the chief of the N.S.K.K., the Nazi Motor Corps, came in.

"This is my oldest daughter," said Mother, introducing me, "the one I sent to a boarding school because she was such a bad influence on her brothers and sister. She had completely spoiled them." Mother was using the old Knittel technique, speaking about me as if I weren't there. Inside I winced but outwardly I smiled broadly, refusing to be abashed. To my astonished delight that uncouth soldier came to my defense.

"It's a sure sign of poor sense when parents send their children to boarding schools to be educated by strangers because they are incapable of doing it themselves. It should be forbidden. The parents need educating, not the children."

Mother was speechless but I could have hugged the man, although at the same time I hated him because he was so rude to Mother. After an hour and a half of waiting Hitler finally made his entrance in one of his blue "country schoolteacher" suits. He looked tired; the bags under his eyes were bigger than usual and his lids were only half open, but he seemed in high spirits about the boycott.

We went into the dining room, enormous like all the others and papered with exotic parrots against a purple jungle. Hitler sat at one end of the very long table set with heavy silver engraved with coats of arms, and looking as if it had been inherited from imperial Germany. Mother sat on his right, Mrs. Hess on his left, and on either side were ranged Brückner, Schaub and other high party members.

During the soup—noodle soup, Hitler ate it every day for luncheon and sometimes again for dinner—Göbbels limped in and sat next to me. He greeted me with a German proverb.

"Well, my dear, are you still fat, lazy and greedy?" (*dick, dumm, faul und gefrässig*), leaving out the "dumb" probably because he thought it less uncomplimentary than the other adjectives.

"See for yourself," I told him, whereupon he grinned broadly, much pleased with his joke.

While his guests sipped German red wine, a concession that Hitler had made both to his thirsty companions and to the German wine industry, and I drank a horrible ersatz orangeade as befitted my years, Hitler began to denounce his Nazi party.

"I'm going to start a new party," he declared. "I don't like the old one any more."

While he continued his unflattering remarks about the Brown Shirts and party members who had brought him to power, I noticed that his teeth had been made over. His curious little moles' teeth had been filled and his whole mouth glittered with a network of gold. His fingernails, however, were still half covered with cuticle and he kept biting them as he talked, scrutinizing one after the other critically, then going vigorously to work on it.

Finally we returned to the living room for our coffee. Hitler went into the next room to have a word with his aide-de-camp, Schaub, and left the door open. A few minutes later he was screaming at Schaub at the top of his lungs. From where I sat I could see him bent forward, his eyes and face bloodshot. He was fairly spitting his words, hurling at the poor man the vilest Austrian phrases he could think of, forcing them through his teeth with an awful swishing noise. Instinctively I looked around for

86

cover, feeling that he had lost all self-control and might start to shoot at any moment.

All this time Schaub stood opposite Hitler, his eyes fixed on the ugly, distorted face flecked with saliva, and didn't make a sound. He was completely paralyzed, unable to move or speak. I glanced at Mother to see if she was frightened too, if she guessed that at this moment Hitler was not sane, but she was sitting quietly with her eyes cast down as though she hadn't heard.

After perhaps ten minutes the storm passed as quickly as it had come. Hitler's body sagged visibly and he began to pant as he walked back and forth across the floor. Finally Mrs. Hess found the courage to tell him that his guests were leaving—all of us, Hühnlein as well as the others, without waiting to discuss the business for which they had come. Although Hitler seemed perfectly composed when he bade us farewell, we huddled together uneasily in the elevator, glad when the heavy doors shut him away from us. Still shaken I kept close to Mother when we left the others, wondering if she would make any comment on the extraordinary scene.

"Poor Führer," she said, her voice gentle with concern. "He is so excitable. Schaub oughtn't to do things to disturb him."

That evening I went to a performance of *Die Zauberflöte* at the Staatsoper. The conductor was Leo Blech and the Sarastro, Alexander Kipnis, both Jews. As I made my way to the director's box next the stage, I noticed the tension in the air and was as nervous as the performers, wondering how the audience would behave. Across from me in the little proscenium box was Otto Klemperer with the same anxious expression on his face.

As the lights faded and Blech stepped into the dark pit, the audience broke spontaneously into such cheers and applause as I had never witnessed in the blasé Staatsoper. He acknowledged the ovation again and again before he was permitted to lift his baton. Then the house fell sud-

denly silent until Kipnis made his entrance. When he
started his great aria, *"In diesen heil'gen Hallen wo
Mensch den Menschen liebt,"* his voice was unsteady but
be caught himself and sang with such warmth and com-
passion that he brought down the house. Mozart was
answering the Nazis. For this moment at least a whole
assembly of German people had the courage to show their
sympathy loudly and convincingly for a Jew.

The next day I heard that Klemperer had left Germany.
Bruno Walter had already gone. In March after he had
conducted a concert at the Gewandthaus in Leipzig he was
scheduled to conduct one in Berlin, but when he arrived
at the concert hall he found the door locked. Scarcely was
the ink dry on the newspaper announcing that Walter had
been forced to resign, when Richard Strauss offered himself by wire as replacement for his old friend and col-
league, a move which did not endear him to the musicians
who were sympathetic to Walter.

The entire Busch family, Fritz, Adolf and Hermann,
had also departed. They were not Jews but went in protest against the treatment of their Jewish colleagues. Fritz
was actually the first conductor to be dislodged by the
Nazis—he and his director of the Dresden opera—because
they would not tolerate loudmouthed party members at
the opera. Later the Nazis tried to woo Adolf and his
chamber music players back to Germany and sent an
emissary to Basel with tempting offers. Adolf assured the
messenger that he would return joyfully on the day Hitler,
Göbbels and Göring were publicly hanged.

But to return to the Eden Hotel and my Easter vacation.
A day or so after the boycott Mother received a wire from
Toscanini saying that he could not return to Bayreuth
after the treatment his Jewish colleagues had received in
Germany. She was desolate; her blue eyes usually so clear
were darkened with worry and her face blanched as she
phoned Hitler the disastrous news. From the half of the
conversation that I heard, I gathered that he felt very

badly treated after he had generously permitted Mother to keep her Jewish artists. On further thought he must have realized what it would mean to have such a powerful voice as that of Toscanini openly denouncing Nazi Germany, for his aides rushed back and forth from the Chancellery to the hotel all day long. Finally it was decided to send a wire in Hitler's name, urging Toscanini to reconsider. The cost of the wire, ninety-five marks, impressed me profoundly; compared with my pocket money it seemed a fortune.

This wire was followed by a personal letter from Hitler which he felt sure the Maestro could not resist. Brückner brought it over and read it to Mother before it was posted. It said among other things, "Until now it has been denied him (Hitler) to hear the great conductor but this year in his capacity as Chancellor of the Reich, he would be especially happy to greet Toscanini in Bayreuth."

When I heard this, I couldn't keep still.

"It would be crazy to send such a letter," I protested. "This is the surest way to drive Toscanini away forever. If you really want him to come, don't send it, because he comes to Bayreuth for Wagner, not for Hitler. It will be sure to make him furious."

Mother glared at me and her temper flared. In an angry voice she reminded me that I was speaking like a child, and advised me to leave the operating of the festival to her until I could show more sense. I bit my lip and smiled but didn't reply, knowing my silence would further enrage her, but I was right. Toscanini's answer came by return post and it was so vivid that it made Hitler see red whenever the Maestro's name was mentioned.

It was impossible for him to conduct in Germany "because of painful events which have wounded my feeling as a man and as an artist," Toscanini wrote among many other biting phrases. Hitler ordered a violent smear campaign in the German papers. At first Toscanini considered suing them, but on second thought he chose the wiser course and ignored them.

As a matter of fact this first boycott was harmless in comparison with the later purges. Hitler Brown Shirts and Black Shirts were posted in front of Jewish stores to keep an eye on Aryans who were not supposed to trade with them. Germans were encouraged to "buy German" which meant, of course, not from the Jews. On that April day people were too confused, too apprehensive to take a stand, especially since it was whispered that the Nazis were carrying concealed cameras and snapping pictures of prominent party members who broke the boycott, pictures which later appeared in the Jew-baiting paper, *Stürmer*, of Nuremberg. Party members soon got around the inconvenience by making working arrangements with nonparty friends to do their shopping for them. In Wahnfried, for instance, two of the maids who were Nazis did their buying through the others who were not.

One often wonders what would have happened if the Jews themselves had taken a stand. There were ten thousand large industrial establishments in Jewish hands when Hitler came to power, many of them essential industries such as food, clothing and shoes. As a Jewish friend said to me later, "What we should have done was to close down our factories immediately when Hitler arrived; then he would have found himself in an awful jam. If we had dismissed all the workmen and simply gone on strike, he would have been compelled to come around and beg us to reopen—and it would have been we who dictated the terms. It might very well have changed things considerably because the Nazis were too weak in the beginning to offer much opposition." This sounded sensible to me—but of course hindthought is always easier than forethought.

Meanwhile I returned to Heiligengrabe which was no longer a cloister remote from the world. Politics had entered its portals; the Hitler Youth movement was in the process of organization and I involved myself in difficul-

90

ties immediately by refusing to join. To do so would have been to desert friends who happened to be of the wrong race or nationality or party. When I did not, one of the mistresses in newly discovered zeal for Hitler, flung at me, "Friedelind is not a National Socialist—she is a traitor." Was I a traitor? I didn't know but I couldn't see why one should change all his loyalties overnight.

With the end of June I was at home again preparing for the festival, helping with the technical rehearsals, checking on the lighting while one of the stagehands played Brünnhilde to a piano accompaniment, or timing the color effects on the waves. The scenery of *Parsifal* was finally falling to pieces and Mother had engaged Alfred Roller to do a new setting. It wasn't to be ready until the following season, but Daniela was hurt and grieved at the whole idea. Although she never entered Wahnfried after the kiss episode she was still wardrobe mistress and had transferred her battlefield to the Festspielhaus. She insisted vehemently that the setting should be an exact reproduction of the old one but this was impossible because of the fire laws.

"Why not?" protested Daniela hotly. She felt so keenly about the desecration of *Parsifal* that she cut herself off from Mother entirely, ceased to be wardrobe mistress and never again set foot in the Festspielhaus. Now there was no intercourse between the two houses. The other children sided with Mother and refused to see the aunts but, although I agreed with Mother about the scenery, they were Father's sisters and I loved them. Mother railed at me and said I had no character, but I still went to Eva's for luncheon and occasionally for tea. Now that Father was gone, the only place in which I found the peace that used to be at Wahnfried was in Eva's pleasant old-fashioned drawing room. Daniela was happy to have me and told me endless stories about the old days when Cosima directed the Festspielhaus and Father ran about with a score in his hand, beating time for the entrance of the swan.

91

Tietjen now had established himself at Wahnfried and before he had been there many days had trained a sparrow to play with him, sit on his shoulder and eat its dinner on the edge of his plate. If it stayed away for a day, he was brokenhearted. In Berlin, he told me, his tame canaries flew about his apartment uncaged. Once he trained a mouse who arrived with her four children in convoy every morning for breakfast. They were entrancing, he said, but after awhile they disappeared and he always suspected his housekeeper of poisoning them.

I was fascinated to watch his work. Wagner's ideal was to combine the conductor, stage director, administrator, all in one person, and in Bayreuth it had always been that way, first Wagner, then Cosima, then Father. Tietjen was nominally "artistic director" under Mother but he soon had things pretty much his own way. Although he was a fifth-rate conductor, he was an excellent musician with wide knowledge, and he was a very great stage director. Here was someone from whom I could learn and I never missed a rehearsal.

Earlier in June Richard Strauss and his clan had moved into the bachelor house which Mother had enlarged, saying she wanted it for a home when Wieland married. The moment Strauss had heard about Toscanini's refusal to return to Bayreuth he had wired Mother, offering his assistance, and as she was looking frantically for a conductor to do the *Meistersinger* and *Parsifal*, she reluctantly accepted. She didn't trust him although he had an old association with Bayreuth—he had been Cosima's assistant in the eighties when he was a very young man and much in love with the Elisabeth in *Tannhäuser*. When he became engaged to Pauline, Cosima was the first one to know about it.

Mother knew that Strauss was a weather-vane, veering with every political wind. Monarchist, Social Democrat, a little pink, a little brown, he got along with all regimes. At the moment he stood high with the Nazis and was president of the Reichs Music Chamber, an organization to which every musician was forced to belong—and pay heavy dues. Hitler wanted to extend the copyright law which protected a composer's work from thirty to eighty years after his death. Strauss managed to make the period fifty years which protected his own works for twenty more years and neatly excluded the Wagners.

However, here he was in the guest house, a tall old man with big ears and a little white mustache; and with him were Pauline, "Bubi" and Bubi's beautiful, delightful but un-Aryan wife. We liked Bubi for all his six feet six of rather childish indecision. He had been a spoiled and dominated only child, but after the arrival of the Nazis he showed enough character to refuse to part with his wife. Pauline who had been delighted with the match because the girl was a rich heiress, would not allow her daughter-in-law to be seen with them in public until the Nazis finally quieted her anxiety by declaring the grandchildren Aryans and making Bubi's wife a sort of honorary Aryan.

Pauline had two complexes, both of them uncomfortable; she disliked dust to such an extent that she made her guests remove their shoes in her house and wear felt slippers, and she was unbelievably stingy. At home she rarely served meat unless Bubi brought game from hunting. Strauss had a big Mercedes car and a liveried chauffeur but the minute they arrived at Wahnfried the car went into the garage; Mother had to turn over one of our cars for the chauffeur to drive—and furnish the gas as well.

The only money Strauss ever saw—this in spite of the fact that his yearly income was something like a million marks—was the money he made playing skat. He played every day and every night, and I have never met a soul who won a round from him. Before we reached the general rehearsals there was a crisis. Strauss played for such high stakes that the few singers and members of the

93

orchestra who played couldn't keep up with him. When everyone refused to play, things looked serious because without skat there was no conducting.

Mother solved the problem in an unorthodox manner; she engaged some of the musicians to play with Strauss every night as usual. In the morning they reported to the treasurer at the Festspielhaus and collected their losses.

Another of Mother's difficulties was the food. The Strausses took their meals with us and Richard liked rich, solid Bavarian cooking. Since we were unwilling to go on a Bavarian diet, she engaged a special cook for him, but even so, we discovered that Strauss fortified himself with a luncheon at a little restaurant behind the Festspielhaus every day before he returned to the meal with the family.

Herbert Janssen had arrived, the same handsome distinguished-looking young Viking. This summer he was devoting his attention to Erna Carstens whom he afterward married, a large flaxen-haired woman, very vivacious and pretty.

Herbert was so reserved and modest that when someone put on one of his records he invariably left the room. Now that I knew him better he told me about his audition at the Staatsoper where he sang his first engagement, an almost unheard-of honor for a young singer. In the auditorium, listening to the audition, sat two impressive-looking gentlemen, who he was told were the director of the Dresden opera, and the director of the one in Hanover. While he was singing, Janssen noticed a man walking back and forth in the wings beckoning to him in an agitated way. It was very disconcerting; he couldn't imagine what might be the matter. After he had finished, Herbert walked over and asked the stranger what he wanted. The man was Max von Schillings, the director of the Staatsoper, who wanted to sign him up before the others reached him.

Frida Leider, who was singing Brünnhilde and Kundry, I remembered from an earlier appearance in 1928 when she fed me frankfurters at a big garden party. Dark, elegant Frida, always beautifully dressed, always serious, always so sure of her technique that she didn't need to wrestle with the score. Whenever she appeared in a new opera house she looked for the prompter at once and told him, "For God's sake, never prompt me." She was a brilliant woman, well read, shrewd about business, alert to all that was going on, and such a diplomat that almost everybody liked her. With her husband, Professor Deman, the former concertmaster of the Berlin Staatsoper, she took an apartment in Donndorf, the little village in which Wagner had lived before he built Wahnfried. Here in a charming garden perched halfway up a mountain, she kept open house for her friends.

Rudolf Deman was an Austrian Jew, and I wondered if Frida were anxious about what might happen to him in Germany, but she told me that there was no need to worry. When Hitler came to power Tietjen had telegraphed to them in Paris that her contract was secure and that everything would be satisfactory.

Frida often talked to me seriously about what I intended to do with myself.

"It's a pity you children have everything," she used to say. "You are all clever enough to make careers but you never will. I made mine because I never knew where my next meal was coming from."

Although now she was so wealthy, so successful, so obviously the great artist, Frida had not had an easy life. When she was thirteen her father committed suicide and she, left penniless, clerked in a bank while she studied languages and singing at night. Sympathizing with my difficulties at home, she was always trying to make life easier for me by saying pleasant things to Mother, telling her how courteous I was to this one and that. Mother would shake her head.

"I can't understand why it is that everyone gets along

with Mausi except me. At home she's a perfect devil yet I am always hearing how nice she is when she's away."

In the dressing rooms, at the restaurant, even at the gayest parties, there was a new undertone of uncertainty and dread. Many of the singers and musicians had Jewish wives or husbands and no one knew how long they would be permitted to live in peace or even safety. Everybody had news from Berlin about what had happened to this musician or the other. Furtwängler had actually taken a stand in regard to the Jewish members of the Philharmonic and by fighting wild battles had so far prevented any of them from being discharged. Even Dr. Geissmar was safe at the moment and it was rumored that Göbbels would have forced her to become his secretary if he could have forgiven her for being a Jew.

All this while my critical faculties were being sharpened by the misfortunes of my friends. While my family never learned to look upon Hitler as anyone but an old friend who was very kind to them now that he had risen to power, never failing to show his gratitude for their loyalty in the early days while he was unknown, I realized that he was two people. The "nice uncle" had nothing to do with the ruler of Germany who decreed the boycott. Although we had no reason to fear, I could not be blind to the uneasiness, the denunciations, the fear of reprisals that had seized Germany, and it made me ashamed to be safe and favored when I saw the misery of others. The little rowdy was no longer kicking blindly against whatever obstacle might be in the way; she had become within a few months an adult with a purpose behind her rebellion.

CHAPTER XI

THE FÜHRER VISITS BAYREUTH

DAYS before the opening of the festival of 1933, S. S. troops arrived in Bayreuth; the place swarmed with blue, green, black, white and brown uniforms. Hitler had leased a house at the other end of the park, one on a dead-end street that could be easily shut off and guarded, and he was coming to the first cycle like a victorious Cæsar. On the drive to the Festspielhaus policemen stood at intervals of fifty yards, and along the main street S. S. men were shoulder to shoulder, holding back the townspeople with a cordon of their leather belts.

Around noon a car of shouting S. S. men blared through the street followed by the Führer's car, and behind it, a convoy of four or five cars full of guards, many of them standing on the footboards and clinging to the doors like ants. At every street corner two of these guard cars shot forward and barricaded the side streets until the Führer's car passed, then fell in line again. While the crowd screamed "Heil Hitler," the dictator's car dashed by with incredible speed, entered the gates of Wahnfried; the aides leaped out and Hitler was with us for the first time since he had "arrived."

We met him on the steps of the big front entrance, and after a sufficient number of heils and handshakes ushered his company into the library. He was wearing a new uniform and seemed relieved to get rid of the military cap that sat too low on his forehead and almost extinguished him.

In the library he looked around with beaming satisfaction.

"It was right here that you received me ten years ago," he said to Mother. "Then I had no idea it would take another ten years to arrive. If the *Putsch* hadn't failed everything would have been different; I would have been the right age. Now I am too old. I have lost too much time and must work with double speed."

The family murmured polite assurances, but Hitler did not need them. The moment of regret had passed; he was fortifying himself with grandiose views of the future which he proceeded to express with no intention of being interrupted.

"I'll remain in power for twenty-two years," he prophesied. "Then I'll be able to retire, but first I must get more power into my hands so I won't have to bother with the Cabinet. Just now they think they have a perfect right to meddle in things that are none of their business."

We went to luncheon. The cook had been saving stale bread for days to make his favorite soup and had taken great pains with the main dish, a concoction of eggs and vegetables. Hitler's own dietitian had arrived earlier in the morning and had made his special salad.

"As soon as I have the power I shall dissolve the monasteries and confiscate their property," he announced with the soup. "It is abnormal for a man to lead the life of a monk—nothing but cowardice and an attempt to escape responsibility. In the next war monks and priests won't be able to hide in their sacred tunics; I'll send them all to the front. And I'll certainly be able to use the money. It's incredible how much these bastards own."

From the wealth of the monasteries Hitler jumped to Gothic script which, although he afterward made it the official German script, he then believed should be banned as un-German because it originated in the monasteries. He was especially annoyed with the German Language Research Association which, it seemed, had had the temerity to send him copies of his speeches with German terms substituted for foreign words. Why, he exclaimed in grieved

98

tones, should he talk about a super-screw-fixer when every child knew what he meant by mechanic. A few weeks in a concentration camp would give these gentlemen the opportunity to find the proper word for this institution. By this time we had reached the dessert—Hitler finished his dish of the inevitable grated apples, swallowed a large white pill, and we were ready for the afternoon. Hitler and his three cars full of aides proceeded to his residence across the park and we went to the Festspielhaus to superintend last-minute details of the opening.

When we reached the theater, driving between walls of S. S. guards, we found two rows of green-uniformed police standing at attention in front of the entrance. At their head, looking distinctly unmilitary and uncomfortable in his new police uniform, stood the old chief of police of Bayreuth who ten years before had threatened Mother with jail. He exchanged glances with Mother who had seen that he kept his job and who now gave him an encouraging smile.

Göbbels arrived first and a few minutes later Hitler's convoy of cars dashed up to the entrance between the policemen presenting arms. Repeating the technique of the entrance to Wahnfried, the aides jumped out of the moving car to cover the Führer from all sides, while Hitler dashed up the few steps to the entrance and turned to lift his arm in acknowledgment of the booming heils. Then Mother started the procession upstairs to the Fürstenzimmer, a drawing room which had been built for King Ludwig of Bavaria, and someone telephoned the stage that the performance could now begin. As soon as Mother's guests started upstairs, I hurried to her big office with its dressing room where I slipped out of my evening dress and into the coveralls in which I worked backstage.

During the intermission Hitler made a dash for the restaurant through a corridor of S. S. men and there, at a long, closely guarded table, entertained his guests. The rest of the audience at the Festspielhaus looked on with curious restraint. In one day the informal friendliness and gaiety of Bayreuth had been destroyed.

This was the first time I had seen Hitler in tails. He no longer wore his top hat on the back of his head like a chimney sweep, but he did not feel at ease in his new elegance. Mother and the family were full of praise, but I noticed that the suit was badly made and that one lapel was fully an inch higher than the other. However, he had made one undeniable improvement in his appearance; his nails were actually manicured and no longer bitten to the quick.

"I wish to God the Prince of Wales would start wearing soft shirts with his evening clothes. Then we could all get rid of these terrible stiff collars," he complained. When Mother, taking pity on him, suggested that he wear his uniform which would be cooler, he looked pathetically relieved and grateful.

On the second day at luncheon Hitler was agitated by the thought of an ordeal that faced him in the afternoon; his old patrons, the Bechsteins, had arrived. Frau Bechstein who had supported him throughout those early years in Munich was the first and most vehement critic of his performance after his accession to power. The "terror of the party," his aides called her. Now she had notified Hitler of her address, and her protégé was honor-bound to make a call. The prospect of a tongue-lashing from this formidable Valkyrie was more than he could face. Throughout luncheon he tried to persuade us children to make the call with him and soften Frau Bechstein's blows, but we were so amused at the thought of Wolf trembling before her that we refused to go.

Hitler sent his aides scouring the town for red roses and, waiting as long as he dared so that there would be very little time before the afternoon performance, he set out in the black Mercedes with his arms full of roses.

The big social event of the week was Hitler's reception to the artists. This first year it was arranged informally,

but in the succeeding years it became known officially as
the Führer *Empfang*. The huge affair was held at Wahnfried with Mother arranging the catering and acting as official hostess. In issuing the invitations she was faced with
a dilemma; should she or shouldn't she invite the performers who were Jews or had Jewish wives or husbands?
This year she solved it by inviting everybody, hoping, the
Jewish halves would stay away. A number of the more
courageous artists, Herbert Janssen among them, left town
for the day and on their return were in Hitler's black
books—the Führer didn't like to be snubbed.

The invitations were issued for nine o'clock on the evening that *Rheingold* was scheduled as it was a short drama,
out at seven-thirty. Mother, the Göbbels, my brothers and
sister received, presenting the guests to the Führer. I
passed down the receiving line with a group of friends and
spent the rest of the evening in a quiet corner of the garden looking on at the party, interrupted occasionally by
a maid who wanted me to settle a crisis in the kitchen,
such as the plight of a poor guard who felt that nothing
but good French cognac would relieve his toothache.

The guests milled about the two long buffets, the drinks
in one room, the food in the other, and carried their sup-
pers to little tables in the garden that was lighted with
Chinese lanterns. The ambitious guests crowded as closely
around Hitler as possible. At first the Führer sat with
the artists, but he couldn't endure a normal conversation·
for longer than five minutes. Leaping to his feet he turned
the casual talk into a two-hour oration on world or artistic
affairs.

A few of the curious who stood around at the beginning
attracted others—they flocked from the far corners of the
garden and were soon packed so tightly that we could
barely see the Führer's forelock. He proceeded to go
through all his paces, starting with his voice low-pitched
and raising it so high that it cracked and emerged from his
throat as hoarse noises. By the end of the speech the audi-

ence was in a state of hysteria. Many of them rushed over to our group, purple in the face as though they were under the effect of a drug.

"It was divine, it was a revelation," they exclaimed, flailing their arms. But when we asked them, "What did the Führer talk about?" they couldn't tell us; they hadn't listened but had been carried away by their emotions. This was exactly what Hitler had intended. I was interested to see how easily he resumed his deep, resonant, natural voice after he had hypnotized his audience.

The performances that year were exceptionally good. Janssen, Leider, Onegin and Kipnis had never sung better and Strauss was a great conductor although with age his tempi had increased to a flabbergasting speed. He conducted the first act of *Parsifal* in one hour and thirty-five mintues against Toscanini's two hours and two minutes, and Muck's one hour and fifty-four. Another record that he broke was the time of Beethoven's *Ninth Symphony* which he conducted at the memorial concert for Father; he made it in forty-five minutes sharp, without so much as a damp collar or a drop of perspiration. Wolfi coined a phrase that swept through Bayreuth: "Strauss's *Parsifal* is wonderful. It's like a waltz all the way through. You actually stay awake."

Hitler was lavish with his praise of the cycle. At that time he was determined to be a patron of the arts: he had just tried to engineer the passage of a law to restore the right of the performance of *Parsifal* to Bayreuth exclusively, as Wagner had wished, but the opposition in his Cabinet was too strong. Only a few people, the members said, could attend the Bayreuth festivals, and if the bill were passed people would hear *Parsifal* in Zürich, Prague, Vienna, or Paris, cities near but outside of the Reich, in which the German copyright law was not effective. Hitler desisted, but he soon came back with another bill to exempt Bayreuth from taxes—it was the only private opera in Germany, hence the only one that was

102

taxed. His Finance Minister didn't agree so Bayreuth continued to pay fantastic sums in taxes, and the Führer gave up the attempt to carve a niche for himself in musical history.

It was a relief when his visit was over and we could relax from the stiffness of official etiquette. Göbbels, however, stayed on and through him mother was able to straighten out some of Strauss's troubles about his libretti. The Nazis resented the fact that all of them were written by Jews and had actually banned the world première of *Die Schweigsame Frau* because Stefan Zweig had written the book. The director of the Dresden opera at which all of Strauss's operas were premièred, made a pilgrimage to Bayreuth and implored Göbbels for permission to go ahead with the work. Finally Mother talked Göbbels into giving his consent, but he made it a law that the name of the librettist must be omitted if he was a Jew. In all future schoolbooks, for instance, Heine's "Lorelei" which had become a national folk song known to every German child, was printed under the words "Poet Unknown."

It was at about this time that Strauss naïvely told Mother about the Göbbels plan to "dethrone the Wagners" by building a rival Festspielhaus on the hill just behind us. The blueprints of the new state theater were already made by an architect who was a member of the Bayreuth staff, and Göbbels had begun to negotiate with the city for the land. Strauss, who was involved in the plan and very enthusiastic about it, assumed that Mother had been informed. She went directly to Hitler and asked whether this had been done with his consent, and he, with fits of rage, put a stop to the scheme.

My only personal brush with Nazi officialdom came on an evening when *Rheingold* had just come to an end. As Frida Leider and I were having supper with a group of friends in the restaurant, Lieselotte rushed up to me and whispered excitedly that Röhm and Schemm were sitting at a table on the other side and as the rest of the family

103

had disappeared, wouldn't I please go over and entertain them? I followed her eyes and saw six men in uniform surrounded with innumerable mugs of beer.

In a little while I went over to the Nazi dignitaries to do the honors of the family. Schemm I knew; everybody in Bayreuth liked him until he developed a mania for expensive cars for which his fellow citizens were none too willing to pay. Röhm was tall and thickset with a full-moon sort of face blotched with innumerable fencing scars. His nose was little more than a stump, and a pair of small steel-blue eyes peered out of his florid face. The others were nondescript—one of them, I noticed, was sucking a fat cigar. We found conversation heavy going; they couldn't think of anything to say about the performance and their jokes were for the most part entirely over my head. Suddenly the fat one with the cigar pushed at me a piece of paper on which were written a dozen or more names.

"Can you tell me," he asked, "which of these are Jews?"

I looked at the list and found on it the names of our greatest artists. I tried hard to control a mounting rage.

"Here in Bayreuth," I answered, "we are not in the least interested in our artists' grandmothers, but if you must know, only two of these names are Jews and they are Americans so it can't possibly matter to you."

Perhaps it was a futile gesture to state my conviction as that of Bayreuth, the real Bayreuth, but I did believe it even though I had no proof. Father, I kept reassuring myself, would never have lent himself to this intolerance and persecution and I wished over and over again that I had some way of establishing his point of view. But all I could do was to hold to my own convictions and never be afraid to fight for them.

Several years later, after I had left Germany, I found by pure chance a letter written by my father for the very purpose of expressing his stand clearly and unmistakably. It was addressed to one of those gentlemen who wanted him to exclude not only Jewish artists from Bayreuth but also Jewish visitors. This is what he wrote as long ago as 1921.

Dear Mr. Püringer,

In answer to your letter, which I found here on my return, I feel bound to tell you that I do not agree with your views at all. Among the Jews we count a great many loyal, honest and unselfish adherents who have given us numerous proofs of their devotion. You suggest that we should turn all these people from our doors? Repulse them for no other reason than that they are Jews? Is that human? Is that Christian? Is that German? No! If we wanted to behave like that, we Germans would first have to become quite a different sort of people and have consciences clear as a mountain stream. But we have nothing of the kind. The lives of all great Germans prove that they have been treated with meanness, indifference, malice and stupidity by the German people.

The festivals from 1876 to 1889 demonstrate the truth of what I have just said. To cover the deficit my father, who was ill at that time, had to travel to England and conduct concerts there. It was not even possible to scrape together the ridiculous sum of a hundred and fifty thousand marks. And then, when later on, thank heaven, Englishmen, Frenchmen, Americans and other friends made the pilgrimage to Bayreuth and helped to bridge over the financial crisis, the German bourgeoisie had nothing better to do than to complain that foreigners were receiving preferential treatment in Bayreuth.

Yes! Why hadn't they found the way there themselves? Not until my father's works had been triumphantly acclaimed in Paris, did our supercilious Germans begin to think that possibly Richard Wagner might be somebody after all, and that they might risk a journey to Bayreuth without compromising themselves too far. And so gradually the Germans began to visit Bayreuth. But without the foreigners we should have been done for long before. Well then, have we Germans the right to exclude others who are prepared to make sacrifices and contribute to the reopening of the festivals? I deny that with all my strength at my command.

And if the Jews are willing to help us, that is doubly meritorious, because my father in his writings attacked and offended them. They would, therefore, have—and they have

105

—every reason to hate Bayreuth. Yet, in spite of my father's attacks, a great many of them revere my father's art with genuine enthusiasm. You must be well acquainted with the name of former Jewish adherents. Who at that time, carried on a press campaign for my father? George Davidsohn and Dohm! You must have heard too of Taussig and Heinrich Porges. Josef Rubinstein arranged "Parsifal" for the piano, and Levi conducted the first performance of "Parsifal." And if among a hundred thousand Jews there should be no more than a single one who is devoted heart and soul to my father's art, I should feel shame if I were to turn him back just because he is a Jew.

On our Bayreuth hill we want to do *positive* work, not negative. Whether a man is a Chinese, a Negro, an American, an Indian or a Jew, that is a matter of complete indifference to us. But we might learn from the Jews how to stick together and how to give help. With envy and admiration I see how the Jews assist their artists, how they pave the way for them. If I were a Jew my operas would be performed in every theater. As things are, however, we must wait till we are dead.

No, my dear Mr. Püringer, it is we who must bear the blame for the hopeless state of affairs in our fatherland because we have no national pride, because we leave our own men in the lurch. Are we now to add intolerance to all our other bad qualities and reject people of good will? Are you really prepared to deny that among the Jews there are people whose enthusiasm for Bayreuth is genuine? They are a people that I will not and must not offend. I am in a position to show you that you are wrong and even to give you the names of a very large number. In selecting our artists we have never taken the racial question into consideration. We have been guided solely by voice, talent and appearance suitable for the part in question, and that is a principle by which we shall continue to abide in the future.

I hope that you will grasp my meaning. Bayreuth is to be a true work of *Peace.*

Faithfully yours,

Siegfried Wagner

106

CHAPTER XII

UNEASY SUMMER

HEILIGENGRABE again, the striped prisonlike
blouses, the white and yellow puddings and the ancient Stifts ladies upholding a vanished glory in their convent residences, shut in by their little gardens! From
Lilliput to the Eden Hotel, from droned hymns at evensong
to the Staatsoper—I had enjoyed the holidays all the
more because of their glittering contrast with my cloistered
life. Winter passed, the snow melted, the apple trees in
the convent orchards burst into bloom and it was the spring
of 1934—time to return to Wahnfried and help prepare
for another festival.

Scarcely had I reached Bayreuth when the whole of
Germany was shaken by the Nazi blood purge. No one
knew what to say, what to think, so people whispered to
each other and the rumors grew. At Wahnfried Mother
instructed everyone to keep silent about it when Hitler
came for the opening of the festival.

"Poor Führer," she reasoned. "What a terrible shock it
must have been to find himself betrayed by his best
friend."

When he arrived the atmosphere was tense, but on the
very first day of his visit, Hitler cleared it by speaking
about the purge with cool detachment. Seeing that he
actually liked to talk about it, the family stopped being
tactful and asked him what had happened.

Hitler swore that not more than seventy-seven people
were executed. It was unavoidable that several people were
shot by mistake, Willi Schmidt in Munich, for instance.

107

The S. S. were a little hasty in arresting the first Willi
Schmidt they came across and having him shot without
trial, but just think how many Willi Schmidts there must
be in Munich. He had ordered a state pension for the
widow and children.

That was Hitler's version, but everybody at the Festspielhaus was talking about the purge in shocked whispers.
"Just imagine, the Führer arrested Röhm personally
early in the morning and found him in bed with another
man." I contributed the only comedy relief by commenting with the worldly wisdom of my sixteen years, "But
imagine how embarrassing it would have been if they had
found him with a woman."

Not until several months later did Hitler tell Mother
the "true" story of the purge. She was always using her
influence to get people out of concentration camps, but in
the case of young Du Moulin Eckhart, the son of the old
count who was Cosima's friend, she had no success. He
had been in Dachau ever since the purge and his desperate
father couldn't even learn the reason for his confinement.

"Don't try to plead for this one," Hitler interrupted
Mother. "He is the worst traitor of them all." He reminded
her that he had suspected a traitor in the Brown House for
over a year because every day the most secret details of
his consultations were published in a Paris newspaper
within twenty-four hours. He had all the doors watched,
all the closets searched—the traitor was bound to be
inside. In the meantime he learned that one of the staff
of the *Münchener Neue Presse* which was owned by the
Social Democrats, had managed to buy Röhm's love letters
written from Bolivia to a young man in Germany and
later known as the Bolivian letters. Frightened by the
paper's threat to publish them, Röhm ordered young Du
Moulin Eckhart who was one of his aides to get them at
whatever price. The price was to make daily reports on
the secret sessions at the Brown House which Eckhart
delivered with the full knowledge and approval of Röhm.

"Eckhart should have been shot with the others," Hitler said, "but he was lucky. He hid in the woods of Wiesbaden until I had ordered the shooting to stop. That's why he is in Dachau and why he will remain."

Another of Hitler's favorite remarks was, "I hope you realize that the first bomb in the next war will drop on the Festspielhaus and the second on Wahnfried. It's only five minutes by air from Czechoslovakia." Altogether, the festival was not a happy one.

It was during the performance of *Rheingold* that Hitler received the news of the assassination of Dollfuss. It was evident to the people in our box that something unusual was going on because Schaub and Brückner kept alternating between the Hitler box and the anteroom of the family's box where there was a telephone. One would receive the news and the other whisper it to Hitler. After the performance the Führer was most excited. This excitement mounted as he told us the horrible news. It was terrible to witness.

Although he could scarcely wipe the delight from his face Hitler carefully ordered dinner in the restaurant as usual.

"I must go across for an hour and show myself," he said, "or people will think I had something to do with this." As if they were quite unaware of the fast-spreading news, Hitler and his whole party sat in the restaurant eating liver dumplings.

With Frida Leider and a group of friends I went down to another restaurant in the city where we would not see the Nazi officials gloating over their beer and seltzer, but we could not escape hysterical people celebrating the murder of the courageous little man who had dared to oppose the Führer. In a loud group Josef von Manowarda, one of our bassos, and his wife were holding a reunion with their colleagues, the Franz Völkers, shouting in their Austrian dialect, rejoicing that finally Austria would be Nazified.

"The Führer promised me that he would send me to

109

Vienna immediately by plane," Manowarda kept shouting. "You will see—by special plane." But nobody seemed to care.

A few days afterward, persuaded by Nickel, Hitler promised to receive Frau von Manowarda in the Fürstenzimmer during one of the intermissions. She made her entrance, red-faced, already in a mild state of hysteria, curtsied twice and when Hitler kissed her hand, was so overcome that she had to be carried from the room by a couple of aides. We didn't know whether to laugh or look away.

Frau von Manowarda was fat, bleached, middle-aged, by no means a Mata Hari, but we heard later that she became one of the most active of Nazi secret service agents engaged in ferreting out Hitler's Austrian enemies. Herbert Janssen and I happened to see her two years later and were intrigued by the huge gold swastika that she wore on her right hand, held in place by chains that were fastened to a bracelet and to rings on her thumb and little finger. Before I could get around to it, Janssen asked her what it was.

"Oh, it covers the spot where the Führer kissed me!" cooed Frau von Manowarda.

"What a pity he didn't kiss you on the mouth," replied the usually reserved, well-mannered Janssen.

The Manowarda performance was not unusual; it often puzzled and disturbed me to see people making fools of themselves when they were with Hitler. I couldn't understand why men and women who seemed perfectly normal otherwise, appeared to lose their senses in his presence, went purple in the face, dropped their cups and saucers and burst into hysterical fits of tears and laughter. One of the most remarkable phenomena was the way their voices were affected by the Führer. Often, quite unconsciously, when they talked to him they raised their voices at least an octave. These things puzzled me. Sometimes I made the mistake of commenting on them.

110

1. Cosima and Richard Wagner, 1872

2. The Festspielhaus at Bayreuth, designed by Wagner for the presentation of his music dramas

3. Wagner with his son Siegfried, 1880

4. Wahnfried, the Wagner home in Bayreuth. The bust is that of Ludwig II of Bavaria

5. Wagner's library at Wahnfried, used during festival seasons for receptions to the notables who gathered at Bayreuth

6. Winifred and Siegfried Wagner at the time of their marriage

7. Siegfried Wagner's children Wolfgang—Verena—Wieland—Friedelind in the costumes in which they performed their version of "The Ring," 1924

8. Friedelind Wagner and Toscanini at the Buenos Aires airport, 1941

"Isn't it disgusting the way so and so behaved?" But the answer I received was always a variation on the same theme, "Why not learn how to behave yourself instead of criticizing others?"

The Führer *Empfang* that season was smaller, more official and more painful than the first. This time Mother invited only the artists, hoping to avoid embarrassing situations, but this arrangement created much discontent.

To add to the feeling of unrest, Hindenburg became mortally ill during the first week of the festival, and Hitler rushed from Bayreuth to his deathbed. On the day of the funeral every theater, opera house and place of entertainment in the Reich was closed. This meant a hasty rearrangement of the schedule at the Festspielhaus which normally played *Das Rheingold* on Monday, *Die Walküre* on Tuesday, *Siegfried* on Wednesday, recessed a day and finished a week with *Die Götterdämmerung*. As Hindenburg's funeral was on a Tuesday in which the Festspielhaus was opened and the service broadcast from a loud speaker on the stage set for the first act of *Die Walküre*, the remaining three music dramas followed on successive days, giving Lorenz and Leider three heavy roles with no opportunity to rest. They met the emergency but vowed they would never do it again.

Hitler wanted Furtwängler to conduct at the funeral but no one could find him, not even the Gestapo. Later rumor had it that he was spending a romantic holiday on a Polish estate and had been careful to leave his address with no one.

After the funeral was over we settled back for a less strained two weeks at the Festspielhaus. All day I stayed at the theater, even when I wasn't busy. Something interesting was always going on, and it was pleasanter than the critical atmosphere at Wahnfried. Strauss, who was back again in the guest house, was a fascinating conductor to watch. There was something disconcerting about his honesty. He would remark suddenly, when listening to a

111

rehearsal of one of his own works, "I like this, it turned out very well," or he would say, "I don't care for this—I didn't do a good job." He commented to me one day with utter simplicity, "People say I'm a plagiarist. Of course I borrow from other composers. Why shouldn't I? So much beautiful music has been written. Why not use it again?"

All the time Wahnfried was like a hotel, guests coming, guests going, guests for luncheon, dinner, tea. Emma was brisk and grim. When three maids couldn't manage the dinners, she put on a uniform and helped to wait on the table. During the festivals Mother doubled her staff of servants and arranged their hours so that they worked in rotation; those who were up late slept late, those who were on duty one day were given free time to attend the performances on the next.

Luckily Mother didn't have much time to discipline me, but the friction was always there. She had learned that her boiling point was much lower than mine and that she usually got the worst of an argument when she lost her temper and I kept mine, so she avoided encounters. When she wanted to tell me anything disagreeable she instructed Lieselotte to tell somebody to tell me, or she wrote a note and laid it by my plate at the breakfast table. I can still feel the constriction in my stomach that the sight of these notes caused: I could never guess what I had done or what the punishment would be.

The friendliest haven was Eva's drawing room in which the aunts always listened to my affairs with sympathy and affection. That autumn Daniela had received an offer to lecture on Wagner in Vienna, and managed to insert in the contract that the date should be within the week of Toscanini's concert and that she should be entertained at the same hotel. Toscanini was her idol. She told me that she asked him why he had accepted an offer to conduct the Jewish Orchestra in Palestine.

"*Per l'umanità*," he answered. Daniela's voice broke

112

when she repeated his words and her thin, sensitive old face flushed with admiration.

It was hard to go back to Heiligengrabe after my summer with Frida Leider, Janssen, Erna Carstens, Onegin and the rest, the gay parties and expeditions, the lively conversation at Bayreuth; something like being demoted from a university to a kindergarten. Affairs were not running smoothly in the convent, and under her calm front the Äbtissin was worried. The royal visits for which she had so happily bought the china, the glass and the raspberry syrup had given the school a bad reputation among the Nazis and the visit of the Crown Prince that autumn was the final proof that Heiligengrabe was reactionary and monarchistic.

The Crown Prince arrived one Sunday morning just before we started to church. I was upstairs in *Mauseloch*, a tiny "mousehole" that I had to myself this year, when Cecilchen appeared in the doorway and said, "Papa would like to see you."

"Where on earth is he?" I asked.

"Don't you know?" she answered blushing—she always blushed. "Everybody is downstairs." Just then we heard noisy hurrahs and I couldn't help laughing because although I was entirely innocent, everyone would think I was staying away on purpose to avoid bending the knee to royalty. The Crown Prince whom I had met a few weeks earlier in Wahnfried, didn't recognize me at first in the ridiculous school cape and beret, but when he did we both smiled. Later the Abtissin said to me, "I was surprised, Friedelind, that you curtsied to His Imperial Highness.' But I told her it was the least I could do in view of the money Mother was spending on my education.

One morning not long after, the Äbtissin called me into her study. Her hands trembled and she was so distressed that she forgot to watch my curtsy with a critical eye. She showed me an official order to close the school immediately and wanted me to call Mother on the phone, hoping her

113

influence might save the school. I was eager to try, but it would be a miracle to find Mother at home; she was most likely driving somewhere along the highway or in a railway carriage or an airplane. All morning I stayed on the phone and finally learned where I could reach her that night. The other girls were indignant.

"When Friedelind feels like talking to her mother she simply takes the morning off," they jibed, "and the teachers don't even say a word." But I kept the secret and that night reached Mother who promised to do what she could. She bombarded the Minister of Culture and Education and the district leader of Brandenburg, telling them that the school was being unjustly denounced by one hundred and fifty per cent Nazis, and that she would certainly not educate her daughter there if she had a single doubt about the spirit of the institution or its faculty.

At last the Nazi officials arrived at a compromise, they removed the old Stifts ladies as teachers and placed in charge a "technical director" who was both a chaplain and a super-Nazi. He was so rude to the Äbtissin that we heartily disliked him and did nothing to help him restore order. For three months, while the Nazis were looking for substitutes, we had no history lessons, no literature, no mathematics. Finally one substitute arrived, but she increased the havoc by immediately breaking her leg.

When she knew that Heiligengrabe was re-established in official favor, the Äbtissin felt it correct to inform the senior grade about the difficulties through which the school had passed, so she assembled us in her study and told us what Mother had done. Without mentioning names, she concluded, "We owe our survival entirely to the kindness and generous support of a very important personage who came to Heiligengrabe's rescue."

Of course every one guessed that the Äbtissin was talking about Mother. From then on my friends thought I should take advantage of the fact that I had the whip hand. When I wanted to get away for a week end they

114

would say, "You have only to mention Hitler and you can stay as long as you please." But somehow I didn't want to take advantage of a favored position, so I remained the only one of the four Wagner children who never flourished an excuse that read, "By the Führer's express wish and order my son or daughter will be absent from school for a period. . . ."

At Christmas Mother was highly amused by my tale about the difficulties of the Herr Pastor among the Stifts ladies and told Hitler about it when he came to Bayreuth for the funeral of handsome Hans Schemm. Perhaps the occasion made Wolf sensitive about health, his own and everybody's, for he seemed to have the subject on his mind. Seeing Mother take a pill at luncheon, he inquired anxiously, "Are you taking it on a doctor's prescription?"

"Yes, of course," answered Mother, surprised.

"Then it's all right," Hitler agreed, "but I hope you never take any medicine unless you know what it is and have a doctor's prescription." Whereupon he told her how he nearly met his end taking pills that weren't prescribed for him. One day at luncheon his old friend, Müller, took a couple of pills and recommended them to Hitler, saying that they were wonderful for the gall bladder. Hitler was so impressed by his friend's enthusiasm that he took them for at least a year until he began to have fits which were something like strokes. The doctors actually gave him up after a rally at Hamburg.

"That night they forced me to name my successor and make my will. I was really a candidate for death and no one could find the cause until one day at the Chancellery my physician saw me taking my pills. He had one of them analyzed and found that it contained nothing but pure ethyl alcohol. Here was I, a teetotaler, poisoning myself with the worst of all alcohols." Hitler gave a frustrated little shrug. "I am still on a diet to get it out of my system."

With his own bitter experiences on his mind he turned his attention to his special favorite, Nickel, who had

115

reached the age when one becomes figure-conscious and was living on a starvation diet. Everybody was coaxing her to eat but without success. She was dressed in her Hitler Maiden uniform and very bewitching she looked in it too, with her straight young figure and her pointed face with its crown of yellow curls. When no blandishments would move her to eat a jelly doughnut, Hitler tried his authority as her commander.

"Look here, my dear, you are wearing the uniform of the Youth movement and have sworn an oath to obey and follow me until death. Yet here I am saying, 'eat a doughnut,' and you say 'no.'"

Verena turned on him her most irresistible smile but she did *not* eat the doughnut.

CHAPTER XIII

GOLD LEAF AND NOODLE SOUP

AFTER my return to Heiligengrabe at the end of the holidays, Nickel went to Jena to see Mother who was very ill at Dr. Veil's clinic, and later came on to Berlin where I met her for a week end. She was disappointed that Mother wasn't able to come along for she had visions of the smart creations she was going to find in the Berlin shops. Her technique was infallible; she did her own prospecting and, after having discovered what she wanted, was particularly attentive to Mother for a day or two. Next came the suggestion that she wanted to show Mother something very attractive which she had noticed in a shop-window. Mother went, the costumes Nickel had chosen were trotted out, and Mother bought them, every one, delighted to see how charming her Nickel looked in them.

As indeed she did—at fourteen Nickel was a slim, adorable little coquette with admirers, old and young, showering her with sweets and flowers.

We stayed at the apartment which Mother had leased, with the housekeeper looking after us, preferring it to a hotel. I took my responsibilities as a chaperone seriously, trying to keep an eye on Nickel.

Nickel was excited to find an invitation from Wolf for luncheon on Sunday. Nickel always kept him informed of her whereabouts and many a ride she took in the Hitler or Göring cars. Into Saturday we squeezed all the engagements a day would hold, a rehearsal of the opera in the morning, luncheon with Frida Leider in her attractive apartment, a dinner party after the opera.

Everybody was talking about some aspect of the same theme, the musical desert that Germany had become. Since such great artists as Kreisler, Menuhin, Rachmaninoff, Heifetz, Schnabel, Horowitz, Serkin and Hubermann—to name a few—had either refused engagements in the Third Reich or were not welcome, the Nazis had no one of international reputation except Walter Gieseking who performed seldom in public, and Elly Ney. Backhaus was at the moment Hitler's favorite pianist, but there were rumors that all was not peaceful between them.

"Have you heard the joke that Erich Kleiber played on the Gestapo?" our friends asked, and "You know about Furtwängler?"

Nickel was entranced with the story of Kleiber's farewell to the Staatsoper. He had played for the last time a few weeks after Christmas, a special command performance of *Tannhäuser*. Knowing that on the morning of the performance the Gestapo would turn the opera house inside out looking for hidden weapons, Kleiber locked his alarm clock in his desk drawer. The Gestapo heard the ticking and went into huddles at a respectful distance from the suspected time bomb. Finally they produced their equipment to destroy the bomb, then ordered a lower

117

Black Shirt whose life was not so precious, to force open the desk, much to the delight of the opera staff who were watching from the corridors.

Kleiber left Germany a few days after the incident. Furtwängler who had been forced out of the Staatsoper at the same time—a "resignation" it was labeled officially—owed his troubles chiefly to the machinations of Tietjen. His troubles with the Nazis began with the creation of Göring's Prussian State Council, a collection of intellectuals upon whom he conferred the title of state councilor, a salary of six thousand marks a year, a huge roll of parchment decorated with a red seal and a red ribbon, and the privilege of traveling free and first class on German railroads. This honor was to compensate for heavy cuts in salaries. At that time Furtwängler was earning only twenty-five thousand marks a year as director of the Berlin Philharmonic Orchestra and twenty-four thousand as musical director of the Staatsoper.

He had managed to survive the dismissal of Dr. Geissmar —she was somewhere in the country and couldn't get out of Germany because the Nazis had taken away her passport; by continual rows he had managed to keep his Jewish musicians in the Philharmonic; but he owed the first step in his downfall to Göring's newly conferred title of *Herr Staatsrat.*

Tietjen slyly placed posters about the Staatsoper instructing all members of the staff that Dr. Furtwängler hereafter wished to be addressed as *Herr Staatsrat.* Immediately the people about the opera house called poor Furtwängler *Herr Staatsrat* with such exaggerated deference that the atmosphere was anything but pleasant. All of these rows Tietjen fostered, whispering to Göring suspicions of Furtwängler, especially because he continued to include in his repertoire the works of his friend, Hindemith, who had long since left Germany. The official "resignation" from all Furtwängler's government positions was forced over the Hindemith issue, but the conductor actually lost them because his enemies were too powerful. The one who was most satisfied with the accomplishment was Tietjen.

On this holiday Tietjen was particularly pleasant to us in the matter of tickets for the opera and all the little attentions that he could devise, because, I suspected, he had incurred the dislike of Hitler and was relying on Mother for protection. She kept telling the Führer that Tietjen was a very great artist and that she couldn't manage Bayreuth without him. She even went so far as to testify for him in a lawsuit brought by a singer whom he had discharged. He was always being sued and always by one means or another winning his cases.

Tietjen enjoyed showing me his offices in the Administration Building of the state theaters and the other in the Staatsoper a few blocks away. At his office on the Oberwallstrasse he pointed to the little button under his writing desk which switched on a dictaphone in the office of his secretary next door and recorded every word his visitors said. These records, he told me, were labeled with the date, the hour and name of the person and filed away in the archives to be brought out when he wanted them. Another interesting apparatus which gave Tietjen great delight was a system of microphones by which he could not only follow rehearsals but catch the lowest whisper backstage or on-stage in every corner of the domain. He switched it on and let me listen to the rehearsal going on at the State Theatre.

One day, according to his story, which he told me with relish, he happened to tune in backstage at the Staatsoper and hear a remark of the famous baritone, Rudolf Bockelmann, who had given Tietjen many headaches since he had turned violent Nazi in 1933 and become the party boss of the opera. One of the singers was asking Bockelmann why he had become a Nazi.

"Why not?" answered Bockelmann. "After all, one has to howl with the wolves." This recording was put on the

119

shelves awaiting the time when it would be valuable to the director.

Officially Tietjen never became a Nazi but he did Göring many services. He boasted that he was the only Federal employee in Germany who had not sworn the Nazi oath, a feat upon which he counted to save his skin in case he survived the Nazi regime.

Hitler had recently moved into the Chancellery which had been rebuilt according to his design, so we were curious to see what he had accomplished as a decorator. At the entrance we were received by countless S. S. men, tall fellows who clicked their heels, heiled and showed us into the huge entrance hall. I looked at the marble floor and the ship models in glass cases along the wall. Here we were turned over to Brückner and Kannenberg who led us through a pale green salon, the only room in which one could smoke, to Hitler's drawing room.

Curiously I looked about this huge, handsome room with its French windows that opened on a garden. It was on two levels; in the far end which was approached by two steps stood the conference table that was always photographed with famous visiting statesmen. At each end precious tapestries covered the entire wall. While we were admiring the room Hitler entered. He wanted to be sure that we noticed the thick carpet which, he said, had been ordered by the League of Nations—he had taken it when the League had run short of money and was unable to pay for it.

In the meantime Kannenberg announced that Hitler's breakfast was ready so we followed him back through the green salon, across a somber room with an enormous fireplace topped by a coat of arms that looked as though it had been left over from the Bismarck period, through the dining room and into a gay winter garden with two walls of French windows and red lacquered furniture set among hothouse plants that reached to the ceiling. Here we watched Hitler take his glass of milk and two slices of unbuttered bread. Kannenberg produced a plate of tempting little sandwiches, but Hitler, noting my interest, advised me not to spoil my appetite as luncheon would be ready in a minute.

We returned to the dining room and took our places at the table which seated about twenty people, Nickel sitting as always between Wolf and his physician. While awaiting the inevitable noodle soup I glanced about at the room, the red leather chairs and red carpet, the walls, cream colored except for the side that was entirely French windows. Behind the enormous buffet was an oil, a feast of Bacchus by Moritz von Schwindt, and in the center of each of the side walls, a semicircular niche in which stood a golden-bronze statue, Eve on one side, facing Adam on the other. Göbbels commented to me that the statues were lighted indirectly at night and very effective.

After the luncheon, a dull one at which the conversation was directed chiefly toward Nickel and her starvation diet, Wolf asked us if we would like to see the whole place. "Of course," we chorused.

First he took us to the kitchen—huge hearths, long tables, immense sinks, any number of electrical machines, all new, shining and modern. Perhaps a dozen cooks, men and women, clad alike in cream coveralls, lifted their arms high and shouted "Heil." Hitler beamed with pride but raised his arm only from the elbow; he reserved the straight arm for official occasions.

We followed Wolf through a comfortable billiard room, a lounge for his guards, to his operating room, complete with every piece of modern hospital equipment.

"This was my idea," he told us proudly. "At a moment's notice every member of my household can be operated on without leaving the Chancellery."

We returned to the anteroom of the enormous drawing room. The Führer explained that he used it as a dressing room for artists when he gave concerts in the evening. Temporarily the upper part of the drawing room was the stage, but he was planning to build a room next the winter garden which would have a real stage and in which he could entertain at least three hundred people at dinner.

Opening another door, Hitler showed us two motion-picture machines and complete equipment, including archives which held hundreds of films from every country. Hurrying us back to the drawing room, he pushed a button that removed the tapestry from both walls and left a perfect screen at one and showed the holes for the projection machine at the other.

"I love to see pictures in the evening," Wolf told us, "especially the French films. They record the life of the *petite bourgeoisie* better than any of the others. I'm almost sorry that they can't be shown to the public."

Hitler looked about the drawing room with an approving air.

"Nickel, you wouldn't believe it, but this room was four little holes of offices. The workmen took out two thousand truckloads of dirt and stucco from the building before you could begin to breathe. I refused to move into it when I first saw it, but finally I thought something could be done. One day when I was inspecting the work, in came some of those old women from the Foreign Office. You should have heard their lamentations. Your mother complains about your old aunts. My God, I have my old aunts too and they are right here in the Foreign Office."

Upstairs we passed through Hitler's library, a dark paneled room with three walls covered with glass-doored bookcases. The doors were lined with green cloth because the Führer didn't like the messy impression of the different sizes, colors and heights of the volumes. Opening from it was Hitler's bedroom which looked more like that of a governess than a dictator—a white iron bedstead, a table, a bed table and a straight wooden chair, all painted white, and nothing else. The single decoration in the room was an oil portrait of the Führer's mother copied from the only photograph in existence.

We looked out of the windows into the garden but we did not see the bath or dressing room because at the

122

moment Hitler's valet, a sickly looking little mouse, emerged from the dressing room with one of the dictator's suits over his arm and gave a start at seeing two women in his master's sacred bedroom. However, we couldn't help seeing one of his closets which stood open when we entered. Nickel glanced at me and I at her. It was like a Walt Disney fantasy, nothing but brown shirts on rows of hangers, one after the other—there must have been thirty-five or forty of them, each with the swastika on the left sleeve. We each put on a very solemn face, the expression that the Führer assumed when he looked at his mother's picture.

By this time Nickel in her high heels was beginning to be restless and I myself would not have scorned a nice soft sofa, but Wolf was fresh as a May morning and thoroughly enjoying himself. We were dragged right through Schaub's office and Hitler's office with the Lembach portrait of the Iron Chancellor over the desk, and we were of course expected to admire the collection of thousands and thousands of scrolls making Hitler a citizen of honor of this town and that.

"Pretty soon I'll be a citizen of every village in the Reich," Wolf said. "Some of these are fascinating, real works of art; I must show them to you later." We both smiled wanly and hoped the moment would never come.

In the cabinet room Hitler pointed to a highly polished table at least fifteen feet long, made of one piece of wood. He seemed to have a mania for these long tables, most of them designed by his favorite architect, Troost. Twenty-four armchairs were upholstered in petit-point, the *Hoheitsabzeichen* ("insignia of the highest order") worked in the Nazi colors, red and black and white. This emblem Hitler had designed himself; he had given Wieland the original drawing of the eagle holding between his claws a round shield bearing the swastika. In front of each seat lay a red leather folding blotter decorated with the eagle and marked with the name of the cabinet member in gold leaf. Beside it were the inkpots, one for blue ink and one for red, and the pencils all sharpened to the prescribed length. High up on the walls were tapestries depicting scenes from the Nordic sagas, and over it all hung a chandelier which again looked as though it were a hand-me-down from Bismarck.

More stairs, the rooms of aides-de-camp, guest rooms. The guest rooms were not very attractive.

"Whenever you come to Berlin and there is no one to look after you in your apartment, you are always welcome to stay here. You know I would be delighted and I am sure Mama would not mind having me look after you for awhile."

We thanked Hitler hastily, and whispered to each other that we hoped the occasion would never arise. Nickel said: "I'd rather die than stay cooped in one of those horrible guest rooms."

I was still thinking about Hitler's expression when he was talking about the old busybodies from the Foreign Office, a flaring of the nostrils that I had seen often when he was annoyed or excited. They had stretched almost to his ears on the night Dollfuss was murdered.

"Did you ever notice," I said apropos of nothing at all, "that Wolf's nostrils are so wide they sometimes reach as far as the ends of his mouth?"

CHAPTER XIV

OPERA BALL

ON MY graduation from Heiligengrabe, Mother came to take me to Berlin for a party on my seventeenth birthday. The holiday was gay but brief; two weeks later she put me in a school in Gross Sachsenheim near Stuttgart, another of Knittel's selections. This one was a domestic science school, a large model farm, with donkeys, a dairy, pigs, chickens, electric brooders, fields, gardens. The entire establishment—instructors, administrators and forty-five pupils—was served by only three maids, so we kept house, fed the pigs, looked after the chickens, shucked the corn, dug the potatoes. In our odd moments we studied theoretical chicken raising, farming, home nursing, civics, economics, as well as practical baby care. For our kindergarten classes and courses in changing diapers, we practiced on the village babies.

Why Mother sent me to such a school I could not imagine, certainly not because I had shown the slightest inclination to become a farm hand or a *Hausfrau*. Mother had always maintained that she wanted to be a grandmother at forty, a pretty sentiment that emphasized her youth, but if she was expecting to achieve her objective through me, she would be disappointed. I was determined to do nothing that would enhance my desirability as a bride.

Her method of leaping from one extreme to another was disconcerting both emotionally and physically. First she brought us up with no restraint, no discipline, prided herself that she was very modern and broad-minded, and then, seeing that we were growing up a pack of wild little Indians, she resorted to iron discipline. After two years and a half in a school for princesses in which the diet was designed to give one anemia and the most strenuous exercise provided for us was an afternoon walk, I was suddenly introduced to the hardest kind of physical labor. It was not surprising that my health gave way and that I spent most of the time in bed.

But summer was not too far away and the long vacation at Lake Constance. Tietjen was there as usual, full of news. Furtwängler who had been virtually a prisoner of the Nazis since he had his passport taken away, had "retired to compose." They were laughing about the blunder

125

the Gestapo had made when they arrested a man on a train near the Swiss border whom they mistook for Furtwängler, but who turned out to be an innocent and indignant clergyman in mufti. Although Tietjen and Knittel were anything but friendly, the two exchanged gossip and the financial manager showed Tietjen an order from the Ministry of Propaganda which forbade the newspapers to print the name of Furtwängler until further notice.

Strauss too, it seemed, had been getting into difficulties. The Gestapo who had been reading his letters to Stefan Zweig, came upon such phrases as "I impersonate here the president of the Reichs Music Chamber," and "Whether they are Jews, Chinese, Hottentots or Nazis— who cares anyway? All that matters is the box office success." His correspondence cost him not only his office as president of the Reichs Music Chamber but also his box-office success in Germany for the Nazis banned his operas for more than a year. So he also had retired to Bavaria and was living in seclusion in his home at Garmisch.

When these days in the sun were over I returned to school, but the little pigs of Gross Sachsenheim got very little attention from me that autumn. After a period in a sanitarium recuperating from the potato season I came home for Christmas.

A day or two after the holiday we were in the small drawing room laboring over thank-you letters. I was in demand as an expert letter writer, an accomplishment which the other children regarded cynically as a sort of mental aberration three hundred and sixty-four days of the year. But on this day when my brothers weren't asking me to help them, Nickel was taking me aside to whisper about her correspondence.

"I've got to see Wolf before Mother sends me to that new school in Dresden. Tell me," she asked with her most seductive smile, "how can I hint it diplomatically?"

"Why diplomatically? If you really want to see him, say it so plainly that he won't misunderstand it." So we wrote

126

her letter. Mother gathered all the "thank-you's" without reading them and dispatched them in one large envelope.

When the phone rang at luncheon three days before the New Year and Mother returned to the dining room in a flurry over the news that the Führer wanted us to have dinner with him that night in Munich, we looked as innocent as unshorn lambs.

"But we have only twenty minutes to catch the last train," gasped Mother. And Brückner didn't say what was planned for us."

Without wasting a moment we dashed upstairs to pack.

"Maybe there'll be opera," suggested Nickel hopefully. "Let's take some evening dresses."

Wieland and Wolfi were already in Munich so Brückner was going to collect them. When we arrived at seven we were whisked to Hitler's apartment in the Prinzregentenstrasse by an enormous S. S. man in one of the Führer's big black cars.

"For heaven's sake, Nickerl," Hitler exclaimed when we were settled in the library (with his Austrian accent he always corrupted "Nickel" with harsh "r"), "you are thinner than ever. Are you starving yourself to death?" Sprawling awkwardly on the sofa, he tweaked her braids while he told her as an awful warning the tale of Lillian Harvey, the idol of German movie fans, who went to Hollywood, was forced to reduce, and never could regain her plumpness although she went to bed and ate six meals a day. Her former picture fans would have none of her, and the government lost a fortune.

"Really, Nickerl," Wolf admonished, "nobody loves a skinny woman."

A few minutes later dinner was announced.

"We must hurry," said Hitler. "We have only an hour to make our train."

Nickel glanced at me exultantly. Berlin, museums, the opera. How glad we were that we had brought along our prettiest dresses.

127

In the blue dining room my eyes wandered to the large mirror over the fireplace and the bronze bust of a young girl reflected in it. The girl, I knew, was the Führer's niece, Geli Raubal, who had died suddenly and mysteriously four years earlier in her uncle's apartment. Hitler had told Mother that a fortuneteller had warned Geli of death by a bullet so she had a hysterical fear of guns and pistols. Nevertheless, since she was often alone in the apartment, she kept a pistol at her bedside. Hitler had left for Erlangen the evening she died. His explanation was that she must have tried to unfasten the safety lock and shot herself by accident. Of course no one would ever know, but we children had heard every sort of rumor and "inside story." The newspapers even hinted that he had shot her in a jealous rage.

Geli, I had always imagined as a beautiful creature, but the girl in bronze had a low forehead, broad cheekbones, a broad upturned nose and a mouth that was much too large. I wondered how she could have so fascinated Hitler that he forswore meat, liquor and tobacco in her memory. For the first few years after her death he refused to celebrate Christmas, and drove about the highways aimlessly all day long. Not until 1934 did he begin to gather his "old fighters" on Christmas Eve in Munich.

The conversation which was still dominated by Nickel and her figure didn't hold my attention so while we hastily ate our hors d'oeuvres—Hitler to my surprise was digging into a pound jar of caviar without offering us any of it— I studied the Spitzwegs, six of them, three on either side of the fireplace. Why the Führer who admired the super-dimensional in architecture and sculpture, should have ordered his agents to hunt down and buy Spitzwegs at any price was one of the mysteries about him; but this artist who painted the little *bourgeoisie* with such tender irony was his special God.

As the dinner progressed, aides rushed into the room periodically to report how much time was left. After a hurried dessert we were turned over to two S. S. men who rushed us to the station at mad speed and put us into car number one of a brand-new four-car train. We were just beginning to examine our compartments when we heard a roaring noise, faint, then louder and nearer—the crowds cheering the Führer.

After Hitler, surrounded by his aides, made his usual dash for our moving train, Brückner came forward and invited us to the drawing room, a large one with a phonograph in one corner, on which sat a silver vase full of rather sad-looking flowers. We crawled along; Hitler explained that he didn't like to be thrown out of place on a curve. The *Reichsbahn* had worked out a plan by which his special train could leave in either direction between Berlin and Munich at four specified times a day without advance warning.

Several times we stopped at a station but we couldn't see anything because the windows were tightly blacked out.

"May I please pull up the curtain and let us see where we are?" I asked.

Hitler jumped to the window.

"Oh no, I must do it. First I must turn out the lights so no one can see me from the outside." He pushed the light button, pulled the curtain and we flattened our noses against the window, but we could see nothing but the deserted station platform of a small Bavarian town.

In the morning when we crept into the Anhalter station, Hitler and his aides made a breakneck exit to the fleet of cars that stood waiting in gear. We, however, made a more dignified trip to the Chancellery where we breakfasted with Hitler at a small table in the state dining room under the niche of Eve; bacon and eggs and goose fat for us, and for the Führer his usual two slices of unbuttered bread and a glass of milk.

Luncheon at the Chancellery, New Year's Eve dinner the following day; when were Nickel and I to find time for our friends? The luncheon was enlivened by Göring who

129

had come in from his estate on the Schorfheide. Nickel and I couldn't take our eyes off this mountain of flesh encased in brown knickerbockers, a silk shirt, a brown suède sleeveless jacket and socks that sagged picturesquely, displaying to our amusement his heavy woolen underwear.

Before we could tear ourselves away, Hitler showed us his latest addition to the Chancellery, the enormous dining room with the stage about which he had told Nickel and me on our February holiday. We entered the huge place full of workmen and noise and sawdust and could see nothing at first but two rows of fat, brownish pillars that cut the room into three sections. Thuringian marble, the Führer explained. Someone had sent him a paperweight of it and he had liked it so well that he had reopened an old marble works that had gone into bankruptcy.

I couldn't help remarking that I thought the marble hideous, but he assured me that the entire room would be toned down to the pillars. Half a year later when I saw the sky-blue mosaic ceiling with its border of golden swastikas, the pale yellow walls, the brown furniture upholstered in petit-point to tones of dull red, green and beige, I acknowledged that he was right. At the round tables about the room dinner guests could sink into their deep armchairs and sleep comfortably through the concert.

The Führer invited us to a performance of *La Fille du Régiment* before the New Year's Eve dinner, but Mother told him we had tickets for *Bettelstudent* at the Staatsoper and would join him later. Why Hitler should want to see this operetta for the nth time I do not know but it vied with *The Merry Widow* as his favorite. Until Hindenburg died he often attended performances at both the Staatsoper and the state theaters in Berlin—he had a little box at the Staatsoper near that of the President and could slip in and out almost unseen—but when he became Reichs Chancellor and was forced to sit in the former royal box as head of the state, he ceased to attend opera. Perhaps, too, he reflected the rapid change in public taste. After a year of puritanism the Nazis went to the other extreme; in later years nudism on the stage and in the night clubs was so usual that a chorus girl who refused to strip was soon out of a job.

When we reached the Chancellery at eleven everyone was still at *La Fille*, but soon Hitler arrived, very animated and pleased with the show. We went in to dinner and at midnight, which was announced by a bang on a huge gong, we made the rounds of the table, wishing each other a happy new year with champagne, all except Hitler who toasted us with seltzer. Then he and Brückner went to the front of the Chancellery to greet the throngs of shouting people on the street, and the Führer returned with an armful of flowers that had been presented to him by little girls.

Finally the aides and satellites escaped to more hilarious entertainment. The butler brought jelly doughnuts and coffee—peppermint tea for Hitler—and we talked drowsily, glad of every telephone call or interruption. One of the boys, to keep from falling asleep, asked what the rest of the house looked like; it must have been nearly three o'clock when we began a personally conducted tour. In his study the Führer stood behind his desk and showed us how he received his ministers and diplomats.

"I always roar with laughter when Mr. X. enters the room," he said. "I must show you what happens." He went to the door and made a stumbling entrance, his body bent forward at the waist, his left hand holding an imaginary monocle to his left eye and the right arm lifted.

"Heil, heil," he said in a high, vague falsetto with a strong English accent. He then spoke about the New Year's reception for the diplomatic corps.

"Don't you sometimes find yourself in a tight spot?" asked Mother, laughing at his accurate impersonation of the English diplomat. "For instance, what do you say to the Russian Ambassador?"

"Oh, that's easy. I simply stare at him like this." Hitler crossed his arms and squeezed his eyes to slits. "When the old Jew gets purple in the face I ask him in the friendliest manner if the climate of Berlin agrees with him and if the construction of the new subway keeps him awake at night."

Five-thirty, the Führer's bedtime, came at last. As we received no invitation for the following day, we knew that we had come to the end of our command visit. But it was not the end of my holiday in Berlin. Next day the family returned to Bayreuth, but I was permitted to stay on for the rest of my vacation. Nickel hinted and cajoled, but she packed her pretty dresses and back she went to Wahnfried.

The gala party of the holiday was Göring's annual opera ball this year, a magnificent affair that set all the tongues in the city wagging about its sensational extravagance. The Staatsoper had been closed for three days in preparation and would be closed for three days afterward while workmen demolished the handsome parquet dance floor that had been built over the entire orchestra floor, and the grand stairway that led down to it and from the boxes. True, every guest was charged fifty marks, but that wouldn't begin to cover the deficit made by canceling six performances.

Tietjen invited me to sit in his box, a small one between Göring's own and that of the diplomatic corps. It was a dazzling show; the pillars, the boxes, the tent for the orchestra on the stage, all were decorated with orange and white silk, an exquisite fabric that the Reichsmarshal had ordered hand-woven in Silesia. In every corner little fountains played, and where there were no fountains there were enormous vases of red roses flown from Holland.

It was a fantastic gathering; in the boxes opposite us sat old Germany: King Ferdinand of Bulgaria and the Crown Prince and his brothers in their imperial uniforms—be-

132

side us sat the Reichsmarshal in his pale-blue air-force uniform.

The entertainment was on the same flamboyant scale. The entire ballet of the opera danced in the traditional white against the orange silk and the soloists of the opera sang a chorus from *The Gypsy Baron*. Downstairs in the banquet rooms the guests found a huge lottery with motor-cars, electric washing machines, cases of champagne—every prize of value that Göring could persuade the merchants to contribute. Champagne flowed ever so much more freely than water and on the dance floor truckfuls of handsome young air officers made attractive dancing partners.

From Tietjen and the artists who gathered in his box I heard blow by blow accounts of the most recent skirmishes in the Göring-Göbbels war. Göring controlled the Prussian state theaters which in Berlin included the Staatsoper, the State Theatre and the Little State Theatre, as well as the opera houses of Hanover, Kassel and several other cities, and he was running them at an enormous profit. The performances at the Staatsoper, the dramas at the State and the comedies at the Little State Theatre were all so popular that it was almost impossible to get seats. True, he depleted the other opera houses for his Staatsoper and soon had so many top-ranking sopranos, tenors, bassos, on his hands that it was difficult to cast them all, but he was producing unsurpassed opera in Berlin. Even the conductor blight was overcome by marvelous ensembles and productions.

Göbbels, on the other hand, as head of the Reichs Music Chamber, was running all the other theaters—but especially considered the German Opera House in Berlin as his own—and at a deficit. He was pouring fantastic sums into productions—two hundred and fifty thousand marks, it was said, into *The Merry Widow* alone. To cover the deficit he took over the German Broadcasting Company, which he squeezed so dry that it could no longer

133

afford to keep the symphony orchestra or the fine artists who had been engaged before the Hitler regime.

However, in the battle for Hitler's favor Göbbels won. After the first two seasons the Führer deserted the Staatsoper and became an ardent fan of the German Opera House which was putting on his beloved *Fille, Butterfly* and *The Merry Widow*, as well as cheap and gaudy ballets. The town was still reverberating with Göring's howl of fury when Hitler canceled a command performance of *Aïda* at the Staatsoper in honor of some Yugoslav mission and took the delegation instead to Göbbels's Opera House to see a vulgar ballet, "The Dance Around the World."

Both of these impresarios were cracking the whip, but Göring's lash flayed the artists of higher rank. My friends were still commenting upon the exit of Lotte Lehmann. Although Lehmann was never a member of the Staatsoper, she had appeared there each year as a guest. A few days before her scheduled performance in Berlin she was giving a lieder recital in Dresden when an S. S. trooper walked down the aisle and held up his hand to stop her in the middle of a phrase. After heiling Hitler in a loud voice he called to Lehmann that Göring was on the telephone. It wasn't even Göring, only an aide ordering her to appear before the Minister.

When Lehmann returned to Berlin she went to Göring's palace, accompanied by Tietjen. After an interminable wait Göring dashed through in riding habit, calling that he would be back shortly. Half an hour later he returned from the garden, hot and flushed, brandishing his riding whip, and gave Lehmann the choice of accepting engagements in Germany only or finding the borders closed to her forever. She told him that her choice was made. After this interview she never again set foot in Germany.

In spite of his plethora of artists the famous conductors were slipping between Göring's fingers. Lamenting his conductor troubles, he said, "If I could only manage to get Furtwängler, Kleiber and Krauss at the Staatsoper at the same time, we could really do something, but one won't come unless the others go. It's terrible."

We agreed that he was in a bad way. Kleiber had left Germany, Furtwängler was in disgrace and Krauss was making himself so disliked that he was soon to be kicked upstairs. But not until after many fights with Tietjen. The wily Tietjen had finally goaded the conductor into a row in the director's office and told Krauss that on such and such an occasion he had made such a statement. Krauss had retorted by calling Tietjen a liar, but when he heard his own voice on the record he turned pale and dashed from the office. Only too willingly he went to Munich which for this very purpose had been declared the art center of Germany. His new position as musical director was labeled the highest in the Reich. Looking at Göring in his mountebank clothes, it was hard to believe that he was actually one of the chief instigators of the evil which had befallen Germany.

CHAPTER XV

THE WOOING OF ENGLAND

IN MARCH, 1936, I took another holiday from the chickens and diapers, this time to meet Mother in Darmstadt for the christening of a friend's baby. When I stepped off the train, the radio and loud speakers were blaring Hitler's voice, crowds of people were milling about, and through the streets marched columns of troops. Hitler had moved into the Rhineland.

As I stood there listening to that rasping voice above the thud of soldiers' feet, I began to piece together unrelated words and events which at the time had had no signifi-

135

cance for me. One was an autumn holiday on which I had driven with several friends to a little town near the Czechoslovakian frontier.

"This is the only part of Germany in which every man has his uniform, arms and ammunitions ready at home," one of them had said. "If the Czechs attack, we can hold them off for twenty-four hours and by that time reinforcements should arrive."

When I asked why in the world the Czechs should want to attack, he looked at me pityingly.

"Surely you can't be such a baby. The Russians have more than an army corps in Czechoslovakia and the country is simply swarming with French officers training the Czech Army. We can't drive to the frontier. The last few miles are an open-air fortress. You probably wouldn't notice anything but there's an antiaircraft gun behind almost every tree."

And then there was Hitler's remark about the motor roads.

"I had great difficulty in making my generals agree to your having one of the new *Autobahnen* here in Bayreuth," he said. "They were dead against it but I insisted. I can understand why they don't want a main highway through here but I managed to get you a branch road."

War! Of course people had been talking about it. Chaotic thoughts buzzed through my mind, formless terrors because I couldn't imagine what war would be like. However, I realized that the road into the Rhineland would eventually lead into war.

Soon after my return from school I was reminded of war again by Wieland and his classmates, who had just graduated from high school and were starting their labor service. It was the summer of 1936; Wieland was only nineteen and frail to be handling a pick and shovel. On the first Sunday that was visiting day, Mother, Wolfi and I drove to Dresden, picked up Nickel and went out to the camp not far from the city. Wieland was almost unrecognizable in a muddy shirt and a uniform that looked as though he had slept in it, as indeed he had. He was embarrassed about the dirt but explained to mother that he couldn't help it. The boys were allowed one clean shirt every ten days and as they were doing heavy road repair and were compelled to work and sleep in the same shirt, they were never clean.

The main room of the camp, a dilapidated old factory, was a dormitory around the walls of which ran a line of little square, barred windows with broken panes that let in a constant draft. The washroom in which two hundred and fifty boys washed in two minutes flat, boasted one plumbing eccentricity. On each of three walls lined with huge watering troughs was one faucet. When the three were turned on at once, the water wouldn't run at all.

Mother asked Wieland anxiously what he did all day. He made a grimace. After eight hours of laboring on the road the boys upended their spades for rifles and went through everlasting military drill in order to make a good showing at the party rally in Nuremberg.

Never had I seen such a disillusioned lot of boys; they grumbled about the food which "wasn't fit for bugs," about their leader, about everything. I glanced at Mother, wondering how she felt about her darling's undergoing these hardships for the Führer. Her eyes were dark with sympathy; she wanted to know what she could do or send to help Wieland endure the place; and after the visit immediately started an unsuccessful campaign against the labor service in Germany. Nothing could be done. Most of the complaints were withheld by the boys because of the harsh treatment meted out to the complainant—it was not unusual for the second boy who complained to be summarily shot. Suicide was rife in all the labor camps.

Wieland finally developed blisters on his feet and collapsed on the road. Given leave at Whitsuntide, he joined us at Lake Constance where our doctor immediately put him in the hospital. Carbuncles had broken out all over his body. Mother indignantly reported the camp to Hirl, head of the *Arbeitsdienst* and, whether as a consequence or not, Wieland was shortly transferred to another camp where conditions were a little better. His labor service was not unrelieved because it was soon time for the opening of the festival during which Hitler ordered his release.

The rehearsals this summer were particularly interesting because we were using Wieland's scenery for *Parsifal* and were anxious that everything should go without a hitch. Already Wieland had made a name as a scenic artist by designing and selling several sets for Father's operas. It was hard that he should be nursing his poor feet in a labor camp while I had the fun of seeing how his sets worked.

Although everything was running smoothly, we couldn't forget for a moment that art was the servant of the Third Reich. Tietjen was constantly on the telephone consulting with Göring or calling up Covent Garden, acting as liaison man between Göring and prominent German musicians who were carrying German culture as well as propaganda to the ouside world. In his spare moments he was organizing the new "Cultural Exchange" by which entire opera companies were sent to countries which were not too enthusiastic about the Nazi regime.

Since Hitler had become a "connoisseur of the arts" his ideas were regarded with a mixture of apprehension and amusement by the old-timers at Bayreuth.

"You'll see," they prophesied, "when he attends *Parsifal* he'll want to strip the flower maidens. You'll be lucky if he doesn't want to rebuild the Festspielhaus."

Since his remodeling of the Nuremberg Opera House the Führer had developed grandiose ideas about the opera; he dreamed of super-buildings with super-stages and audiences that numbered tens of thousands.

"It is stupid," he said, "to hàve such small stages. They hamper the acting of the singers and limit the scenery."

He tried to force the smaller cities to build new opera

houses, outsized ones with enormous stages, and was annoyed when the city fathers explained to him that a theater built to hold ten thousand requires a huge orchestra as well as a chorus of a hundred to a hundred and fifty singers. How could a small city meet such heavy overhead? They couldn't sell enough tickets even at popular prices.

"This is all nonsense," Hitler insisted, and refused to give government money for opera projects unless they met with his expansive ideas. In consequence Nuremberg was the only city that rebuilt its opera house.

Fortunately Hitler seemed to consider the Festspielhaus sacred.

"But you'll see," said the staff, he'll have a lot of fantastic ideas about the production."

Sepp Dietrich, the chief of Hitler's bodyguard, had arrived at the beginning of the rehearsals, with his special guards who organized the protective measures for the safety of the Führer. Bayreuth was proclaimed a prohibited area for aircraft, and antiaircraft batteries were hidden in all the hills and slopes around the town. Nearer Bayreuth, police officers were stationed on every road leading into the town, to hold up passing cars and question the occupants. All of the staff and artists connected with the festival had "Free Passage" stickers pasted on their windshields. The police, who picked up these stickers from a long distance through their field glasses, let us pass and gave us an immunity that covered many a sin of omission. I was always forgetting my license, a serious offense in those days, but the formidable officers looked at the "Free Passage" and waved me on.

This year Hitler was to be in residence in the rebuilt bachelor house at Wahnfried and the whole place was in a state of tension. A few days before his arrival police and plain-clothes men swarmed over the grounds. The milkman, the butcher, the grocery boys, all the tradespeople who had access to Wahnfried, were furnished with passes bearing their numbers and photographs. We were in-

139

structed to carry them too and warned that we would have to show them every time we wanted to enter our own house. As for guests—they would be allowed to enter only when escorted by two heavily armed S. S. men.

On the opening day an entire staff of servants arrived from Berlin to take over the bachelor house; S. S. men paced up and down under every window. Suddenly, quietly, Hitler drove up from the airport and was in residence. It seemed queer to be invited to dine with him in one of our own homes and be ushered into Mother's study by a butler from the Chancellery.

Entertaining a ruler, especially one with the habits of the Führer, is not all roses and champagne. The entire routine of Wahnfried had to adapt itself to Hitler's fondness for staying up all night and sleeping half the day. In the morning nobody could speak above a whisper until the blinds in the Führer's bedroom were raised, indicating that he was awake. We weren't even permitted to start a motor. The gardeners had to push our four cars out of the garage and down the driveway to the street. As a great concession the dogs were permitted to stay, with the understanding that they would be kept indoors until noon. I liked nothing better than to go into the garden in the morning and call my English sheep dog, Toby. Instantly a dozen S. S. guards leaped from behind the bushes and put their fingers to their mouths.

While Hitler liked to give the impression that during his week in Bayreuth he forgot everything except music, in reality he seldom wasted a moment. Before he went to his box and from four to eleven did public homage to Wagner, he had already spent several busy hours with his ambassadors, cabinet members or generals who arrived by plane and were whisked away again before the performance started. From Nickel's bedroom we could see them walking in the garden hours on end, talking—that is, Hitler talked and the others waited for a chance to slip in a word. Sometimes the Führer waved his arms about

and stamped, but Toby who followed him around de-
votedly, taught him restraint. When the Führer gesticu-
lated, Toby thought he was being encouraged to jump on
his friend, and in consequence Hitler's white jacket was
ruined.

To Nickel and me the most interesting aspect of the
visit was the arrival of Unity Mitford about whom we had
heard many stories. Mother had met her a year earlier in
Munich with Sir Oswald Mosley whom Hitler was welcom-
ing as a brother Fascist. She admitted that she had been a
bit disappointed in the girl, thought her too naïve for the
position of Hitler's wife, and doubted if such a marriage
would improve the relations of the Third Reich with
England.

I wondered what Hitler would do with a wife, but I
was curious to see Unity who arrived during the opening
performance with her sister Diana.

Mother asked the Führer if he would like her to invite
Unity for luncheon. He was delighted.

"It would make me terribly happy," he assured her.
"You know Unity lives on little more than a mark a month.
Her parents have cut off her allowance to force her back
to England. She has returned once or twice but she always
runs away again."

Unity was an attractive girl, ash-blond hair, gray eyes,
very much like a Botticelli, until she smiled and displayed
the ugliest set of teeth I have ever seen. She spoke German
fluently with a broad Bavarian accent and made conversation by ridiculing her family and everything English. Her
sister, Diana, the divorced Lady Guinness, was truly beautiful in a cool blue-eyed English way. The low-necked
dresses of the girls and their lipstick made the Führer's
party stare.

The idea that Unity was performing a sacred mission by
bringing about a German-British understanding was without foundation—quite the contrary, for the girl tried to
prejudice Hitler against England by giving him the idea

141

that most of the English were stupid. His entourage despised her, perhaps because they were jealous, or more likely because they found her very wearisome. They called her *Mitfahrt*, because she trailed Hitler everywhere, to the rallies, to Munich and Obersalzberg, traveling on his special train. In Berlin Mrs. Göbbels was detailed to chaperone her. The two were invariably late to meals while the ministers waited and grumbled.

Nevertheless, in spite of Unity's discouraging example, Hitler was busily courting England.

"We must be friends," he said not once but a hundred times. "The two nations spring from the same race. It is unnatural for England and France to be friends, a contradiction both racially and historically. The Germanic races belong together."

When the Führer had made an expansive gesture toward England a year earlier by inviting Sir John Simon, then Foreign Secretary, and Anthony Eden, Lord Privy Seal, to Berlin for the discussion of the naval agreement, he had invited Mother to the banquet, seating her next to Sir John Simon in order to impress him with the fact that the English-born daughter-in-law of Wagner sympathized with Hitler. When she came home, we plied her with questions.

Sir John, she said, kept exclaiming about Hitler's hands and eyes, but Mr. Eden stared through his horn-rimmed spectacles with complete detachment. Once in awhile he would take off his glasses and lay them on the table until one or the other of the ladies would attract his attention, whereupon he put them on again, had a good look at her, and then proceeded with his dinner. Hitler toasted his guests in silence but in champagne instead of seltzer water, making a grimace when he took the sip. This was the greatest compliment he had ever paid a guest.

The banquet was served by S. S. guards in their black trousers and white linen jackets. At a signal from Kannenberg these conspicuously tall and fair-haired troopers rushed forward in close formation, brandishing their dishes as though they were about to take the table by storm.

After the official visitors had disappeared Hitler kept with him a small party of friends with whom he rejoiced over his diplomatic success, slapping his knees and clapping his hands like a schoolboy.

"I'm so happy I've got to let myself go," he exclaimed. "Everything's going so wonderfully. Grand fellows, the English. Even when they lie they do it on a magnificent scale, not a bit like the niggardly French."

For the rest of the night he told funny stories about Göbbels and Göring to which they listened with roars of laughter.

"Do you know what a Göbbels and a Göring are?" he demanded, and when nobody ventured to guess his riddle, he answered it himself. "A Göbbels is the amount of nonsense a man can say in an hour, and a Göring is the amount of metal that can be pinned on a man's breast."

At Bayreuth Hitler was still full of plans for wooing England, one of which centered about a diplomatic assault on Sir Thomas Beecham, a friend of the new king. As Beecham was expected at the festival, he was given an invitation to share the Führer's box. The days passed—Hitler waited—messages were sent—but no Beecham appeared. Then Hitler saw a performance of *Lohengrin* and was inspired with a fantastic idea although it didn't burst upon us until after his departure.

Meanwhile he and Göbbels and Göring sat through the performance, took supper at the restaurant, discussed art or rather listened to Hitler's theories. The Führer did indeed advance a number of ideas about the productions that gave Tietjen the jitters. To avoid displeasing him by disregarding his scheme to light the sky in the second act of *Tristan*, with a moon and innumerable stars, Tietjen made the woods so dense that not a bit of the sky could be seen.

Both Hitler and Göbbels indulged in speculations about

143

how much more beautiful *Parsifal* would be with the flower maidens entirely naked. The Venusberg in *Tannhäuser* would be much more effective, they agreed, when Nazism had bred a super-race which would furnish a nude ballet. Wagner, they were sure, would be delighted.

One of Hitler's ideas, however, was so good that I once tried it out in a miniature stage set. He insisted that it would be very impressive to place the three Norns in *Die Götterdämmerung* on top of half a globe and there let them sing about the end of the world.

During these eternal discussions the most concerned member of the household was Verena who didn't want to go back to school and had extracted Hitler's promise to ask Mother for an extension of her vacation. The days went by and he did nothing about it. One afternoon she edged me into a corner of the music room and whispered gloomily, "Wolf is almost ready to go away again and he hasn't said a word to Mama about my vacation. I don't dare remind him. What shall I do about it?"

"If you really want to play hooky," I promised, "I'll fix it for you."

Hitler and Göring had retired to the lilac salon after luncheon for a conference, but I took a chance on interrupting world affairs for a moment. Opening the door, I made my entrance with a loud cough. The Führer and Göring looked up sharply and stopped talking.

"What is it, Mausi?" Hitler asked.

"This is very urgent," I assured him. "You promised Nickel that she might stay away from school for the rest of the festival."

"Of course I did." Hitler smiled and Göring gave me an amused grin.

"Have you talked to Mama?"

Hitler acknowledged that he hadn't, but promised to do it immediately.

"It will be pretty tough going," I warned him. "If I were

144

you, I'd go after it in a very convincing way, make it sound important, as if you were really concerned about it."

"Oh, I hope I will manage." Hitler burst into a laugh, and as I retired, the huge bulk of the field marshal was shaking like custard. In the library I nodded to Verena that it was all arranged.

When Hitler and Göring finally returned to the library and the guests had made their adieus, the family gathered in the music room.

"What is going to happen about Nickerl?" Hitler asked Mother. "Have you written to her headmistress that she won't be back before the end of August?"

Mother admitted that she hadn't. With a huge gesture Hitler put on his loudest public-speaking voice and began to thunder.

"Once and for all I want everyone to understand that it is the sacred duty of a Wagner to be present in Bayreuth during a festival. There can be no question about Nickerl's returning to school. Attending classes cannot be compared with the performing of this most important of all duties."

Hitler kept this up for a good twenty minutes, talking himself into a rage, standing in the middle of the floor, making wild gestures with both arms and spitting his words excitedly all over the place. My family stood with shaking knees, unable to move or say a word. At the first moment I too was bluffed; Hitler was turning out this nonsense with such convincing fervor. Then I remembered my urging him to go about it in a convincing manner. This was it, elephant-sized and no acoustics spared. I burst out laughing. He was getting a diabolical pleasure out of calling on heaven and eternity and everything else he could think of while his audience grew limper and limper.

Suddenly he stopped and turning to my mother said in his normal voice, "Come now, do give the child her holiday."

After several attempts to speak, Mother finally managed

145

to answer in a voice a third above her natural tone, "Of course, if that is the way you look at it. Certainly."

I gave him a loud "Bravo," but no one paid attention to me until the Führer had retired to the bachelor house; then the family tore me to shreds for daring to laugh in the Führer's face when he was so excited. I kept quiet. It would have been impossible to convince them that he was putting on an act. Anyway, Nickel got her vacation.

As the first cycle drew to a close I was so weary of the stultifying atmosphere about Wahnfried with everybody doing reverence to the Führer, that I wanted to get away for a few hours, anywhere out of Bayreuth, so one morning when Hitler's plane went to Berlin to bring several guests for *Rheingold*, I went along without asking Mother's permission. She would be furious, but the junket would be worth a tempest.

Nobody else was in the big plane except the two pilots, a radio operator and a lone man, but on the return there were half a dozen guests. One of them showed me how to open the little red lids which covered the mouths of the tubes that furnished fresh air. The breeze felt so cool and refreshing that I put the tube in my mouth.

"Don't do it. You'll make yourself ill," he warned me, but I didn't see how fresh pure air could hurt me. However, he was right; by evening I had lost my voice and was squeaking on a single high note. Mother fumed and raged. I didn't like her doctor and refused to swallow his sprays and glycerine so before the festival was over I was walking about with a painful case of sinus.

Meanwhile Hitler, who had departed with his guards, his Gestapo and shrieking sirens, learned that Sir Thomas Beecham had arrived for the second cycle. Immediately he rang up Mother and unfolded to her his marvelous plan.

"I've got it now," he told her. "*Lohengrin* must go to London as a coronation present for Edward." Mother was completely flabbergasted; so were Tietjen and everybody else at the Festspielhaus.

146

"It's impossible," Mother told Hitler. "Covent Garden is much too small; we couldn't get the scenery in without taking off the roof. Besides, the scenery, which was never built for packing, would be ruined by the time it arrived in London. And what about the members of the company recruited from fifty different cities and engaged for only the period of the festival! The expense would be astronomical!"

Hitler swept away all these objections. Day and night he telephoned until everyone in the place began to loathe the thought of *Lohengrin*. The scenery could be rebuilt in London, he insisted, to the exact proportions of Covent Garden. He would order all members of the chorus and orchestra as well as the principals released from their other contracts, and as for the cost, we needn't worry about that; we could begin by estimating double salaries for the musical and technical personnel.

Mother went to work; she estimated that the cost would be between one and two million marks. Patiently she listened to Hitler's telephoned suggestions and tried to carry them out, but her heart was not in it and neither were those of the staff at the Festspielhaus. Luckily, before we had gone too far, it occurred to the Führer that it might be a good idea to ask King Edward if the present would be acceptable. His Majesty was duly appreciative but "hoped no one would expect him to be present at the performance because opera bored him to death."

Not at all discouraged by Edward's lack of musical appreciation, Hitler continued to pursue Sir Thomas Beecham who later in the autumn made a tour of Germany with the London Philharmonic Orchestra. In Berlin he could not escape Hitler, but we very soon heard reports that at the audience the Führer came off second best. Accustomed to guests who "heiled" briskly, then waited in silence for his monologue, Hitler was overwhelmed by the dynamic Englishman who completely monopolized the conversation, even taxed the speed of the poor gaping in-

147

terpreter. As to Sir Thomas' impression of the interview, he summed it up in the laconic phrase, "Now I know what is wrong with Germany."

The Nazis gaped at the conductor as though he were a rare animal at the zoo, but they rallied to give him a magnificent welcome. The first concert was attended by all of the high-ranking officials with Hitler at their head and it was broadcast by the German radio stations. After the first number which went with a swing, there was hearty applause. Suddenly, above the hand clapping, I heard an aside in English, unmistakably in Sir Thomas' voice.

"The old bloke seems to like it."

Everyone in Germany who understood English thought it a marvelous joke. Sir Thomas, I heard later, hadn't known that they were on the air and had made the remark casually to his first violin. Before he left Germany he had become a legendary figure.

Hitler's wooing of England through Beecham never progressed any further and with the abdication of Edward who he had hoped might be induced to attend Bayreuth on an unofficial visit the next summer, his dream faded. Later that year I asked the Führer at tea what he was going to send as a coronation present to the new king and queen.

"Nothing at all," he said crossly. "I'll send an official representative and nothing else. They don't interest me."

CHAPTER XVI

BACKSTAGE

WHEN the shadow of the Führer's invasion was lifted from the Festspielhaus we gave an audible sigh and relaxed over the week end in anticipation of a brilliant

148

second cycle. Tietjen lounged in the garden without fear of troopers leaping from every bush and played with his tame sparrow. Frida gave a supper party in her apartment near the hill, everybody seemed to feel positively light-headed.

In spite of Mother's anger about the stolen plane ride, which was holding over longer than usual, my spirits were singing too because this year Tietjen took me on as an assistant and gave me real work to do, superintending the entrances and exits, following him with a notebook, taking down and checking on the execution of his instructions. I was eighteen and serious as a bishop about my duties.

Watching him at close range, I concentrated on learning everything that he could teach me. As a stage director I considered him great although I was sorry when he fell a victim to the lavishness of the Reinhardt school. He was no longer satisfied unless he had at least eight hundred people and a dozen horses milling around on the stage. Comparing his manner with Father's, I was finally convinced that many of his productions were too elaborate and a departure from the inner meaning of the music dramas.

The rehearsals ran with smooth efficiency. Long before the singers arrived, the schedule of performances had been arranged so no one would sing two days in succession. Every day the lists of coaches and the appointments for coaching were posted on the bulletin board as well as on the dressing room doors. The German custom, unlike the American, is for the management to furnish the coaches and assign the singers to them according to the director's best judgment.

While the technicians, the electricians, the stage manager and the manipulators of the scenic effects practiced with a piano on the stage, the orchestra rehearsed in the lower part of the restaurant with the conductor on a

149

platform and the musicians grouped as usual. The schedule
for rehearsals read something like this:

Rheingold

Monday	9 to 11 o'clock	wind instruments
	11 to 1	strings
	10	stage with piano
	3:50 to 5:30	full orchestra
	5:30 to 8	stage with piano
Tuesday	9 to 11	full orchestra
	11 to 1	stage with piano
	3 to 7	stage with piano
Wednesday	10 to 1	stage with orchestra
	4 to 7	full orchestra

While this was going on at one side of the theater, on
the other side Rüdel was marshaling the chorus, and upstairs in the new addition, the flower maidens or the Valkyries were rehearsing. Everywhere the musical assistants
were dashing about, prompting, rehearsing, accompanying, always with score in hand, beating time for the
singers, giving them the cue, giving light signals. At odd
moments they played any extra instrument for which the
score called, the anvils in *Rheingold*, the thunder, the
organ in *Lohengrin*. Usually there were more than a
dozen assistants and among them some of the outstanding musicians of the past sixty years. Humperdinck,
Strauss, Mottl, Knoch, Seidl, Weingartner, Father, all
served their apprenticeship in the Festspielhaus.

All this bustle and activity was the very breath of life
to me whether I was hurrying back to the dressing rooms
where sometimes as many as fifty dressers were dashing
about with crowns and spears and flowers, side-stepping
frantic hairdressers, sniffing grease paint, or carrying messages to the sceneshifters, I thrilled with the electric tension that precedes every performance. Yes, and holds
until the drawing of the last curtain. Even the curtain
lowering is timed; the heavy, graceful folds close from the

sides of the proscenium, quickly, sharply, for the first two acts of *Tannhäuser*, and slowly, almost reluctantly, on all the acts of *Parsifal*.

At performances of *Rheingold* and *Götterdämmerung* there was always a special urgency because both of them were nightmares to the director and the stagehands. *Rheingold* called for three complete changes of scenery without any intermission. The first act of *Götterdämmerung* also has three! In *Rheingold* the Rhinemaidens and Alberich go down on the big elevator while the huge rocks of Valhalla are wheeled in. Scenery for the cavern of the dwarfs, Nibelheim, drops from the flies, to be pulled up again in the end to disclose the rocks. The possibilities for a slip-up in the timing are limitless.

Götterdämmerung is especially nerve-racking. Once during this cycle somebody neglected to put the ladder behind the Valkyrie's rock on which Brünnhilde is left gazing after Siegfried. When Frida turned to climb down in that second before the stagehands started to wheel back the rock, she saw that she was trapped. She waved them to go ahead and had a perilous ride backstage while Deman leaped from the wings and ran shouting beside her, cursing the stupidity of the careless fellow who was trying to break her neck.

To cross the stage before it has been cleared after the last act is a hazard. The pillars and the walls of the hall actually collapse. The *Versunkungen* are open, Tietjen invented a brilliant device for throwing lights on a waving blanket to simulate the Rhine flowing over the ruins.

A playmate of mine who cared nothing for opera told me years later that when he was in his teens Father once gave him a ticket to *Götterdämmerung*. The boy passed it on to his brother, an opera fan, for the first half of the performance but decided to look in himself on the last act. When he saw Brünnhilde leading her white horse across the stage he remembered having read in the local paper that the horse had recently kicked the prima donna.

151

Then the hall began to collapse. He jumped from his seat in a panic, to be jerked down by his neighbor who whispered that it was supposed to be that way. However, he was so appalled by the destruction of the hall of the Gibichungen that he never indulged in opera again.

In addition to the work backstage I was always being impressed by Mother to help with her guests. At intermissions I tore off the coveralls, jumped into an evening dress, and entertained whatever guests she left to my care. Before the performance of *Die Walküre* Mother asked me to meet Sir Thomas in our box at the first interval, take him to tea, invite anyone else I liked, and bring him to her at the beginning of the second interval. "I have no time, so don't bother me with him—you can take care of him in the intermissions." Although she had never instructed me in so many words, she expected me to present to Beecham a picture of Nazism in roseate colors. Better, I thought, talk with him myself than have the Nazis talk nothing but politics.

As it turned out, I needn't have worried for Sir Thomas was in no mood for political philosophizing.

"Ah," he exclaimed, looking from me to Verena, "on one side I see young Wagner in a champagne-colored gown and on the other young Liszt in white ruffles."

Sir Thomas had taken a charming little hunting lodge where he entertained Furtwängler and others of his friends and began to engage singers for the approaching coronation in London. Dr. Geissmar, now Sir Thomas' secretary, acted as his hostess, adviser and interpreter; it was amusing to watch people who had avoided her a year earlier, flock around her. As I often entertained her and Beecham for tea and supper at the Festspielhaus, Sir Thomas made it a habit to invite me for luncheon. Thus I saw a great deal of him and of Furtwängler whom I learned to like almost in proportion to the dislike my mother bore him.

Furtwängler was conducting in Bayreuth again that year

152

in spite of the fact that he and Tietjen were still busily accusing each other of dark intrigues. Furtwängler had achieved a comeback of a sort. This year his new symphony had been performed and had received such a panning from the Nazi press that it was never heard of again. Nonetheless he was offered every big orchestra in Germany but he refused them all, deaf even to the pleas of Göring to return to the Staatsoper. Whenever he wanted to conduct the Philharmonic, he engaged the musicians himself at a cost of twelve thousand marks a concert. His profits averaged twelve thousand, thus in two concerts he earned as much as when he was the holder of the highsounding titles.

To the feminine swooners he was as irresistible as ever, but they didn't get a fair opportunity to worship him at the Festspielhaus on account of the shell that hid him from view. Curiously enough his famous gymnastics at the desk were absent when he couldn't be seen. The musicians used to say that in Berlin he was impossible to follow because he "beat out the sixty-fourth notes." Nickel teased him in her guileless way and so fascinated him that she could say the most outlandish things. He was always inviting her to sit in the orchestra when he conducted but she managed to avoid being his inspiration.

This year for the first time anti-Semitism was making an unhappy change in the once friendly atmosphere of Bayreuth. Instead of all gathering for intermissions or supper in one careless informal family, the artists began to separate in little cliques and look suspiciously at everyone who didn't belong to their group. Everyone knew who was high in Nazi favor, who was toppling and would be a dangerous acquaintance, none knew who was a spy, so they regarded the world with caution and distrust.

As for actual deeds of violence, even boycotts, we had seen little of them in Bayreuth and if it hadn't been for the horrible atmosphere of uneasiness and suspicion we might have been unaware of the things that were happening in Germany. We didn't know anybody in Bayreuth who had suffered; none of our friends were persecuted or in concentration camps. In this kindly little city the pre-Nazi officials were taken over by the Nazi organization and the local government didn't change. Nobody persecuted his neighbors; the Jewish doctors and merchants and lawyers didn't lose many patients, customers or clients until later when an ardent Gauleiter who was imposed upon them complained that the city officials were patronizing Jews. Even then they gave shamefaced undercover assistance to their old friends—there was never any baiting.

Mother's own attitude was as puzzlingly inconsistent as that of the other Nazis I knew. She believed in a vague theoretical anti-Semitism and spoke detachedly of the Führer's plans to use Sir Oswald Mosley to arouse the British lower classes against the "Jewish menace," but in her private life she never gave it a thought; she bought in Jewish shops as usual, went openly to her Jewish tailor for fittings and enjoyed poking fun at the local party leaders. Like many ardent followers of Hitler, she believed in him implicitly but laughed at the party organization. Everything good in National Socialism was Hitler's idea; everything evil was the fault of the party and done without the Führer's knowledge.

In Mother's own case she lived above the law. None of the restrictions bothered her and she went along in her usual way without paying them the slightest attention. To the winter relief, the sports contributions, the multitudinous drives for funds, she was expected to contribute generously according to her income even though she had heard Hitler boast many times that he was converting the money into armaments; but she never could resist putting facetious answers on the forms that had to be filled out to prove that one was a pure Aryan and worthy of the honor of "contributing."

In regard to these collections the musicians were embellishing a story about Strauss who was still in retirement

154

at Garmisch where the winter Olympic games had just been held. The Nazis, discovering that in the eyes of the world Strauss was the greatest living German composer, approached him on the subject of writing an impressive Olympic hymn for the occasion. He did it, and further-more, he waived all royalties, thus installing himself again in the good graces of the party. But this magnificent gesture was his utmost act of charity. When the party chieftains began to levy contributions for the games they put on a special drive in Garmisch which would benefit from them. Knowing Strauss's reputation, the Reichs Sports Führer himself called on the Strauss family. But he never got beyond the entrance door where he was met by Pauline who told him in her worst Bavarian that she was not to be bothered with their silly collections.

"My husband composed the damned hymn for nothing," she said and slammed the door.

These were the winter games. The summer games which were held that year in Berlin made many additional diffi-culties for Mother because they necessitated the breaking of the festival into two parts: the last two weeks of July as usual, a two-week interval for the games, and a conclud-ing two weeks of festival during the latter part of August. They also complicated my life for they focused her pent-up wrath on me. All the little irritations that had accumu-lated during the first weeks of the festival, Lieselotte's talebearing, reports that I had slighted Mother's guests, Knittel's hostility, Tietjen's sly insinuations, gave her material for her anger, but the real cause was Hitler's tickets for the games. She had deferred to him about Nickel's vacation against her better judgment, and she was even more disturbed when he insisted that she let us attend the games.

She opposed the trip to Berlin bitterly because she wanted us to go to Lake Constance with our brothers. We needed the vacation, she said. We would certainly get no rest at the games, our apartment was closed; the whole idea was absurd, but she could do nothing but consent.

Nickel escaped her tongue-lashing which fell on me whom she considered the chief culprit, the instigator of the whole affair.

Mother arranged for Nickel to stay with friends and expected me to be with Frida; but as I thought it might not be convenient for Frida to have me I went to the city information booth and found an attractive room in an apartment not many blocks from the stadium.

Just as I was beginning to enjoy the games, Frida telephoned.

"Did you know that Lieselotte has had a terrible automobile accident? Your mother is there alone. Shouldn't you go back and stay with her?"

Of course, I would take the next train; my heart leaped at the thought of Mother's needing me, but Frida, coolerheaded than I, suggested that we phone first. From her apartment I called Mother; we both talked to her, but she was cold and definite.

"Don't bother to come home," she insisted. "I don't need you."

So Nickel and I stayed the two weeks and trooped back with the performers and guests for the last two weeks of the festival. Mother met us with an angry frown and, perversely enough, blamed me for not disobeying her and returning at once to Wahnfried, although it was true that there was nothing to be done about Lieselotte who couldn't be moved from the hospital in Bamberg to which she had been taken after the accident.

The only pleasant incident of the remaining weeks happened at supper one night after the performance. As there were no curtain calls at the Festspielhaus, a custom Wagner inaugurated and to which Bayreuth always conformed, the supper guests in the restaurant made it a habit to applaud their favorite artists whose performances they wanted to praise by cheering as the singers came down the stairway to the dining floor. I had been in Frida's dressing room while she changed into an evening dress after a magnificent performance of *Siegfried*. When she reached the stairs

156

every diner in the place rose and gave her such a thunder of applause that she almost dropped her enormous bunch of roses. After stopping for a few minutes on the balcony to chat with friends, I went downstairs to join Frida and was greeted with a burst of applause that almost equaled hers. Pink with embarrassment I hurried to her table.

"It's your smart hat and gown," Frida said to me. "You do look lovely." The words were balm to the hurt that Mother was always deepening, making me feel like an awkward ugly duckling.

The appearance of Professor Schultze-Naumburg at Wahnfried also furnished several lighter moments. When the professor was remodeling the Nuremberg opera house he often stopped for tea on his way between Nuremberg and Weimar, where he headed the Department of Arts and Architecture at the academy. A year earlier, when Hitler unleashed one of his violent rages at the inspection of the building, we felt sorry for the architect. When the official party arrived at the new opera house, Hitler was at first enthusiastic about the building until Mrs. Troost who was always a member of such parties, began to whisper to him. This sinister woman was the widow of the architect who designed the new Nazi party buildings in Munich and soon after completing them committed suicide, driven to it, the scoffers said, by Hitler's interminable speeches of praise. Whatever his motive, his widow, who is herself an architect and decorated the interiors of the Munich buildings, managed to keep his memory green by prejudicing Hitler against everyone else whose work pleased him.

After Mrs. Troost made her comments on the Nuremberg building, the Führer burst into an uncontrolled flow of curses and vituperation, accusing Schultze-Naumburg of being so occupied with his new wife that he had slacked on the job. For a long time he flew into a rage whenever the man's name was mentioned although he did admit to Mother later, at one of the rallies, that he thought the opera house a beautiful building.

Far from being discouraged by the Führer's displeasure,

157

Schultze-Naumburg remained an ardent Nazi and specialized in extolling the Nordic race. Indeed he liked the type so well that he married four blond Nordic women in fairly quick succession. Influenced perhaps by his friend, Günther, who was writing pseudo-scientific books about the Aryans, their characteristics and their eternal mission to mankind, the professor went one better. He had just published a book which gave infinite details as to the traits of the Aryans and illustrated it with photographs. One chapter was devoted to the Nordic breast and maintained that there was no future in Germany for a woman whose nipples were darker than the true Nordic pink. His photographs of the Aryan and non-Aryan breasts were very popular.

The first time the architect and the fourth of his strictly Nordic wives stopped·for tea after the book appeared, Wieland and Wolfi razzed him unmercifully, quoting sentence after sentence about the nipples, to the delight of the other guests. Even Mother could not be too annoyed with them for she herself had laughed about the book. She was as quick as anyone to see the amusing aspects of the guests who trooped through Wahnfried.

CHAPTER XVII

LABOR CAMP

WHEN the festival was over and there was no longer an excuse to stay at home, Wieland returned to the' labor camp. Nickel and Wolfi returned to school; there was no one at home except Lieselotte whom I had brought from the hospital at Bamberg when she could be moved. Her face was almost unrecognizable. All of her teeth had

158

been knocked crooked. Every day she had to go to our dentist who believed he might be able to reconstruct her mouth, but her pretty, vivid face was ruined.

Mother came and went. Sometimes when she was at home we were in accord for a few minutes—she treated me as an adult, even a friend—but these times never lasted; something that set her on edge always made her return to the role of dictator. Then she would hurry from the room to avoid a scene. At these times I regretted that there was no one, not even Tietjen to act as buffer between us.

I was more restless than ever, ill although I didn't realize it, and poisoned by the drainage from my sinuses. I was full of apprehension, wondering what Mother intended to do with me now that I had finished school. Surely she didn't expect me to sit at Bayreuth and twiddle my thumbs all the year around. Gradually it dawned upon me that this was indeed just what she intended. I was expected to conform to the old-fashioned pattern of the well-brought-up German girl and adorn the home until I married. In that case I must certainly get away and as soon as possible. But where and how?

After considering everything that my imagination suggested, the best move seemed to be to volunteer for women's labor service; it would both get me away from home and make the service easier. Volunteers were permitted to choose their own camps, with the right to ask for three transfers during the six months, while those who waited for the compulsory service which was just beginning, had no choice and, it was rumored, were sent to the worst camps in villages near the Silesian-Polish border.

In September I applied and on the first of October reported to Camp Elisabeth-Höhe near Berlin. This was the truck-garden district which supplied the Berlin market, handkerchief-sized farms that the government had offered settlers as homesteads in a drive to get them out of the cities and industrial occupations. As the soil was

159

almost entirely sandy, the settlers specialized in tomatoes, fruit and strawberries.

The camp, I found, was a small old farmhouse which, when it was built, must have had some pretense to elegance. In the dining room, and the reception room that had been the living room, the floors were parquet, and a large fireplace—they are unusual luxuries in Germany—would have made the dining room a cheerful place if there had been wood to build a fire. Upstairs I was assigned to the largest of three dormitories which I shared with fifteen of the forty girls.

As we used our Christian names only, I never did learn who these girls were, but before we went to sleep that night I knew many of the intimate details of their lives—where they lived, what they liked, and especially their relations with their boy friends. One of them had a passion for sardines and sour herrings. She spent the evening reading a book of etiquette to us from the top of a double-decker in the corner. The girls laughed at the ridiculous idea of wearing gloves or paying attention to table manners. The description of the proper way to eat crabs and lobsters which was greeted with howls of derision, reminded me of a humiliating experience with crabs in a fashionable Berlin restaurant. Afterward I never chose them from the menu, at any rate not with sauce.

The three blankets over our straw mattresses looked luxurious but as they turned out to be ersatz and there was no heat and all the windows were wide open, I lay awake all night shivering. In the morning we washed in a deep cellar downstairs. The water was cold—in the afternoon only was there a little hot water in the huge washtubs. Upstairs there was a bathroom and we were promised a bath once a week as soon as the central heating system began to work.

At six o'clock in the morning we put on our overalls and ran downstairs for setting-up exercises, after which we dressed, made our beds in military style, then hurried out

160

into the garden for a ceremony about the flagpole. The camp leader read quotations from Hitler and other Nazi prophets. While we saluted, one of the girls hoisted the swastika; then it was time for breakfast.

After a session of Nazi songs that occupied us until half-past seven, we started to our working posts at the farms of the settlers or at the offices of the N. S. V., the woman's organization—the *Krampfaderngeschwader* ("varicose vein squadron") we called them. The offices were in the village and there we mended or wrapped bundles for the poor, not such a bad assignment as others, I learned. The worst one was a farm on which the mother of eight children was in bed following her last confinement and needed a helper to wash the baby's diapers as well as the family clothes.

My first assignment, which was to finish out the last two days of the week at the farm farthest from the camp, wasn't so bad according to the girl who went part of the way with me. The twenty-five minute walk each way pleased me for it meant nearly an hour less of work at the settlement. At the little farm I discovered a woman alone with a thin, putty-faced little girl in bed with infantile paralysis. The father, she told me, worked in an airplane factory in Werder and wouldn't return until evening. The mother hurriedly showed me the strawberry field that must be cultivated and went back into the house without another word. All morning I dug and it was not unpleasant turning over the soil in the field, alone under the crisp autumn sun. At two o'clock I brought the hoe back to the house and walked to the camp where we rested for an hour after lunch before we began work on our own fields.

The actual work wasn't so bad but during the first two days we had unending political lessons with our camp leader. After supper we sang for an hour and devoted another to practicing folk dances for the big weekly Wednesday evening meeting when the settlers and their wives visited the camp, danced with the girls and listened

161

to political speeches. We were obliged to dance with everyone who asked us, the girls told me, to encourage the new
spirit of *Volksgemeinschaft*. At ten o'clock, when everything was over, we raced upstairs for our coats and again
stood at attention in the freezing garden, our arms raised
while we sang the national anthem and someone lowered
the flag.

The second day I picked beans at the same little farm
and, since it was Saturday, collected my wages from the
farmer's wife—the camp charged the settlers twenty pfen-
nings a day for our services—and turned it over to the
camp commander. On Sunday which was Germany's
Thanksgiving Day, the whole camp went to the village to
celebrate and dance with the villagers. Most of the girls
were up early chattering as they pressed their uniforms,
for they were expecting to meet their boy friends at the
village inn, but I stayed in camp, wrote letters and lay on
my bunk trying to ease my swollen throat which the cold
of our dormitory had inflamed.

That evening after the celebration the working schedule
for the following week was announced. It varied from
week to week to give the girls an even chance to work at
the less arduous places. I was lucky enough to draw settler
Blum whose farm adjoined the camp. Another girl and I
reported on Monday morning and were set to work helping the farmer and his wife pick tomatoes.

Mr. Blum was a sociable fellow who after he had
stumbled over the pronunciation of my name, told me that
he was a retired naval officer and that he spoke Polish,
French and English. His home was originally East Prussia,
and he wanted to know where I was from. Bayreuth, wasn't
that where they held the festivals? Had I ever seen any of
the famous artists or the Wagner family?

Although I gave him the briefest possible answers, he
chatted on happily about his adventures in the hotel business before the war. He had bought a hotel at Zoppot near
Danzig on the Baltic and during the summer festivals in

the resort he had entertained many artists—his descrip-
tions of some of my friends were hilarious—but when the
business collapsed, he finally descended to nursing tomatoes and strawberries. When he learned that I spoke English he asked if I would mind giving him a little practice
during working hours in the garden, so as we pulled out
the sticks that held the bunches of tomatoes, we discussed
art and music in English.

The next day Mr. Blum was full of praise for his new
field hand and eager to continue our discussions in English. By the third he had picked up the news in the village
that I was one of the Wagners and received me most ceremoniously. He wanted to spare me the hard work and
spend the time discussing music. But that seemed much
more laborious to me than the work which wasn't bad fun.
Now that it was spoiled I was not so sorry that this was,
temporarily at least, my last day. The camp leader noticed
that I was suffering and, although the local doctor who had
examined us had declared me in excellent condition the
day before, agreed to let me go to Berlin for treatment by
my own doctor.

The specialist who had taken care of me during the
school days in Heiligengrabe and had always been generous about writing excuses for a few days extra in Berlin,
examined me and said at first glance that I had a sinus
infection which was poisoning my whole system and would
require treatment for at least three weeks. He drained it
daily and also prescribed a daily baking by a violet-ray
lamp. As there wasn't one to be borrowed in Berlin, I
went for the treatments to Dr. Steinhardter, who had one
in his office on the Nürnbergerstrasse near our apartment.

"Aren't you being very bold?" he asked, amazed that
I should walk into a Jewish doctor's office in the uniform
of the labor service camp with its swastika arm band. I
wasn't conscious of being particularly daring but the uniform was so ill-fitting and hideous that I was delighted

163

when the camp leader gave me written permission to return to civilian clothes.

No sooner had I begun to feel like myself again and enjoy my cure, with opera every night and pleasant hours with my friends, than Mother made one of her visits to Berlin, and sent me for treatment and for punishment to Professor Veil's University Clinic in Jena.

The very thought of that loathsome man filled me with horror, but my protests were useless. For a few days, while Mother engaged my room and made the necessary arrangements; the apartment was a gloomy place, the two of us shut in together with our angry wills clashing.

It was useless to try to make Mother understand how I abhorred Dr. Veil. She thought I was a contrary, ungrateful child, making things difficult when she was trying to give me the best medical attention, so she cut my objections short by handing me a railroad ticket and calling the car to take me to the station. I had no alternative. Clutching my suitcase packed for the hospital, I boarded the train for Jena.

CHAPTER XVIII

"BE TOUGH, MY DEAR"

HOPELESS, rebellious, smarting from Mother's tongue bludgeoning, I sat in a corner of the express, too miserable even to look out the window. When the train pulled in at the Jena station, I met on the platform my grandfather's friend, Hans von Wolzogen, the poet, who was taking this train to Bayreuth. There he was, kind "Uncle Hans," past eighty-five but delighted to see his "niece." He put his old arms around me, gave me a hearty kiss and warmed my heart with a word about Father. In the flurry of greetings and good-bys he introduced me to another of his "nieces," Margot von Wulffen, who lived in Jena and had come down to see him off. As we were going the same way, we walked along together. When she learned that I was bound for the hospital and alone, she went with me and stayed until the nurse took charge. For the entire ten weeks of my internment she visited me each day.

Dr. Veil looked at me with his flickering green eyes, and I stared back with all the strength of my aversion for the man. He was as gross as ever, with his red hair roached stiffly back from the forehead like bristles. As he was not a specialist, he turned me over to a nose and throat man who peered at me with his jaunty headlight and advised an operation. Three times the staff prepared me for it but each time when the instruments were laid out and everything was ready, Professor Veil rushed into the room and insisted that the operation wasn't necessary, that daily drainage would work a cure.

So there I stayed in this gloomy place, sick, poisoned by the infection, hopeless. There was nothing ahead except disagreements with Mother, frustration, endless struggles to do the slightest little thing I wanted to do. Tired of being misunderstood and shoved around, I lay on the bed, submitted indifferently to the treatments and wanted to die. Death was the best solution, the only way out of it all.

While these black thoughts inhabited my mind, I presented outwardly an appearance of hostile aloofness calculated to irritate everyone who had to come near me. It was better to hit back before anyone had a chance to hurt me. This, at eighteen, was the only defense I knew against a world that, it seemed to me, had given me nothing but kicks and bruises.

After five weeks of this grim brooding, relieved only by the visits of Margot who watched me with an anxious face, the nurse suddenly told me to get dressed; we were going

165

to a Turkish bath. Why dress, I inquired, weren't the baths in the building?

"Oh Lord, no," she answered. "They are down on the river about a half mile from here."

As I wobbled unsteadily to my feet—this was the first time I had been allowed out of bed—the nurse busied herself packing a bag with several hypodermic needles and a number of ampules. What was she going to do with them I wanted to know. She told me she would stand behind the door of the Turkish bath and have them ready in case of a heart attack. A cheery prospect, but I was sunk in such depths of hopelessness that it didn't seem to be worth while to protest.

We went out into a raw November day, drizzling and so foggy that we could not see very far ahead. I peered into the mist, thinking there might be a taxi waiting, but no, the nurse walked me through the town to the river where I took a Turkish bath in the municipal house—and without a heart attack. Back again, shivering in the cold fog. Next morning my head was so much worse that the professor consented to an operation.

"Since the bath didn't kill me, I'm afraid nothing will," I said to him. "Too bad, isn't it?" A childish way to vent my dislike but I wanted to make his green eyes cross and flicker in that peculiar way they had when he was angry.

Finally I began to get better. Perhaps it was the kindness of Margot and her husband or the fact that I was permitted to go out in the afternoon and eat palatable food in the town, or it may have been a score of *Tristan* that I had taken along but had been too miserable to read; whatever the reason, I heard a faint voice whispering inside me that it was a cowardly thing to want to die.

"Why don't you fight back?" it asked. "What right have you to give up when there are so many people who have greater miseries to bear? Why don't you try to help them? Misunderstood? What of it? Nobody has actually beaten you. Nobody has directly, physically interfered with your life.

"What about Bayreuth, your responsibility, your promise to your father? Aren't you tough enough to put up a little fight?"

Every day the persistent voice grew louder and louder until it didn't need to prod me any more. In no time I was absorbed in my favorite dream of starting my career as a stage director with a production of *Tristan*. I wrote long letters to Frida Leider, drawing layouts for her, going into minute details about wigs, costumes, scenery, lighting. I put down on paper long dissertations about the acting, the interpretation, the people who should sing the various roles.

The fatalistic, melancholy youngster disappeared, and with her went my indulgence in biting juvenile sarcasm. Nothing seemed discouraging any more. Amazing how much easier it was to laugh at things than to take them seriously. This discovery that a smile or a laugh can often turn what might have been a tragic moment into a funny incident has stood by me in many a tough situation.

Margot and her husband made me one of a group of pleasant young doctors and assistants who, after I had been in the hospital for a couple of months, planned a party for me on a Sunday afternoon when they would be off duty. But we reckoned without Professor Veil. In spite of the more attractive food, the pleasant times with Margot and the lift of my spirits, I was losing as many as nine pounds a week and had become frightfully anemic. The professor found my blood count down to sixty and ordered a transfusion. The nurse told Margot when she came to fetch me for an afternoon in town, "Miss Wagner should be much more careful. She doesn't seem to realize that she is seriously ill."

On Friday the new blood was pumped into my veins, and the entire staff breathed easier, hoping I would stay quietly in bed and not upset the ward with my fun making,

167

but five minutes after the doctors had left, I was up again. Everybody stared at me as though I were a ghost, why I couldn't imagine. They certainly didn't expect the transfusion to kill me.

On Saturday, the day before the party, another transfusion was ordered, and this one did put me in bed for a couple of days. No permission was granted for the few hours of absence on Sunday nor could I have gone although I would rather have died than admit it.

On this very Saturday of the second transfusion a friend of Mother's paid me a visit. With a natural impulse to make the details of my limited existence as interesting as possible, I showed her my view of the university morgue, more politely called the Pathological Institute. From the window we watched the big black car driving back and forth, taking the corpses to the cemetery after they had been dissected.

"Have you been looking at this all these weeks?" she asked.

"Yes." I hadn't missed a single corpse. The stretchers, I told her, were covered with a rubber sheet under which you could see plainly where the head and feet stuck up. Since one of the carriers was short and the other very tall, the corpses always tipped up and down.

To speak lightly of this daily view was easy but, although I would not admit it to myself, it had filled me with an increasing horror, an obsession that had been transformed into a fear of germs. I found myself opening doors with my elbow and rushing to wash my hands at the first possible moment after shaking hands with anyone. To this day my elbows serve as door openers although no one knows better than I that it is a very silly habit.

Mother's friend who was not inured to hospitals, called Mother the instant she left and in a fit of hysterics begged her to take me away from the place—do something— change my room at least, and find out about the necessity of all these transfusions. Mother, it seemed, had known nothing about the transfusions. She had trusted Dr. Veil blindly, and he had not felt it necessary to inform her about them. Over the phone Mother raised quite a commotion in the clinic, demanding to know how Dr. Veil had dared to give me transfusions without her permission.

When the doctor paid me a visit on Monday morning he was flushed with rage and shouted that I was a vicious little liar to tell such stories about the hospital after all the care I had received. In return I looked him straight in the eyes until they began to flicker and told him all the unpleasant things I had heard about him in Jena. It was something of a triumph for I was moved into another room within an hour. A few days later Mother came and got the doctor's permission to take me to Dresden for Nickel's birthday party. Almost eagerly Veil assured her that I was cured, that I could go home to Bayreuth and need return only for a final checkup.

"How amazing," I thought. "A week ago I was practically dying; this week I am completely cured." It gave me a tremendous thrill to feel that I had fought my way out of imprisonment on a sickbed. The words that an old friend of Father's had often said to me when he saw me in a tight spot kept singing in my heart. "*Landgräfin, bleibe hart.*" ("Be tough and stay tough, my dear.")

In Dresden Mother did everything she could think of to give Nickel and me a pleasant time, everything except letting us do the things we wanted most. Although Nickel got around her in a dozen pretty ways, Mother was adamant in the matter of rouge or lipstick. She considered make-up cheap and vulgar, and the women who wore it, almost as disreputable as prostitutes. This was all very well in her case for she had one of those delicious, glowing English skins that shame cosmetics. Even when she drove for hours in the sun and wind with the top of the car turned back, as she loved to do, she just burned to an attractive tan with never a blister or a shiny nose. But Nickel and I had Cosima's pallor which, we believed, was

169

much improved by a discriminating use of color. So we borrowed a little rouge and powdered our fresh young faces when we were away from home, even though we knew we risked a scolding.

Wahnfried again for Christmas. This year although we performed all the accustomed rites, we were none of us particularly happy; the aunts away; Father gone; the boys hostile, Mother genuinely puzzled at my obstinacy. Whenever I came home, Wieland and Wolfi had to be won over afresh. While I was away they looked upon me as an outcast, a strange, outrageous creature as interpreted by Knittel and Tietjen, but after I had been at home for a day or twó, Wieland would acknowledge rather sheepishly that Mausi was a pretty good fellow.

The first break in our Christmas truce came when it was time for me to return to Jena for a final checkup. In a long and bitter argument I told Mother that I would rather die the most horrible death than have Dr. Veil treat me again. Outraged, Mother demanded my vow in writing, and declared that since she had done her very best for me and I had refused to accept it, she would no longer be responsible for my physical welfare. She hadn't believed that I was serious until I gave her the statement, typed and properly signed, looking impressively legal. After that day I chose my own doctors when I needed them for a toothache, a cold or so, and one or two attacks of flu, and she was relieved of the fantastic bills that her doctors used to charge.

After the holidays Mother decided that it was time for me to do something about the labor camp from which I had never been discharged, and, much to her relief, I offered to report to it immediately. My plans were all laid. From Berlin I drove out to the camp and instructed the driver to wait while I spoke to the commandant. My health was temporarily normal, I told her, but I needed care which, of course, the camp could not be expected to give.

The minute a draft touched my throat the trouble returned, so it might be wiser for me to get a release paper now and reapply during the summer months. This the commandant gave me willingly for she wanted no suffering invalid on her hands. With the precious release in my bag I returned to Berlin where I phoned Mother that the camp had rejected me.

So far, so good. Now it was necessary to find a good excuse for staying in Berlin and setting about the preparation for my work. The musical studies on which I had set my mind while I lay in the hospital in Jena must be kept secret, for Mother had the idea that music was a pretty accomplishment for a girl, but that her career was to make a proper marriage. A part-time job might seem innocent and temporary enough, so I wrote that I was going to find one as a doctor's assistant or something of the sort.

But Mother would have none of it—working in an office was, if anything, more unmaidenly than studying at the university. She telephoned from Dresden where she was visiting Nickel and invited me to meet her there for the opera ball. When she was assured that I had no intention of coming, she lost her temper and ordered me to come home.

"No, I am not coming home—I never intend to come home," I told her bluntly.

"But why?" she kept insisting, "Why don't you want to come home?"

Why? The words tumbled hot into the mouthpiece. It was an utter waste of time to stay at Bayreuth with nothing to do all year long except bite my fingernails. She had always promised me that as soon as I finished school I might choose a profession and now I intended to do it. No, I wasn't coming home to Bayreuth, and she couldn't force me back with threats.

"But why not come to Dresden and talk it over?" Mother urged, trying to hold on to herself.

The Äbtissin had invited me to Heiligengrabe for the

week end and I couldn't disappoint her. It was the quickest excuse that came to mind, and Heiligengrabe was a safe retreat, still farther away from Dresden and Bayreuth than Berlin.

With the status of an "old girl" who could do as she pleased, Heiligengrabe was so pleasant that I stayed on for a week and probably would have lingered if it hadn't been for a phone call from Mother.

"I am in Berlin," she told me, "and if you want to stay here, come back at once for I am leaving tomorrow night and there are lots of things to talk over."

On the station platform in Berlin I saw a porter carrying my name printed on a tall pasteboard banner as he shuffled through the crowd calling, "Telegram for Fräulein Wagner." As I hurried toward him I met Mother.

"That's only my telegram," she said. "I was going to Hitler's Reichstag address this morning but decided to meet you instead."

She was no longer angry—Mother didn't harbor anger when she had everything arranged and was eager to get on with it. As she did not want me to stay in the apartment with no one but the cook and maid as chaperones, she took me to a pension. The charming young woman who greeted us almost, but not quite, dismissed my suspicions; she was the widow of a distinguished poet who was trying to educate her young son by boarding and chaperoning young girls.

After we had dropped my bags we started home to our apartment for luncheon. When we came out into the street there was not a taxi or a moving car in sight, not even pedestrian. The few cars that sat by the curb were parked and deserted. The place had been swept clean of all movement, all human life, and yet this ghost city was full of sound. As we walked along Hitler's voice followed us from every loud speaker, every window; we couldn't get away from that rasping, barking fusillade of words. We walked

172

along without speaking, forced into a temporary truce, as if we were the last two people left in a deserted world.

In the quiet, familiar atmosphere of the apartment, Mother told me that she had entered me for a course of shorthand and typing at Rackow's, the outstanding commercial school in Berlin, and after a month would expect me to take bookkeeping also. She thought by that time I would find it easy to manage all three. Instantly I clamped a mask over my face. This was the last thing in the world I wanted but something whispered to me, "Don't object. Mama is going home tomorrow and won't be back for at least a month. You can still do what you want."

Before she left I had another fight to win. In the morning, without saying a word about it, I went to the hairdresser and had my hair bobbed. How much better it was to avoid all the threats by surprising her with the accomplished fact. Of course there was a storm—that was to be expected—but out of it I emerged with the promise of a monthly dress allowance. No longer would I be compelled to wear the dresses that she considered suitable for a young girl. If I appeared unattractive, if I dressed outrageously, at least I would have only myself to blame. After a tempestuous but exultant day I saw Mother off at the station and drove straight to the opera, returning to the pension very late.

What would my new mentor say? Even in the intoxication of this new freedom I did care because I wanted peace. But during the following weeks this delightful woman became a close friend.

"You frightened the wits out of me that first day," she told me. "Never have I seen such a look of distrust and suspicion on anybody's face. You thought I was your mother's accomplice, so I prayed hard that I would be able to win your confidence."

The day after Mother left I called up Frida and told her what had happened.

"Rackow's?" she asked. "That's where I learned how to support myself."

After that I felt better about it. The lessons were from eleven to one in the morning six days a week, but it didn't take long to discover that I could keep up with the class by attending only twice a week. This left plenty of time for a course in the history of art at the university and for the opera and theater rehearsals every day and performances every night.

Tietjen was kind that winter; he gave me the freedom of all his institutions and taught me the *abc*'s of reading scores and conducting. Watching him direct dull modern operas which were ordered by the Nazis and saved only because of his perfect directing and lavish production taught me even more than following him at Bayreuth where I was familiar with the productions. It made me very proud that he relied on my judgment and sometimes engaged people solely on my recommendation. When I attended performances in other cities I always made a minute report to him. On a few occasions he sent me as an official scout for Bayreuth and accepted my verdict in regard to engaging artists.

With all these activities there was also time to explore Berlin. This was the first time I had ever lived in a big city with freedom to wander about the streets, poke into book and art shops—the museums, the lovely surrounding country where we often went for Sunday drives with Tietjen, the opera, the theaters, the fashionable shops and hotels.

At that time the city was being remodeled according to Hitler's twenty-year plan and looked as though it had been half demolished by an earthquake. The Berliners said jokingly that if the Czechs should fly over with the intention of bombing the city, they would look down and save their bombs, seeing it already in a state of ruin.

Hitler designed for the future Berlin one wide avenue straight through the city with ministries, a public library, an enormous new concert hall, theaters, museums, lining either side. Near the grounds where the Olympic games were held he planned to build the world's largest university which would absorb all the others in the city. The attractive modern residences in this section were bought and torn down by the city, but their poor owners couldn't build anywhere else as there was no longer any private building in Germany. The demolition had been going on merrily; it took almost four times as long to drive across town, but the only work actually accomplished was the widening of the main driveway, cutting down the trees which, according to the Führer, hindered the big parades, and the work on the Tempelhof airfield (it was to be the biggest in the world) from which one could reach the leading hotels in ten or fifteen minutes.

Hitler was fascinated by blueprints and was always carrying them around as he dreamed about his paper city. If the Vienna Academy hadn't denied his application, he was confident he would have been a brilliant architect. I have often seen him seized with a kind of ecstasy when he talked about the grandeur of his schemes.

"Just think how terrible it would be if in a couple of thousand years people started to dig up ruins of our time and found the Reichstag building as representative of our age. But I intend that they shall judge it by my new buildings." Sometimes he nodded his head with satisfaction. "My old man wanted me to be a petty office holder as he was. He didn't think much of the idea of my being an architect. Well, he got his wish and I got mine, but wouldn't he be pleased and amazed to see what is happening in this city!"

Possibly, if Hitler's father liked to lean over heaven's bar and see his son sign orders of execution and watch the buildings tumble.

Frida and I spent many a spring afternoon wandering about the city, going to the museums or the galleries, taking in Hitler's "Exhibition of Decadent Art" in which he was showing for the last time the works of the great impressionists that he had collected from the museums or confiscated from Jewish owners and intended to sell on the foreign market to bolster Germany's exchange. Or sometimes Frida took me to a week-end cottage she had built outside Berlin, a delightful place among the pines, with a garden that was just beginning to show a little timid yellowish green. She had planted the garden herself, bringing in every bit of topsoil to enrich the native sand. It gave her a comforting feeling to look at the crisp ruffled curtains in the windows, the gaily painted chairs and tables, the flower beds, and think, "I made these, I accomplished all this with my own hands." She was such a stimulant that she made the things I dreamed seem possible, almost within my reach.

Among them was my long-cherished plan to go to England that spring. Frida was due in London after Easter for an engagement at Covent Garden. Mother had always promised to let me return but when it came to the test, had said no. Now I didn't want to wait any longer and it meant so much to me that I mapped and remapped my strategy, considered and discarded dozens of plans without thinking of a single one that might persuade her.

CHAPTER XIX

SPRING AT COVENT GARDEN

BEFORE I had hit upon a good idea, Mother paid another visit to Berlin and took the initiative from me. One of her first objectives was the Rackow School where she looked at my attendance record and returned to blast me.

176

"It isn't how often I go to classes but how much I learn that matters," I tried to argue, but Mother couldn't see my logic. Puzzled and outraged by my incomprehensible behavior, she asked my friend and chaperone to keep an eye on me and discover what I was doing with my time. Madame S. told her that I was old enough to know what I was doing, and that she could not be responsible for my actions. She tried to protect me and did her hopeless best to persuade Mother that I was an adult.

This, I saw clearly, was not the moment to broach the subject of England, so I bent my head to the storm and waited for Mother's return to Bayreuth. The next month was so full that I was still unprepared when she made a second descent. Sir Thomas Beecham was in Berlin as guest conductor at the Staatsoper and Tietjen had kept me busy entertaining the redoubtable Englishman in his box, helping him arrange a dinner for the visitor and acting as hostess for it.

Mother asked me one day at luncheon, "Now that you have learned shorthand, typewriting and bookkeeping, may I ask what your plans are? What are you going to do with your future?"

"You know as well as I do what my plans are," I answered, jumping to the attack. "You promised me long ago that you would send me back to England to improve my English. You told me yourself that I must have languages for my work at Bayreuth."

"No, I won't have you go to England," snapped Mother, taken by surprise. "Not under any circumstances."

But I pressed the matter.

"What made you change your mind so suddenly? Weren't you going to ask Sir Thomas Beecham to advise you about the arrangements? He is here in Berlin now, and this is the best chance in the world to ask him."

Mother's color began to rise and her voice to take on a sharp, angry edge.

"I've decided against it. Now do forget about it."

177

"No, I won't forget about it. I'm tired of having you promise me things all the time and then tell me to forget about them. I'm going to England," I flung at her. "If you won't help me, I'll get there anyway."

Mother was really angry; to avoid scenes she ignored me during the few days that she was in town. After she returned to Bayreuth I learned she had deliberately neglected to give me Beecham's invitation to dinner at the Esplanade. The guests waited over an hour and put me down as a boor for sending no excuse.

At Easter the school gave a week's vacation but to avoid so long a time at Bayreuth I told Mother we had only a short week end. I must be at school early Tuesday morning for a class in bookkeeping which was still Chinese to me. This ardor for school puzzled Mother; she didn't know that Leider was singing in *Die Walküre* on Tuesday.

On the desk in Mother's study lay a folder for an English school. So she was relenting! But not too far—on closer examination the school appeared to be for children from six to sixteen. But a breath of opposition might ruin everything—after all, the idea was to get out of Germany. When Mother told me she had selected a school, she was thanked with a convincing smile.

"Emma will get together your outfit. As soon as you produce a diploma from the Rackow School you may go, but not until you pass the examinations satisfactorily."

That was easy. Returning to Berlin I took the examinations and surprised her with the highest marks in the class.

It was hard to leave Nickel; we had grown very close to each other, but otherwise I was glad to rush through the preparations and get away from Wahnfried. Frida was to take me with her in early May when she went to London for her season at Covent Garden. Mother did not soften before I left, but she did write to the headmistress of the school, giving me permission to go up to London when Frida invited me.

That school—it was the only cloud in a perfect heaven.

178

The German teacher was to meet me at the station—we hoped we might miss the person but there she was.

"Never mind," Frida promised me, "it won't be long." She did not invite me for her first engagement which was during Coronation Week, a difficult time to find quarters, and altogether hectic, but in early June she was returning to sing in *Tristan* and for that she expected me to come. As if I would miss it! Hadn't I contrived to stay in Berlin and hear her Good Friday performance of Kundry in *Parsifal* and her singing in *Die Walküre* at the Staatsoper! I wouldn't have missed her Isolde for plague or hailstorms.

The children were away on a vacation when the German teacher took me down to the big, endlessly rambling old brick school in Sussex. It was perhaps originally the country house of one of the local gentry and pleasant enough, surrounded by woods and rolling meadow. In the good library I began to brush up on my English and wait for Frida.

Toward the end of May the newspapers announced that Toscanini had arrived in London. With an uneasy constriction about the heart, I wrote him a letter, sending it to Queen's Hall for I didn't know where he was staying. Would he remember me after these six years, and if he did would he identify me with the Nazis and all the unhappy things that had grown out of his clash with Bayreuth over Hitler? Day after day I watched the village postman make his leisurely way up the drive, but no answer. Maybe Toscanini didn't receive my letter. Or maybe—I didn't want to believe it—he preferred not to answer.

I counted the days until it was time to go up to London. *Tristan* was scheduled for the first week of June. Telling the headmistress that Frida had invited me for the week end, would meet me at the station, and all the proper things, I got her permission and took the train to the city.

It was a Saturday afternoon. With the name of an inexpensive but eminently respectable little hotel in my purse,

179

I found a taxi and asked the driver to go slowly, wanting to look out the window and discover some place that was familiar, a street, a park, a building that Father had showed me seven years before. But nothing stirred a memory, nothing except a huge flat building that suddenly marched into view. The British Museum! Father and Mother standing on the doorstep chatting with a friend, handing me over to her for luncheon; the picture remained clear and vivid in my consciousness.

At the hotel I telephoned Frida and learned from Dr. Geissmar that Toscanini was staying at Claridge's. A call failed to reach him so I went to the hotel, found everyone out and wrote a little note to leave for him. I was sure he would want to see me. And this time he would surely get my letter.

Sunday evening in Piccadilly Circus with Frida, lingering over the dinner table, talking about home; it was a lovely day and we were content even though her news was not too cheerful. Tietjen who had made so many promises to lure her back to Germany when Hitler began to persecute the Jews, was failing to keep them one by one and making life increasingly difficult. In the beginning he owed much of his security to Frida whose voice was influential at the Staatsoper and who upheld him against Hitler's dislike. Now that he felt more sure of himself he was forgetting his obligations.

Frida had been ill, worrying about the safety of her husband and the friction at the Staatsoper, but here in London she breathed free air; no furtive intrigues—no dread of what might happen tomorrow. For a week at least life was normal and predictable as it should be. On Monday she was singing Isolde. It would be a gala evening for me who had never heard her Isolde, so we forgot our troubles and enjoyed the hour.

Early next morning the telephone rang. Mrs. Toscanini invited me to be at Queen's Hall at nine forty-five. With my heart pounding I jumped into clothes, swallowed a cup

of tea, had a quick breakfast and reached Queen's Hall on
time. But getting in was quite another matter. The entrances seemed to be numbered so I started at No. 1,
coughed loudly to stir the sleepy doorman, and told him
that Toscanini was expecting me.

"This isn't the door," he said languidly, waving me on.
At No. 2 it was the same story, and at numbers 3 and 4.
On I went, circling the building—finally at No. 15 the
haughty doorman told me that this was the orchestra
entrance, but he didn't seem at all sure that Maestro Toscanini wanted to see me. Reluctantly he stumped downstairs while I waited, my knees wobbling with excitement.
A few minutes later the doorman returned and asked me
to follow him in a tone that almost approached cordiality.
Downstairs we went, through a dim, narrow passage to the
artists' room. Mrs. Toscanini saw me first and smiled at
me.

"Here is Mausi," she said, beckoning me to come in.
The Maestro turned and held out his arms.

"*Cara figliola,*" he called, planting a kiss on my cheek.
I embraced him warmly. Once again I had a deep inner
feeling of security.

After a week with Frida and Toscanini, opera, museums
and concerts, a week crammed full of enough happiness
to last until they should return to London I went down to
Sussex, back to school. Most of the time I devoted to English in some form or another, literature, history of art, history, elocution and privately I started to brush up on my
French. During September Frida Leider would be in Paris
at the Exposition with the company from the Staatsoper
which was representing Germany. All my friends would
be there, the music would be unsurpassed and I planned
to hear it since I wasn't going home for the festival. I had
never seen Paris. It cost no more to live there than in England—in fact the exchange rate was much better—so why
not spend several weeks there and see the Exposition?

With a friend who was a party to the secret I wandered

over the downs practicing French on the birds and cows. And of an evening there were the accounts. It was going to be possible, just possible, to make the trip. My student permit from the German government granted me a very small allowance and it couldn't be augmented even if Mother weakened, for there was no way of getting money out of Germany. Every month I sent my passport to the bank in Bayreuth which returned it with the check after it had been stamped by the Devisen Amt. By counting the pennies I could manage three weeks in Paris without a word to anyone.

Early in September I crossed to Paris, found through Cook's a tiny room in a small hotel near Rue de Rivoli and looked up my friends. Mother and the four of us children, I learned, had been invited to attend the Exposition as the guests of the commission, but she had declined. It was a bit ironical to think that I might have been living in splendor at the Crillon, but it was just as much fun, probably more, to do what I pleased and return at night to my own tiny, independent cubicle.

That first week during which the Staatsoper covered itself with glory, I spent every moment with the company, dining at the restaurant atop the German pavilion, listening to the gossip, to the latest stories of intrigues and persecution. Frida sang magnificently and for the moment seemed to feel that everything was peaceful.

Tietjen included me in all of his parties as usual, but he hadn't overcome the old habit of supervising my conduct. When he happened to hear Furtwängler ask if he might talk to me, he called me into his office and admonished me, and managed somehow to prevent Furtwängler from seeing me. The conductor wanted, I imagine, to unburden his mind about what had happened at Bayreuth during the summer which, according to all accounts, had been a particularly hectic season. Furtwängler was a very unhappy man; although the Nazis had finally returned his passport they had held it until he lost his engagement with

182

the New York Philharmonic and was thoroughly discredited outside of Germany as a Nazi. Inside Germany he was constantly harassed and spied on because he wasn't one.

At the Exposition to which he had been sent as Germany's greatest conductor, he was forced to join Tietjen and a high government official in placing a wreath on the grave of the unknown soldier. A news picture of the Nazi delegation giving the salute, showed the official holding his arm very high in the air, Tietjen extending his satisfactorily, but Furtwängler holding his arm at an embarrassed angle against his shoulder. Later I learned that Tietjen showed this picture in the proper quarters as evidence of Furtwängler's treacherous anti-Nazi sentiments.

After the German delegation departed, having won any number of gold medals, I spent my remaining two weeks exploring Paris. Someone had given me E. V. Lucas' *A Wanderer in Paris* and I discovered the city by retracing his footsteps. Up bright and early in the morning, I outdistanced the English friends whom I often met for lunch. "We can't keep up with Mausi" they protested. "She must have feet of cast iron." Whereupon they retired for an hour or two of rest while I continued my quests until time for dinner.

Back in London I did not return to the school but took a room with a charming family in Hampstead. It was an intoxicating autumn; daily visits to the museum, courses in history of art, and permission to attend the rehearsals of the London Philharmonic through the kindness of Dr. Geissmar and Sir Thomas Beecham. A music critic who was a friend of mother's took me to the Sunday concerts at Covent Garden, the Queen's Hall concerts and those of the B. B. C. This was my first intimate acquaintance with symphonic music, which so fascinated me that I lived with my head in a score.

In November Toscanini returned for an engagement with the B. B. C. and found time for the *cara figliola*. He gave me tickets to the concerts and also to the rehearsals and I didn't miss one. After them I went back to the artists' room where the great and the near-great gathered to do homage to the Maestro. It was a kind and friendly world; even the burly old doorman thawed out. I was finally living in an atmosphere which gave me complete happiness, doing all the things I wanted to, seeing the people I loved and breathing deep of freedom.

On the morning of the day Toscanini was to rehearse the *Ninth Symphony*, Dr. Geissmar phoned. After some irrelevant chat she suddenly said, in an agitated voice, "Something terrible has happened. Don't ask me what it is; I can't tell you. I'll see you at rehearsal." And she broke the connection.

All the way to rehearsal my mind was filled with questions. I was going over the unstable positions of my friends in Germany upon whom the ax might have fallen. Suddenly the name of Janssen flashed through my mind. That nagging little sixth sense of mine kept telling me: It will be something about Janssen. The rehearsal hall was filling rapidly when I arrived but Dr. Geissmar was not there. The orchestra assembled; Toscanini came out of the anteroom and tapped the desk with his baton; the rehearsal started and still no Dr. Geissmar. Not until just before the intermission did I hear her slipping into the seat behind me and realize that with her was a tall, gaunt figure. It was Janssen.

So, whatever terrible thing had happened it had not kept Janssen in Germany. But it was bad enough; Janssen had been in the baths at Bad Kissingen when a friend had rushed in to warn him that he must get out at once, that his arrest had been ordered for that day and there was no time to be lost. In some miraculous manner he escaped, with only ten marks in his pocket. And that was all. Like all good Germans at that time, he had brought back into the Reich every cent that he had earned so now he was penniless and frightfully worried about Erna who had stayed to settle their affairs and salvage what she could.

We assured him that Erna would be safe; she was both clever and knew how to play dumb. Later Erna herself told me that when she was summoned to Tietjen's office he tried hard to catch her in an admission that Janssen had resources outside.

"Herbert must have money outside. Nobody in his right mind would walk off without a penny," he kept insisting.

"Not Herbert," she answered lightly as if she had never heard of the death penalty for that offense. "He never thinks of anything practical." When she left through the outer office, she noticed Tietjen's secretary hurriedly closing the lid of a dictaphone.

Although his friends wanted to help Janssen, he didn't need aid. Sir Thomas engaged him immediately for a Sunday concert and "His Master's Voice" presented him with a fat check for recordings. Not more than two or three days afterward he was engaged by the Vienna opera, the Teatro Colon in Buenos Aires, and finally the Metropolitan.

CHAPTER XX

ARYAN BLOOD

CHRISTMAS again—1937. The visit, for that was the way I thought of it, was something to be dreaded although Nickel tugged at my heart. The boys had been ill, both of them, in the hospital, and Mother was worried. This time I promised myself to watch my tongue and give her not the slightest cause for disagreement. By trying hard enough surely I could get through the holidays without a storm.

185

The plane that flew me to Berlin set me down in a strange city. These were the same familiar streets, the same houses, but the people were changed, even my closest friends. Perhaps because I had been "outside" for so long they began to whisper criticisms that never before would have passed their lips. Hitler, to my utter amazement, was no longer sacrosanct. They told me bitterly of fantastic parties in the Chancellery, of fortunes paid to dancers and incredible sums for champagne, of the fabulous amounts this minister paid for his villa and that one for the jewels of his mistress. Germans are not luxury-minded and are inclined to be sharply critical of extravagance, especially when the money for it is being drained from their own pockets.

Amazed to discover that Hitler, the "saintly aesthete," should have begun to rock even lightly on his pedestal, I called up the Chancellery to say that I was in Berlin and would like to see the Führer. My purpose was to tell him what a mistake Ribbentrop was making in London. Everyone in England was honestly anxious to be on friendly terms with Germany but Ribbentrop's antics at the Embassy did not help.

When I arrived at the Chancellery, Kannenberg indicated that I was to lunch alone with the Führer who came to meet me at the foot of the stairs, looking much better, less bloated and sallow than when I had seen him last in March. He led me to a new small dining room, a distinctly elegant room.

"Do you like it?" asked Hitler watching me glance about admiringly. "I want to see my guests alone occasionally without having all these men around."

Yes, I did like its intimate charm but it was a woman's room. The pretty rococo lady on the wall, smiling down in her powdered wig and daringly cut blue gown seemed a bit out of harmony with the loud-voiced S. S. butler. One thing I liked especially—the room was free from the oppressive Hitlerian atmosphere. He belonged in it no

186

more than I; we were a couple of guests and could speak freely to each other.

As we attacked the gigantic platters of pea soup I began to tell him what an unfortunate muddle Ribbentrop was making of German-English relations, and emphasized the German Ambassador's blunders by comparing him with the Austrian, Frankenstein, who was the most popular and at the same time the most respected of the diplomatic representatives in London. I even went into details about some of Ribbentrop's mistakes, his rudeness and his gaudy parties that invited the criticism of the very guests who guzzled his champagne.

The Führer abandoned the pea soup and stared at me, his color beginning to mount.

"You are wrong," he thundered, pointing his finger at me. "That's a lie. Ribbentrop told me differently."

"Why should Ribbentrop tell you the truth?" I inquired.

As he waved his hands about and glared at me with those blue, hypnotic eyes I wanted to laugh at myself, for whatever I might say of Ribbentrop, certainly I was no diplomat. We changed the subject and harmony was restored; and before I realized it the S. S. butler charged in with the Führer's pill and a glass of water. The luncheon was over. This was the wrong moment but since I had bungled everything in my zeal to inform Hitler about conditions in England, I had to seize it to fulfill a promise to a friend.

"I want to ask a great favor of you, not for me but for my best friend." How I wished I could look up at him appealingly through my eyelashes the way Nickel would have managed it, but my only method was to plunge straight ahead.

"Her fiancé is the head surgeon of a big hospital and medical officer to the S. S. Now it turns out that she is one-fourth Jewish though you could never guess it to look at her. She's a perfect Nordic type. And as for the Jewish grandmother, she was awarded the highest decorations for her work as a Red Cross nurse in the Franco-Prussian War. Even though my friend could marry her doctor according to the Nuremberg laws, in practice it would ruin him unless she gets a waiver from the government. He would have to resign from the hospital and the S. S. and lose all his patients. It only needs one word from you to quiet those small-town busybodies."

Hitler could be extraordinarily sentimental and I had known cases in which he had given decisions in a human way. Then, too, I had counted on his not wishing to refuse me a favor.

"I must see what the law says," Hitler answered in an evasive tone. "Please have the whole case typed out and sent to me so it can be investigated."

This was the worst thing that could have happened. I had been warned that these famous typed cases never got any further than the wastepaper basket, but I couldn't abandon my friend's case without one more try.

"Who grants these permissions for half-Jews to marry Aryans? Does Frick decide?"

"No, I do," answered Hitler, looking annoyed. "Only in the most exceptional ones where there is clear proof that the Aryan half is dominant, do I give permission."

"Where there is clear proof? . . ."

"Oh, that is simple," answered Hitler. "I have my blood tests. My scientists deal with such matters." His tone warned me that he wished to hear no more of my friend and her heart affairs.

I clamped my teeth to keep from blurting out that not even the blood of a gorilla can be distinguished from that of a human. We murmured a few strained pleasantries as he walked with me to the top of the stairs.

"Good-by, Mausi. I am always so pleased to see any of you. Give my love to Mama and Nickerl and your brothers."

So that was that. When I went out into the chill winter

188

sunshine I almost ran to get rid of the angry thoughts that were churning about in my mind.

It was time to dress for dinner and the theater with the Passmanns who had been very kind to me during the winter in Berlin. Peter tried to chase away my depression with his funny stories, but I felt as if nothing in the world would ever lift my spirits.

"I wish I knew where I belong. I don't belong here any more. Tell me, Peter, where do I belong?"

Father's old friend made no answer; he only patted my hand.

The next afternon Tietjen had a long talk with me in his office, trying to prepare me for conditions at home. Nobody had told me how serious the illnesses of the boys had been. All autumn Wieland had stayed in the hospital in Bayreuth where he had undergone an operation for an old lesion that had never bothered him until he strained himself at the labor camp. On the day he was well enough to get out of bed it was discovered that he had a double embolism of the lungs. The doctors had promised that he would be at home for Christmas.

Wolfi had come home from the labor camp in a miserable condition. The authorities had held the boys for an extra month to get in the harvest but had issued them no warm clothes, so Wolfi returned with a bad case of inflammatory rheumatism plus a poisoning of his whole system; Emma had taken him to the mountains to recuperate, and he too would be able to come home for the holidays.

"You will find your mother a changed woman," warned Tietjen, "uncertain and distrustful. When Wieland was so ill and she was opening his letters she came upon several from Knittel advising the boy to break away from his mother and live his own life. You know how she has always trusted Knittel blindly. In the depths of her troubles she called for you. She asked me 'Shall I send for Mausi?' Although she probably won't tell you these things because

189

you have always disliked Knittel, she needs you. See what you can do for her."

It was kind of Tietjen. I promised him to do my best and on the very next day started home. When Mother saw me at Wahnfried she threw her arms about me and wept. We were close again, but the moment passed as had all the others, leaving us politely wary of each other.

The holidays passed much more smoothly than we had expected, chiefly because of little Betty, who I found was the adorable tyrant of Wahnfried. Mother had discovered her at the clinic in Bayreuth when she was visiting Wieland and had become attached to the pathetic little three-year-old wisp who was suffering from a dietary skin disease. The doctor, who was also the public health officer, had brought her in from her peasant home because her parents were both too poor and too ignorant to give her the proper diet, but her little crib was being shoved around from one ward to another and nobody could give her proper attention.

"I have plenty of room and food and time," said Mother. "I'll take her home."

Betty was so frail, so backward physically that she could scarcely walk, so we took her out in the baby carriage, sometimes Mother, sometimes Emma or I, while the townspeople speculated about her parentage. She blossomed in Wahnfried and was soon so bright-eyed and entertaining that Mother's friends were eager to come for tea and listen to Betty in her high chair beside the table.

During the day Betty did not scratch her rash but at night no matter how well she was bandaged, she always managed to dig at a few of her scars. In the morning she presented her little behind with the demand to be spanked. Finally Mother discovered that the child was afraid she would be sent home when she was well, so she was determined to keep a few unhealed scratches. When Mother made her understand that she could stay as long as she wished, Betty stopped scratching and enjoyed Wahnfried.

The maids, the gardener, the cook, everybody was her delighted slave except Emma who, when Mother dressed Betty in some particularly attractive little frock, reminded her that after all this wasn't a Wagner child.

As Wieland was about the house most of the time, we became good friends again. He told me how he had turned on the radio one night while he was resting in the guardhouse during his military service. The tune he got was a march with a fine swing to it so he turned the dial full blast for the benefit of the boys on guard outside. Suddenly an officer threw open the door and shouted above the music, "For God's sake, turn off that tune. Don't you know it's the 'Internationale'?" Wieland was innocent and surprised but disappointed to miss the end, so I promised to bring him a record of it from London on my next visit. Between us we should have some fun.

Another story that he told me, one which had evidently become one of the family legends, was the saga of Prince Chichiboo's visit to Wahnfried. The Japanese Prince, a brother of Hirohito, had been Hitler's guest during the autumn party rally at Nuremberg, so Hitler had asked Mother to evacuate Wahnfried for a week and let the Prince and his aides move in. Mother was to stay near by and act as hostess. The Prince spoke broken English but no German, and Mother of course, no Japanese, so conversation was a bit difficult between them. When she asked him how he liked his eggs for breakfast, poached, boiled, fried, scrambled, he replied with a polite smile, "everything." So Mother ordered "everything." In the morning when she joined the Prince at breakfast, she saw him happily eat them all, every style of egg the cook had been able to contrive. She had not been warned that the Japanese guest must finish all the food his host sets before him, so while the Prince ate heroically, she marveled at his gustatory powers.

The first dinner went smoothly enough with conversation supplemented by the sign language, until the dessert

191

was reached. When all was finished, Prince Chichiboo gave a mighty belch followed by his aides in a chorus of belches, likewise fortissimo. Mother nearly jumped from her chair but remembered that this was the way a Japanese says "What a delicious dinner."

After a week of eggs and belching, the Prince departed. When little Betty came shortly afterward and, like all babies, belched, the whole company shouted "Chichibooooo!" Next time Betty was ahead of them all. "Chichiboo," she cooed proudly, looking at Mother for approval.

This Christmas I managed to get away without the usual storm, but Mother was so harassed, so distrustful of my hidden motives, that it was difficult. London in which no one suspected me, no one told fantastic stories about the things I did and didn't do, was a sort of paradise. Hurrying back to London I worked hard at my studies until March when Mother sent me a plane ticket to return for the performance of one of father's operas in Berlin, *Der Schmied von Marienburg* in which the heroine was Friedelind.

Momentarily I caused a sensation in the dowdy, cosmetics-pure hub of German culture with my gown, a rich embroidered black silk with a train. Over it was worn an evening jacket made of a piece of lacquered silk that Frida had given me in Paris, red, green, blue flowers and gold; the effect was chiefly gold, on a black ground. Red lacquered toenails showing through the sheerest of stockings, gold French sandals; with these and my blond hair burnished and curled by a good hairdresser everybody stared at me that night.

Mother gave me one horrified look and didn't speak to me the entire evening, keeping as far away as possible, behaving as though I were a public scandal. The friend who came to my rescue was Peter Passmann. Age sat lightly on Peter. He took me to his table as though he were entertaining a great lady. Margarete told me proudly how gorgeous I looked and after awhile our dentist in Bayreuth who was pursuing an operatic songbird came over and paid me a pretty compliment.

Peter was in high spirits. He told me all of the things that had happened to him since we had seen each other. Göring, the mighty hunter, had appointed hunt masters for each district and because of Peter's fame as a sportsman, had given him the district of Berlin.

"What do you have to do, Peter?" I asked curiously, "shoot the field marshal's game for him?"

"He hunts a lot in this district, of course, so I'm always invited," said Peter with a chuckle. "The field marshal takes good care of the deer. The game laws are really intelligent and humane."

"But you should see him in his uniform," added Margarete. "Göring designed it and it has so many gold and red stripes that it makes him look like a toy soldier in a comic opera."

It was a warm and friendly party. The artists who were by no means horrified by my lacquered toenails, joined us, and we exchanged news of what was happening inside and outside the fortress. Already Germany was beginning to feel like a prison from which the people inside asked eagerly for news of "the world." The only one I missed was Frida. She had not been well but even so it seemed unnatural not to see her at the opera.

The next morning Tietjen sent for me. Frida, who hadn't sung all winter because she was suffering from a breakdown was singing Isolde in Bremen the following night, her first appearance since Christmas. He had promised her half of the Brünnhildes as usual at the 1938 festival and also all of the Isoldes, but he was doubtful about her voice so he wanted me to go to Bremen and check on it. Considering what close friends we were, I thought it rather low of Tietjen to make such a proposal, but as I wanted to go anyway, it was good luck to have my expenses paid by the "festivals," in other words, Mother.

The next day on the street, the train, in the hotel. the

193

air was full of the *Anschluss* with Austria. Nobody talked of anything else, some exultantly, others with ill-concealed dread. That night I again wore the black gown and the lovely jacket but didn't send word to Frida. When the performance was over—her Isolde was perfect as usual— I went back and threw my arms around her.

"You elegant child," she exclaimed, noting her lacquered gift from Paris. We had supper with a group of artists, a jolly supper at which the talk was of the performance and such musical gossip. Nobody spoke of the *Anschluss*. Afterward, early in the morning, the three of us went back to the hotel and talked in Frida's room. She and Deman were grave and subdued, wondering what the news would mean to them. So far her Austrian citizenship had been a protection to Frida; now nobody knew what would happen. However we looked at it, the future was black. Finally she kissed me and sent me away to bed.

The musical world in London was full of news and rumors about what was happening in Austria. Janssen luckily had concluded his engagement with the Vienna opera and left with Erna the very day before the *Anschluss*. Kerstin Thorborg who had always refused to sing in Nazi Germany, broke her contract with the opera and left within twenty-four hours of Hitler's arrival. Later Felix von Weingartner told me the story of the Nazis' efforts to get rid of him. As he had just signed a new contract with the opera and was a Swiss citizen, they had to do it very legally and properly so that it wouldn't offend a neutral government. They studied their law books. On the ground of "unreliability" they could break his contract, but even they saw that it was going to be difficult to prove him unreliable, so they looked further. Another paragraph that permitted the cancellation of contracts when it was necessary as a measure of economy, seemed more plausible, so the Nazi government, suddenly poor, canceled Weingartner's contract and refused to pay him a cent.

Many of the artists who had left Austria came to London and made the spring season exceptionally brilliant. Toscanini returned and told me he was playing the "Siegfried Idyll" in Tribschen in August. He invited me to join the family there after the festival.

Finally Leider and Deman arrived but neither they nor the other German singers felt the holiday spirit that usually made the London engagement a festival. Things were getting worse and worse, Frida told me. This year she was restricted to nine pounds a day as expense money and was busy all day long counting, trying to stretch the amount for entertaining friends. With them all it was the same problem. In other years they had taken advantage of this engagement to buy a few clothes, eat well, recuperate from the dietary ailments caused by food shortages in Germany and enjoy a few of the luxuries that were non-existent at home except for Hitler and his ministers, but this season they could spend only a small percentage of their salaries, some of them as little as two and a half pounds a day. The rest was accountable directly to the Nazi government through which their contracts were made. Frida looked ill; her splendid vitality was dimmed. I begged her to stay out of Germany, to save herself while there was yet time, but she gave a tired little shrug and pointed out that everything she had built during her whole life was in Germany, her mother, what she had saved, her career. She was no longer young for a singer, not young enough to start over without a cent.

"You are lucky, my boy," she reminded Janssen with a tragic note in her lovely voice. "You are lucky because you are young."

To me she said, "Now come the difficult years." She put her arms around me and added, "Our friendship is beginning a new chapter."

CHAPTER XXI

PATRON OF THE ARTS

NORMALLY 1938 would have been the year between the festivals, but the taxes on the Festspielhaus were so high that the only way Mother could meet expenses was to give one every year. She expected me to return in June. I went unwillingly. I knew it would be my last visit because in March I would be twenty-one and of age. My passport might be revoked at any time so I began to explore ways of crossing the border illegally in case I had to get out of Germany without legal papers.

I was told of two easy routes: one through Switzerland and one through Czechoslovakia. The latter, Wolfi and I had discovered by accident during the course of one of our long walks in the Erzgebirge Mountains when we were on a holiday together and crossed into Czechoslovakia without knowing it until we came upon the strange road signs.

This time, in spite of apprehensions which kept me in a state of uneasy nausea, I was flying to Berlin in the usual way. Remembering my promise to get a record of the "Internationale" for Wieland I got one from Fred Gaisberg, director of the big English recording company, "His Master's Voice." Uncle Fred even gave me a couple of red labels reading, "Sir Thomas Beecham and the London Philharmonic Orchestra playing Schubert's *Unfinished Symphony*." With these plastered over the correct title it would be easy to get the record through the customs at the Berlin airport unless I happened to get an official who was a "beefsteak," outside brown, inside red, and he should take it into his head to hear for himself what the record played.

196

However, nothing happened, the record traveled safely in my hatbox and in the apartment I amused myself by playing it for the cook and the maid. When they learned what it was they were terrified lest our neighbors recognize it and report me to the Gestapo who would hurry me off to jail.

On the way to the Kurfürstendamm the next morning I found the word "Jude" painted in red letters on the windows of many shops, and on the pavement in front of these same shops a clumsily daubed Star of David, often with insulting unofficial additions. This new humiliation of the Jews made me feel so uncomfortable—almost embarrassed as if I had been staring at a cripple—that I turned away my head. Miserably I looked up at the airliner streaking across the sky, wishing it were carrying me back to London. Within twenty-four hours I had realized what a mistake this homecoming was to be.

That evening the housekeeper met me with a troubled face.

"Did you go into town?" she asked and "what did you think of it?"

"Of what?" I answered, pretending not to understand her meaning.

The color rose in her cheeks.

"It's a filthy business. I'm ashamed to go out and have to look on at such things." She flicked a bit of imaginary dust from the hall table and went back to the kitchen without another word. The chauffeur, too, whom I had always known as a simon-pure Nazi, cautiously sputtered his indignation. The change was almost unbelievable.

During the week in Berlin I heard that Mother was ill over the scandal about our financial manager. The Nazis had thrown Knittel into jail, and accused him of having embezzled part of our fortune. Tietjen, no doubt, would tell me all about it. This news should have shocked me, but I was bitterly aware that I was not surprised.

In order to avoid a trainful of Nazis whose remarks always goaded me into hot and unnecessary rejoinders I

197

told Mother that I would fly to Nuremberg and asked her
to send a car for me. When she learned my reason for not
taking the train she grew very angry and refused to send
one. So it was nearly eleven o'clock when the cab deposited
me at Wahnfried and to emphasize my disgrace everyone
had gone to bed instead of staying up to greet me.

The next day was the twenty-third of June, Mother's
birthday, a day we had always celebrated with presents
and special treats. When I came down to breakfast, Wolfi,
Wieland and little Betty were at the table—Nickel was
still at school. Although the sun was pouring into the room
and Betty called "Mausi, Mausi," quite happily, the
place was as gloomy as a mausoleum. The boys gave grunts
of welcome and continued to drink their tea in silence.

Mother came in from the hall. Her face, usually so live,
so vividly colored, was gray; her eyes were almost black
with an expression that looked like fear and her hair, her
lovely bright hair with the lights in it, was dull and laced
with a few threads of gray. Without giving me an opportunity to wish her a happy birthday, she began to upbraid
me in a voice so hoarse that it was a rusty whisper.
Wieland kept his eyes glued to his plate but he was not
eating, and Wolfi, although he consumed his breakfast
with the usual gusto, made no attempt to enliven the meal
with conversation.

After breakfast I found Tietjen in the garden before he
went to the Festspielhaus and asked him about Knittel.

"I doubt if your mother will discuss the matter; she is
still too shocked," he said. "The boys have not been told
the whole truth. As a matter of fact your mother can't face
your probable satisfaction." Emma told me how Mother
had had a second shock when Tietjen refused to stand by
and help her; he had said that he could do nothing about
the unsavory business.

During the next few days I unearthed further details
about Knittel. Although he had gone to a hospital when
he learned that an investigation was pending, he had been

dragged out of it and put in a prison near Karlsruhe. The most serious of the charges was *Verschiebung*, transferring money to foreign territory.

The state charged that all these years while he was serving as financial manager of the Festspielhaus, ostensibly giving his services to music, Knittel had been pocketing Wagner money; that two hundred and fifty thousand marks had gone into his publishing house; that about the same sum had been spent for living, including extravagant parties for his victims; another two hundred and fifty thousand marks had not yet been traced nor had the government been able to determine the amount that he was alleged to have taken over the border. Large sums that Knittel had deposited with friends were said to have been uncovered.

But this was not the final disaster. The authorities charged that Knittel had covered himself by making it appear that he had done everything with Mother's full knowledge and consent. As the grim days slid by and Mother told me not a word, the knowledge kept haunting me that I was the only one who could prove her innocent if the matter came to trial. Every month I had seen her send Knittel several hundred sheets of her business stationery, blank except for her signature at the bottom of the page. During the festivals she signed hundreds of papers with her initials "W. W." and never bothered to read them because she trusted him completely.

The German state, I learned, had impounded our entire fortune for the investigation. Hitler, however, had instructed the courts to release the amount of cash that Mother needed to run the festival.

When it became evident that no one, not even Wieland whom I tried to lift out of his depression by taking him about in the car, had the remotest intention of telling me a word, I called on Knittel's successor at the Festspielhaus, a rotund, pleasant, middle-aged businessman who received me ceremoniously. As the very sparrows in Bayreuth were whistling the Knittel story from the roofs, didn't it seem ridiculous to him, I asked, that I who was almost of age and had a quarter interest, should be kept in the dark?

He nodded in embarrassment, indicating that he saw my point. When I asked him to use his influence with Mother, try to persuade her to tell me all about the affair, he gave a hesitant promise that he would ask her about it.

That was the last word I had with Mr. Sawade. Whenever he saw me during the festival he made wide circles around me. A few months later, when I was telling the Janssens about the affair in Paris, they laughed.

"Don't you know what happened?" they asked. "Max Lorenz told us about it in Buenos Aires. Sawade really did talk to your mother and Tietjen and the poor innocent dear got such hell that he nearly had a heart attack."

In this atmosphere the festival started. Janssen wasn't there, of course, nor several of the other principals who were familiar to Bayreuth. Tietjen, had engaged Norma Gadsden, the Australian soprano, and for Kundry he produced Germaine Lubin, prima donna of the Paris Opera, whom he had engaged for "political" reasons. When Mother asked him about Lubin's voice, he replied, "She is not up to Bayreuth standards, but she is a very beautiful woman."

And indeed she was; tall, elegant, blond, looking like a Roman madonna. Before the rehearsals she had written asking Mother if there were any objection to her bringing her Negro chauffeur. As we had never seen a Negro in Bayreuth, in the whole of Germany for that matter, except in circuses and during the Olympic games, mother consulted the mayor who could see no reason why the Negro shouldn't come. So the handsome Clement arrived with Lubin and her Hispano Suiza. He was married to a white Swiss wife and had always associated with white people in Paris, so he saw nothing unusual in the furore he caused among the Hitler Maidens. They battled so strenuously for the privilege of dancing with Clement that he made a sensation even greater than that of his mistress.

During the rehearsals her colleagues ignored Lubin because she was French and spoke no German, but when Hitler arrived and began to pay her marked attention—they all courted her.

At the beginning of the first cycle all the principal streets of Bayreuth were plastered with swastika flags; the famous old houses were completely hidden and at the foot of the hill leading up to the Festspielhaus the Nazi party had erected two columns draped in red and surmounted by two golden Nazi eagles. I was so furious that I kept thinking what a glorious fire all this bunting would make.

At Wahnfried Mother played hostess with the gracious gestures that had become second nature, but her vivacity was forced and her voice was still husky. On one of the first evenings when she was recounting to Hitler the recent histories of her children, she told him about the record.

"Don't you think Mausi's an outrageous girl to bring home the 'Internationale'? She even plastered it with labels of the *Unfinished Symphony* to fool the customs."

Hitler looked startled, as though he didn't know whether to be angry or to laugh. As there was one of those little dead silences which plague a hostess, I leapt in.

"Yes, and you may need it some day. You never know. It's probably the only recording now in Germany."

Mother looked at the Führer's stormy face and gave me a frown—but then, she needn't have started the conversation.

That same evening Hitler told us about his recent visit to Mussolini and his first contact with the ceremonials of a royal court. When he wanted to retire on the first night of the visit, the Lord Chamberlain with an elaborate branched candlestick in one hand, led a slow-motion procession through miles of regal halls including the throne room. The next day Hitler told Mussolini that if this nonsense wasn't stopped he wouldn't stay another night. In the meanwhile he had discovered a little winding staircase that led from his suite directly to the court. The next night

201

he retired by these stairs, three steps at a time, with the Lord Chamberlain panting behind.

"It was the most ridiculous court you could imagine," concluded Hitler. "The only human being around was Maria (the youngest daughter of King Victor Emmanuel) and she was charming. How Mussolini endures it, I don't see. I told him again and again to get rid of all this royalty, but he says the time hasn't come yet. Even for a few days it was unbearable. I still don't see how I stood it."

At luncheon with his ministers the talk was chiefly of the new decrees against the Jews.

"My Führer," reported Göbbels, beaming with satisfaction, "my Berlin boys thoroughly enjoyed themselves. They stopped Jews in the street or rounded them up in cafés and said 'Show us your pocketbook.' When one of the boys found three hundred marks or so, he would order, 'Come with me. You have no proof of your right to this.' It all sounded wonderfully legal."

"What happened to the Jews?" I asked.

"What happened to the Jews! They were detained, of course, and were sent to concentration camps." Göbbels added with a boastful smile, "We caught about twelve hundred with that trick."

"And when will they be set free?" I questioned again.

Göbbels made a wide and royal gesture.

"Never in this world."

Everybody was busy with the dessert. I poked at the ice with my spoon, feeling a horrid faintness in my stomach. The shrill voice of Mrs. Göbbels cut through my discomfort.

"Look at the girl; she's quite pale. You mustn't pity them, my child. Never feel pity."

Hitler raised his eyes and gave me an amused glance, then returned to the dessert which he ate greedily, listening to Göbbels with evident satisfaction.

At a word from the Führer his S. S. attendant charged the table with another bottle of beer. Hitler had recently

202

taken to beer drinking in a manner of speaking although his special dark beer which was brewed for him at Holzkirchen contained only one per cent of alcohol. Hitler looked at the bottle suspiciously and called Kannenberg. "Are you sure this is my beer? Are you positive it is in the original bottle? I won't be poisoned by any of your stronger stuff."

Kannenberg swore, but Hitler would not be satisfied until the attendant produced several other bottles to show him that they were exactly alike. Finally Hitler took a cautious sip and agreed that this was indeed his special brew. At every dinner and every luncheon while he was at Wahnfried the Führer enacted this little scene with Kannenberg.

In spite of his feeling of camaraderie with the artists (he always insisted that he was at his best with them), the effect of Hitler's visitation was more depressing with each successive year. The audiences at the Festspielhaus didn't, however, suffer as they did in Nuremberg, Munich and Berlin. We children had been amused when mother told us about an incident at the opening of one of the Nuremberg rallies. The conductor and orchestra of first rank and some of Germany's best artists performed to a completely apathetic audience of snoring Nazi officials, until Hitler sent his aides through the aisles with the order to applaud. The noisy military ovation that followed was even more disturbing than the former silence.

This year, 1938, Bayreuth was invaded by the "Strength through Joy" organization that bought up the entire house for two performances. Aside from some slight overindulgence in Bavarian beer, they behaved quite well. Hitler himself respected Bayreuth. Although he did not try to quiet the noisy crowds screaming "Heils" outside of the Festspielhaus, he did order the distribution of little cards to the audience forbidding demonstrations in the theater, and he never entered his box until the lights had gone down. The spontaneous friendliness of the festivals, how-

203

ever, was destroyed beyond recapture by the heavy official atmosphere.

Everyone of the cast and the staff endured, and waited for the second cycle, everyone except the ardent Nazis who seemed to live only for a glance from the Führer. He gave the singers a final opportunity for adoration on the last night of his visit by inviting them to supper in the restaurant. After the performance of *Götterdämmerung*, Hitler took his place halfway down one side of a long table that seated perhaps thirty guests. His aides filled the surrounding tables; S. S. men crowded about. The zealous Nazis among the artists scrambled for seats close to the Führer and hung upon his words. Others at the far ends consoled themselves with champagne whereas the pure souls about the Führer went thirsty. It was growing later and later; the guests were stifling their yawns. Mrs. Göbbels was pulling secretly upon a cigarette that she kept under the table. To stay awake the guests around me began to give an animal concert. Mother gobbled like a turkey, Germaine Lubin gave a masterly performance as a cooing pigeon and I did my best as a duck. Finally this palled and still Hitler talked. Being out of favor anyway, I volunteered somehow to dam the flow of his words. Several times I started to rise but was restrained by my friend. The commotion attracted Hitler's attention.

"What's the matter, Mausi?" he asked, pausing in the middle of his dissertation on German Art.

Putting my hand to my mouth I yawned with all my might. The Führer glanced down the long table, noticed the twilight that had descended on his guests and asked his adjutant what time it was. After two o'clock! Heels clicked and "Heils" filled the air as the Führer disappeared.

But for the Wagners the day was not yet over, we still had to say good night to the Führer at Wahnfried. The drive home in the night air revived us so we were wide awake when we went into the garden room where Hitler was talking to one of his aides. He sent the officer away and we sat in what resembled a peaceful family circle, discussing the performance. We spoke of this singer and that one.

"Isn't Fuchs good?" commented Wolfi.

"Hmm, so so," Hitler dissented, imitating the lady's Swabian dialect. "A pity she's a theosophist; she shouldn't dabble in such nonsense. But the Swabians are a peculiar people."

When we finally said good night it was nearly six o'clock. Before going to our rooms Nickel and I sat by the empty grate in the drawing room and each ate an apple. The sun was beginning to chase the mist and light up a new day untouched as yet by humans.

"Let's not go to bed," I suggested to Nickel. "It would be a lovely time to take a drive."

Hitler was gone and peace of a sort returned to Bayreuth, but at Wahnfried we were not to forget his visit so easily. Unity Mitford remained in the city. This year she had bleached her hair to a more Nordic gold, but she was no longer Hitler's shadow. She did not walk through the cordons of S. S. guards but saw the Führer only when she received an official invitation and was conducted to his table during the intermissions by an aide-de-camp.

Nobody thought much about her in Bayreuth until she fell ill. Our doctor who attended her for a slight bronchitis, discovered her pouring her medicine out of the window, standing there in a thin nightgown courting pneumonia. When she grew worse, he removed her to the clinic. Her father, Lord Redesdale, had attended the performance but had left.

One night, or rather morning at four o'clock, we were awakened at Wahnfried by a violent ringing of the bell. The urgent caller was Hitler's physician looking for Unity whose address apparently the Führer did not know. We sent the doctor to the clinic and he attended Unity constantly until she was well. Hitler paid the bill and also sent autographed pictures of himself for her to give to the nurses.

When Unity was able to leave the clinic, Lord Redesdale took her to Obersalzburg where he gave Hitler the amount of his daughter's bills. One heard very little more about Mitford until the now famous shooting attempt after which she was returned to England.

CHAPTER XXII

GOOD-BY TO WAHNFRIED

THE festival dragged along, on the surface brilliant, successful; underneath, a bitter guerrilla war, full of alarms, ambuscades, angry shouting behind closed doors. The fear of a trial had been lifted from Mother—Hitler had decreed that one would involve too many people— but she had not recovered from the shock of the Knittel affair. She still wore a frightened look and spoke in that strange, hoarse voice. My brothers who still didn't know the extent of the disaster but enough of it to understand what Mother was suffering, banded against me instinctively. Only Nickel was my friend.

Leider, with whom I spent most of the time, tried hard to make things easier for me at home. She thought it a pity that we four children weren't closer together so she invited Wieland and Wolfi to dinner with Nickel and me.

"It will never do," I warned her. "When we are alone Wieland and I understand each other, but in the family group he always joins Wolfi and the opposition. The boys will be horrid and disagreeable."

I was right; the evening was a dismal failure. The boys spent the time making unpleasant remarks about me, echoing the opinions of Mother and Tietjen. Every day I was becoming more obviously the black sheep, the nonconformer. But in spite of it all the bond between Nickel and me was strengthening. As it became clear that I must make a break with Germany and home, I wanted her to feel safe with my friends who would protect her if the need should ever come.

To increase the gloom at home, Lieselotte returned from Dr. Veil's clinic in Jena. After our dentist had been unable to reconstruct her jaw, Mother had sent her to a plastic surgeon in Munich who had built a new face, but it was no longer the delicate, pretty one that had attracted Frank "Zwei." He never divorced his wife as he promised, but kept on patriotically fathering a child a year by her while he put off Lieselotte with hopes.

For five weeks Dr. Veil treated Lieselotte, giving her a sleep cure for a nervous heart condition, keeping her under the influence of luminal day and night. When she returned, the once intelligent woman seemed to have the mentality of an underdeveloped child. She could no longer follow a conversation but giggled and chatted continuously in a foolish way. After a few days she developed a skin disease that looked at first like nettle rash but soon became more serious.

Mother put Lieselotte in the clinic of our Bayreuth physician and brightened a little when the girl was out of the house; nevertheless, Wahnfried was no pleasanter for me. At Frida's there was more peace but her troubles also had reached a climax. Tietjen had given her every possible assurance that she would not be affected by the laws against the Jews, but as the last of June approached, the day on which all Jews were ordered to declare—and probably lose—their property, he did nothing. This was in addition to his defaulting in March on his promise that she should sing all the Isoldes.

In this atmosphere of recrimination and distrust Frida had come to Bayreuth. After her first performance she collapsed and Deman reported to my mother first, then to Tietjen that she would have to cancel her "Ring" performances. Tietjen screamed at him that Frida wasn't ill. Deman in turn cursed Tietjen. We could hear them screaming threats at each other behind the door of Tietjen's office.

While Mother tried to make peace, Frida went to Berlin to her doctor. Every day after luncheon I hurried to the restaurant at the Festspielhaus to telephone where nobody would overhear me. She returned to sing two Isoldes at the end of the season, but no one was happy.

Tietjen's complacent plaint, "I can't imagine why Frida behaves so strangely toward me," infuriated me beyond endurance. We had clashed earlier in the season over his production of *Tristan* which was overdone, extravagant in both acting and costumes, and which violated the score in dozens of ways. He admitted that he had blundered with the first act and didn't know how to save it. When he accepted my suggestion and suavely presented it as his own, I was so indignant that I stayed away from the stage during the performances. Everything about the Festspielhaus was so polluted by Nazism, by false emphasis and false values, that I had an almost uncontrollable impulse to burn the place. But there was always the hope that this blight would not endure forever, and that if I couldn't save Bayreuth by staying in Germany I might somehow do it from without. Strangely enough, Mother's friendship for Hitler which was so embarrassing for Bayreuth had saved the Festspielhaus from being nationalized and might, I thought, have saved it for the future.

But Tietjen—he was a symbol of all the evils that plagued the theater. When he persecuted Frida so flagrantly, I threw myself into her defense and recounted to him hotly all the ways in which he had betrayed her. From that moment he avoided me and I refused to extend the olive branch.

208

"Have you said good morning to Heinz?" mother would ask in a harassed tone at breakfast.

"Why should I?" she was answered. The hostility was so apparent that I was at home only to dress and sleep, coming in late after everyone had gone to bed.

The third cycle was drawing to a close and my immediate objective was Lucerne where Toscanini was scheduled to give a concert in the garden at Tribschen, the "Siegfried Idyll" and a program in commemoration of my grandfather's wedding anniversary. His telegram inviting me to come I snatched from the delivery boy to keep the family from knowing that I had promised to meet him at Tribschen.

The only way of getting there that seemed even remotely possible was offered by the mother of one of the musical assistants, an attractive young Austrian whom Mother regarded hopefully, believing she detected a spark of romance between us. If Mausi were only safely married she could wash her hands of this unruly daughter. The musician and I lent ourselves to her plans in that we spent much of our free time together. His mother, a dashing Viennese baroness, appeared for the last cycle with a big English car, a chauffeur, a secretary and a general air of importance. Hearing my lament about Tribschen, she suggested that I drive to Venice with her and her son for a fortnight's holiday after the festival and quietly stop for a couple of days in Lucerne. When this strange and rather overpowering woman approached her in the office and proposed the trip, Mother was dubious but so pleased with the idea of my wanting to spend a holiday with the son that she consented.

We planned to meet in Zürich after my friend's visit to Berlin for a performance of *Lohengrin* in honor of Horthy—a strange choice we thought, since in the opening scene the king protests at the top of his voice "Lord protect us from the Hungarian Fury." As it was impossible to take out money, we had made an exchange by which

209

the baroness was to finance the trip outside of Germany. She had not arrived when my plane got in. Although I had but a few marks in my pocket I went boldly to the hotel at which we were to stay, took a room, ordered luncheon which I charged, and prayed she would have no motor accident to prevent her from appearing in time for dinner.

She arrived; next day we drove to Lucerne and I spent two completely happy days with the aunts and the Toscaninis, licking my wounds in the contented surety of their affection. Then on to Venice for a sight-seeing holiday after which I parted from the baroness and flew to Berlin. I was astonished to learn much later that she was arrested for high treason a few days after I left Germany. She and all of her family were jailed by the Gestapo.

After visiting Frida for several days while the Foreign Office visaed my passport, this time for France, I went to Bayreuth. Mother and the family were at Lake Constance so this was the opportunity to get away from Wahnfried with no angry scenes. It is almost impossible to decide what to take, what to leave behind when one is going away forever and doesn't want his departure to look like the flight from Egypt. My scores, the books that I needed— these were packed first. Most of my summer dresses were left hanging in the wardrobes to look as though they were awaiting my return.

These were days of enchantment in a muted key, tinged with melancholy: dinner with the aunts who had returned before me, walks in the garden, afternoons in the library drifting from book to book that I had discovered in my childhood. Sometimes I forgot what I was reading when the late sun gilded the portraits of Cosima and our great-grandmother in her green silk snood, and fell to dreaming about the shadowy and almost forgotten little girl, Friedelind, who had lived here years ago. Or I walked along the chestnut drive with Toby at my heels and said good-by to the bust of King Ludwig with the girlish haircut and

210

Wotan, the ravens, Freia and Fricka, on the frieze above the entrance door.

For five precious days the house was mine. Friends came in the afternoon and we had tea before the fire in the salon. We listened to the radio through which Hitler was screaming about the wrongs the Czechs were inflicting on the poor innocent Germans, the shadow of war once more loomed over our existence. I was in a hurry to get out of Germany in order to be able to fight against Nazism openly.

During these few crowded days I had not neglected to inquire about Lieselotte. The doctor told me that after several weeks of frantic urging on his part he had finally succeeded in getting Dr. Veil to come and see her. The girl had swollen to twice her size and turned copper-colored as a result of sepsis of the liver and, he suspected, all the glands. She had been transferred to Jena in a hopeless condition. Next morning Emma wakened me with the news that Lieselotte was dead.

It was plainly my task to do what must be done. With the nurse who had taken care of Lieselotte in Bayreuth I drove to Jena. To keep up my spirits I wore a bright green leather jacket that would be stowed in the car before we met the parents, and speeded much too fast down the new highway. The Schmidts tried hard to be brave. I took them to luncheon and gave them wine which helped a little, then drove to the hospital where the nurse packed Lieselotte's things. Outside in the long hall I encountered Dr. Veil.

"I am desolate. Miss Schmidt's death is very sad. We hoped the operation on her glands and the transfusion might save her," he said, trying to outstare me with his green eyes.

"Perhaps you can tell me the cause of her death, Professor," I asked, avoiding his proffered hand.

"Yes, an infection that started in the fractured bones. We had a great deal of it after the last war."

211

"You may call it that," I said. He flushed purple and turned away to Mrs. Schmidt who was coming down the hall. He took her into a room to talk to her.

A few minutes later Mrs. Schmidt returned with the professor who bade me an icy good day.

"He's such a kind man," murmured the old lady, fumbling in her bag for a handkerchief. "When he talked about the child there were tears in his eyes."

Later in the afternoon I drove the Schmidts to the funeral parlor through a gloomy autumn drizzle. After we said good-by to them at the hotel, I pulled out the green coat and a bright red scarf and felt better even though I couldn't see them in the dark. It was ten o'clock when we arrived in Bayreuth.

That night I phoned Mother at Lake Constance, telling her that the funeral was to be on Saturday. She didn't want to go, she had a horror of funerals, but it was an obligation from which there was no escape. Without mentioning it to me she planned to spend the night at Wahnfried and arrived with Betty in time for tea. My trunk had already left but two suitcases were packed and waiting in the front hall. For fear she would try to stop me I slipped into the entrance, extracted my passport and tickets from my purse and stuck them in the front of my blouse.

Tea, however, passed calmly enough with little Betty sitting beside Mother, pretending to help her pour, and Emma serving while she told Mother about what had happened in Wahnfried during her absence. The storm did not break until after dinner when we went into Mother's study to do accounts. She scolded me furiously for going to see Toscanini, for being extravagant, for wanting to go to France.

"I cannot let you go," she stormed. "You have no feeling for decency left in you and spend your time associating with international Jews and traitors. I cannot let you leave Germany. Every day and every night I would worry about the disgrace you bring to your name. No, I will never let

212

you out of my sight again. I cannot be responsible for what you do."

"But you needn't be," I answered, keeping my temper, "and I'm very sorry but I must go to Berlin tonight."

"Why Berlin?" she demanded hotly, changing her point of attack. "You can go to Paris directly from here." This was the moment of weakening and I seized it, explaining that I had an appointment with my dressmaker and would stay in Berlin for a week. A week! I could see her thinking this would give her time to consider.

"Very well," Mother said icily, pushing back her chair and straightening the desk, "Good night. I will order the car but won't stay down to see you go." That was the memory of her I carried away, beautiful and flushed and unforgiving. At midnight I slipped out of Wahnfried as though I were a thief, not a daughter, and as I rode for the last time between the ghostly chestnuts, wondered what was this fierce emotion that we aroused in each other. Under the storm and fury there was respect, I knew, and admiration.

For the next winter and summer and winter again, life was like a collection of picture postcards, except that some of the views were grim: a parting with Frida in her cottage, both of us silent, weeping a little with the unexpressed feeling that we might never see each other again; Paris in September, the leaves turning in the Bois de Boulogne and the booksellers along the Seine dozing in front of their stalls; Germaine Lubin's country home, luxurious and beautiful; a drive back to Paris against a stream of people fleeing the city at Hitler's threat to invade Czechoslovakia, automobiles packed with mattresses and trunks and baby carriages; mobilization notices at every corner, women kissing their soldiers in railway stations, troops everywhere, and over it all the terrible expectancy of war.

Friends warned me to get out of Paris while there was time so I hurried to Zürich where Frida was staying. It was

213

thrilling to meet after having tacitly said good-by forever, and Frida and Deman were relieved to see me. Switzerland was bursting with foreigners, people sleeping in hotel lobbies, sitting on their suitcases, concerned only to get away from countries in the line of Hitler's wrath.

"You must go home, Mausi," Frida urged. "This is different; this is serious. You will need your family. No matter how you disagree, you need their backing. In Germany you are a Wagner; you have a background that will protect you. Outside, you will have nothing to stand between you and the hard knocks. You will be kicked around and you never have been, Mausi. You don't know a thing about life. You'll be sorry if you don't go home."

Perhaps she was right; she wanted to protect me, but I couldn't go back. In exasperation at my stubbornness, she bade me good-by again.

In Zürich I had written to Mother about the flight from Paris and the things I had seen along the way. One morning early she telephoned, blazing at me over the wire.

"We laughed ourselves sick over your letter. You are a hysterical spinster and a terrible coward. Don't you think I know that not one soldier has been mobilized in Germany." Then leaping to a *non sequitur* in the way I remembered so well, she demanded, "Why didn't you come to Cologne? You would have been safe there, and Cologne is several hours nearer Paris than Zürich."

At that very time the Munich conference was decreeing that there would be no war so I returned to Paris and sublet an apartment from Norma Gadsden, a studio at the edge of Montmartre high up under the eaves and looking over the roofs to Sacré Coeur on the hill. Studies at the Sorbonne, nights at the opera, visits to the Louvre, concerts, long days at the piano, studying scores, or occasional holidays wandering about the streets; but in spite of all I felt terribly homesick for London. At Christmas Mother expected me in Wahnfried as usual but I had no intention of going.

214

During the holidays Furtwängler was in Paris to conduct *Siegfried*.

"Tell me," he asked over and over, "how did you get out? How did you manage to make such a decision? What can I do? How can I get out of Germany?"

Every time I answered, "You are outside of Germany now. Throw away your return ticket." But I knew he would never do it.

The gossip about Tietjen and Berlin and Wahnfried that he repeated to me made me boil with indignation. How could Tietjen say and how could Mother countenance his stories that I was involved in the high treason of the baroness who had taken me to Venice? In a furious letter I asked her why such reports originated in Wahnfried. She answered with heat that she couldn't be responsible for what was said about such an undisciplined daughter. This letter I didn't answer and I never wrote again. There seemed to be nothing to say except recriminations, and I didn't want to be rude to Mother.

In March, on my twenty-first birthday, Mother and Wieland suddenly paid me a visit. Hastily I put away Toscanini's photograph and the books that were considered treasonable literature in Germany. It was an uneventful three days, each of us walking warily, determined that there shouldn't be a sharp word between us. We explored Paris, went to the opera, the theater. Wieland wanted above all to see a news reel at which the audience hissed Hitler, hoping to produce an account of it for his friends as a sort of "believe it or not" phenomenon, but the only news reel showing the Führer that we could track down was playing in an almost empty house, and the few loungers in the audience were too apathetic to hiss.

Mother told me about little Betty who was growing into an amazingly pretty child, and about Nickel's stay in Rome.

We went shopping, Mother bought presents, everything

215

was amicable, but when she left I was relieved. We had both been so cautious, so politely distrustful. Did she ever once, I wondered, want to throw her arms around me and take her turbulent child to her heart?

London in the spring; Toscanini and the Janssens; reunion with all my friends; the Nazis from the Staatsoper refusing to share dressing rooms with "traitors"; bitterness and turmoil and lots of music, but this season no Frida. In July I went to Tribschen and joined the aunts, and attended the Lucerne festival with Toscanini. It was wonderful to be with one's own again.

In August Nickel suddenly appeared for a couple of days. She had told Mother "I want to go to Tribschen to see Mausi."

"No, I won't have it," forbade Mother, "I won't have you spoiled by Mausi." Then she weakened and added, "I suppose you want to drive to Lake Constance and take the train there, but you must take someone with you. I won't have you driving so far alone."

In those two days Nickel was so charming to the aunts that they forgot their dislike.

"Yes, she really is beautiful," admitted Daniela who had never before acknowledged that Nickel was lovely. Eva was beginning to see that she looked like the young Liszt.

On the first of September Hitler marched into Poland. This was war and there would be no Munich. The aunts began to pack unhappily. Their friends urged them to stay in Switzerland, but Eva had a maid and a cook to look after and numberless obligations. One afternoon the mayor called to ask what he could do to help with their arrangements.

"As for Miss Friedelind," he said, "she will make her home in Tribschen and be the guest of our city as long as it may be necessary."

That afternoon the Maestro and Carla Toscanini called on us.

216

"Don't worry about Mausi," Toscanini said, kissing Daniela and Eva on the cheek. "As long as Mausi is alone and has nobody in this world, Carla and I will be mother and father to her."

CHAPTER XXIII

·

"SHE IS YOUR MOTHER"

MOTHER, I had been warned by Nickel, planned to make me a surprise visit after the festival. The prospect filled me with such dread that I told the aunts it might be better for me to go away from Lucerne and hide where no one could find me. So much had happened to push us even farther apart since our meeting in Paris that I couldn't trust myself or her. Daniela put her arm around me.

"I can't advise you about your mother, my dear. Go and talk to the Maestro."

So I did. I told Toscanini how I felt about seeing Mother and how completely useless such a meeting would be. He listened to me thoughtfully without once interrupting. Then he shrugged and said, half in Italian, half in French, "Ma . . . elle est ta mère."

Toscanini was right I knew in my heart. He made sense. Above all else she was my mother and I would somehow endure the meeting. Then came that September day when war broke out and the aunts departed. To my great relief Mother was unable to leave Germany.

In Lucerne I waited for my visa to return to England. Indeed I had already put myself at the disposal of the English government which considered me of "unique propaganda value." But the French transit visa was everlastingly slow in coming and I could not move without it.

217

One Friday afternoon in early February, 1940, I answered a phone call from Zürich. Mother was in Switzerland.

"I couldn't send you a wire because it is forbidden. Will you take the next train and stay until Sunday with me at the Baur au Lac?"

My throat contracted. I urged her to come to Lucerne, fearing that there might be something more behind her plan to stay in Zürich than the wish to avoid seeing people and making the official visits which would be expected of her. But as she insisted, I took the afternoon train.

Remember, she is your mother. With that thought held fast I stepped out at the Zürich station, exchanged dutiful, reserved kisses with Mother and drove with her to the hotel. Covertly I looked at her beside me in the taxi. She was heavier, no doubt because of the potato diet, her face looking more English than ever, vivid, distinguished, indestructibly beautiful. We might have been strangers, polite strangers, for no warmth flowered between us.

After we unpacked I suggested a walk and dinner at the Veltliner Keller where the food was especially good. To be moving, doing something, was easier than to sit and face one another for the showdown that I guessed was behind her visit. She seemed to think so too; as we walked along we kept up an aimless and determinedly friendly chatter. I asked if she must return on Sunday. She explained that she had permission to stay until Monday but couldn't get a sleeper so it was easier to go back Sunday night.

"Whose permission?" I asked curiously.

"Himmler's" she answered, and launched upon an amusing description of her surprise when he corrected her naïve assumption that she could walk out of the Gestapo office without a couple of aides to get her past the guards.

"I had to take my passport to him personally," she explained. "We had a long talk. 'It is high time you put sense into that child of yours,' he said. 'She's playing with fire

218

and doesn't know how dangerous it is. Of course I have read her letters and had my doubts about sending them along to you and the aunts. She should come home. If she doesn't, we'll have to do something about it." Mother chattered along; from her tone she might have been telling me about a bon mot that somebody had made at the festival.

"And what would he do?" I tried to keep my voice casual too, as though "that child" meant anyone else but me.

"You know," continued Mother. "The Führer is really angry with you. We have sent so many messengers to you, so many people. Every time he believed you would come back, that this time you wouldn't argue but would do as you were ordered. But you never came. Finally he said, 'Isn't there one reliable person in the whole of Germany who will go to Switzerland and talk to that girl and *not* return to tell me that she is right?'"

"'Why don't you send Furtwängler?'" I asked. You know what he thinks about Furtwängler's reliability. That made the Führer laugh and when he felt more cheerful he suggested, 'Why not go yourself?' That's how I happened to get permission."

So now I knew. Thinking back I remembered that any number of Mother's friends had visited me in Lucerne and some of them had pleaded with me to come home, but not one of them had said he had been sent by Hitler. Mother, I guessed, was carefully laying the groundwork for a definite order from the Führer. Hoping to postpone whatever it was and spend one amicable evening with her, I veered the talk from Hitler to news of Wahnfried.

We lingered over the dinner which Mother was enjoying to the last drop of coffee.

"The other day the Führer made me a present of two pounds of coffee. Ibn Saud sent him forty sacks and he gave two pounds to each of his friends. It was wonderful!"

What about my brothers, I asked. Wieland, she told me, had been exempted from the Army to preserve the Wagner

219

line, one of five whom Hitler had so honored, but Wolfi
had been called up in August and had been seriously
wounded in Poland. He was only twenty but one of the
oldest in his company. He and four of his comrades were
captured on patrol. They were all injured by grenades and
received very little attention as the Poles were already in
full retreat. The Polish doctor did his best but the medical
equipment had given out completely. For three days they
were constantly under fire of the Germans. Finally the
commander of the company told Wolfi that his troops
could no longer take along the wounded, the Germans
and twenty-five of their own men, and asked Wolfi if he
would attempt to return to the German lines with the
wounded Poles as his prisoners.

Wolfi agreed. With the wounded loaded on six wagons
and the whitest shirt among them for a flag, they wandered
for four hours before they reached the German lines. The
commanding officer at first shouted at Wolfi that he was
crazy to do such a thing, but after he understood what had
happened he ordered my brother and two wounded comrades to the Liegnitz field hospital by plane.

Now Wolfi was in the big Charité hospital in Berlin.
Dr. Sauerbruch, the famous surgeon, managed to save his
arm and hand. He had acute blood poisoning, and when
they finally dared to operate, they could not give him an
anesthetic on account of his weakened heart. But he would
get well although his wrist and finger joints would always
be stiff. Wieland went with him on the hospital train and
stayed until Mother arrived in Berlin.

Mother's voice began to fade and her eyes were almost
black. She took another drink of coffee and smiled across
at me.

"The boy in Wolfi's room is only nineteen. He had
a bullet in his heart muscle but Sauerbruch took it out,
and he will live even though he has to stay in bed a year.
And the Führer—you know how he dislikes hospitals—he
has come to see Wolfi five times and once he brought pink

roses. Wolfi persuaded him to go through the wards and
visit the wounded soldiers."

The Führer again! People were glancing at Mother.
Hitler's name wasn't too popular in the Swiss restaurants,
and I wished she would talk of something else.

"What about Nickel?" I asked. The child was taking a
nursing course in Berlin. Betty was starting to school in
April, and Toby, my English shepherd—he had been
called up for military service but after he had knocked
down the examiner twice, the soldier said to Mother, "You
may take your dog home, Frau Wagner."

Tietjen had been assigned new, very confidential work
in addition to his other duties. He was questioning British
spies.

"Don't get into their hands," warned Mother. "You
might easily be used as a spy without knowing it."

The German high command didn't hold its meetings in
Tribschen, I answered, laughing. But Mother was getting
serious. We had finished dinner and were walking along
the Zürich streets that dazzled Mother with their lights.
I told her how I had been caught in a practice blackout on
the way to a concert and had walked for miles.

"How silly of the Swiss," Mother remarked. "Whoever
would want to invade them! I was amazed to see soldiers
all about when I crossed the border."

Yes, I told her, the Swiss were fully mobilized. They
were taking no chances.

"It's ridiculous. You are all war mongers. You don't
really believe Germany could do such a thing?"

I tried to distract her with a shop window, but she was
launched on the subject in her mind.

"The whole of Berlin is buzzing about you, saying you
are employed by the British Secret Service and the international Jews. You are being foolish, Mausi, and thoroughly selfish. You don't stop to think about the unhappiness you're causing your family. Your brothers burn
with shame when people talk about their sister and they

221

have no means of defending her. If you will only come to Berlin for a couple of days and be seen with your family; if you will lunch with me at the Bristol, let people see us together, all this talk will stop. You will have shown where you stand. Then you may come back to Switzerland. I won't mind. Just show yourself."

"So I could come back as easily as that?" I said to myself. How naïve they must have thought me.

Aloud I answered, "You know very well where I stand."

"You really have your mind completely poisoned by enemy propaganda," Mother cried bitterly, then checked herself and tried to smile. We walked along in silence, each thinking dejectedly that we must find some way to bridge this gap.

At the hotel Mother was tired and went immediately to her room. So was I, wearied with the tugging of my emotions. But I dared not go to sleep. Mother was feeling her way and hadn't yet told me everything that had brought her. There were so many stories of people being kidnaped by the Gestapo that my friends were always warning me to be careful where I went and what I ate. I actually searched my room, looked under the bed and in the closet.

Saturday we spent the morning shopping. It was strange to hear Mother, whom I had watched so often running her shapely hands through the finest American silk stockings, demanding now the thickest wool. The government had forgotten to ration woolen bathing suits, she told me, and they had become the most fashionable winter underwear. We bought cheese and chocolate and window-shopped for things that Mother wanted but couldn't make up her mind to buy until too late. The stores closed early on Saturday.

One could still eat well in Berlin, she said, if one spent the money, and told me about a new restaurant on the Kurfürstendamm where Hjalmar Schacht and his bride, the sculptress, Barbara von Kalkreuth, enjoyed the caviar and lobsters. The Russians, she commented, were neglecting to send Hitler the supplies he needed badly but were keeping Göring and the other gourmets happy with caviar.

In the late afternoon we returned to the hotel, both of us tense, knowing that we could not put off the explosion much longer. We were in my room; I was sitting in the big armchair near the window and Mother was opposite me on the bed. The pale green shimmer of her dressing gown, a lovely prewar oriental silk, brought out the gold tints in her skin.

We were still talking about the Russian pact; she was boasting about Hitler's shrewdness, repeating his version of the deal with Stalin. Unintentionally I set off the explosion by remarking, "You don't really believe he is telling you the truth? He lies to you just as much as to everybody else."

Mother sat up straight, the friendly, animated expression on her face was wiped out by one of horror, then of cold hate. She wouldn't have been so outraged if I had doubted the integrity of God.

"Until this moment," she flung at me in a choked voice, "I didn't want to believe what the others said. They reported from Paris that you were talking your head off against Germany and I wouldn't believe them. But now I see for myself. What a fool I have been. Believe me, I am your mother, I cannot longer permit you to walk about freely. You belong behind lock and key."

She bent forward and fixed me with her eyes.

"For one last time I ask you to come home. Your brothers command you to return and spare them further disgrace."

"How Teutonic," I commented. "And when did I ever obey my brothers?"

Mother's voice hardened.

"I was sent to give you a choice. You need not decide immediately. You may have time to think, but you must make your choice. You may return to Germany immediately where you will be kept in some safe place behind lock and key for the duration, or you may stay in neutral

223

territory and behave yourself. But you must stop your talking. If you do not agree then you will be kidnaped and taken to a safe place."

I started to speak, but Mother had more to say.

"And if these measures fail the order will be given; you will be destroyed and exterminated at the first opportunity. If you should actually dare to go into enemy territory, you know what that will mean. You will be deprived of your German citizenship, your property will be confiscated and you will be forbidden to see your family or have any contact with us for the rest of your life."

I could feel the blood leave my face as I listened—not to the threats but to the language Mother used. "Destroyed" and "exterminated," they were Hitler's terms, of course, or Himmler's. She seemed utterly unimpressed by them, unmoved that she was using them against her own child, her own flesh and blood. *Austilgen und Ausrotten!* No, I had not forgotten my German. They had no other meaning except "destroy and exterminate."

"Think it over," Mother said in a more normal voice, "and let me know. Write me when you have made up your mind."

"But I *have* made up my mind. For a long time I have had a visa for England. I am only waiting for a French transit visa and then I am going to England and from there to America. It is being arranged."

Perhaps it was dangerous, but I took the note from the English Foreign Office out of my bag and showed it to her. Mother's face froze.

"What do you do for the English government that you can travel through enemy country into enemy country? We are at war. What do you do for Germany's enemies?" Her voice was stricken, almost a wail. "How can you, a German, travel into enemy country?"

I tried to tell her that this was not so much a war of nations as it was a war of ideologies. It was useless. Mother's

224

voice rose in high crescendo, "But the Führer—the Führer, what am I to tell him?"

There was no possible answer. Further talk was out of the question. I got up quietly and went out, closing the door softly behind me. At the desk I found an official letter, forwarded from Lucerne. It was my French transit visa. My breath left me.

When Mother came down to dinner I was sitting there remembering Toscanini's words. In spite of everything I wanted so badly to tell her what she could do if ever the moment came when she wanted to flee Germany. But when she stepped into the lobby she was composed and gracious; encased in an armor of surface friendliness that I could not pierce, and which held throughout the evening.

That night the brutal words, *Austilgen und Ausrotten* ("destroy and exterminate"), rang in my ears. With my precious visas clutched in my hand I spent another sleepless and alert night.

Finally we stood together on the station platform. In those few last minutes we would have done anything to wipe out the past, anything except the one thing we could never do, yield to each other. The train pulled in.

"Think things over. Take your time and let me know," Mother repeated as though she would not give up hope. She kissed me good by, took a step toward the coach and turned back. Her voice broke.

"Do come home, Mausi. Please come. I need you."

But it was too late—the answers had all been given. This was farewell. Farewell to all that I had loved in Germany. As the train pulled out my eyes blurred. Toscanini's words rang again in my ears, "After all she is your mother." I turned away from the station aware of a most horrible feeling of loneliness.

Then as I walked the familiar Zürich streets I had an odd feeling of not being quite alone and I remembered that my grandfather too, had come as an exile to Zürich.

It was strangely reassuring.

INDEX

227

Frank, "Zwei" ("butcher of Poland"), 79-80
Frick, 188
Fuchs, 205
Furtwängler, Wilhelm, absent from Hindenburg's funeral, 111
at Bayreuth, 61-64, 67, 71, 152-153
discredited by Nazis and as a Nazi, 182-183
makes comeback with Nazis, 152-153
maneuvered out of Staatsoper, 118-119, 153
Paris visit with Friedelind, 215
protects Jewish musicians, 96, 118
"retires," 125-126, 135

Gadsden, Norma, 200, 214
Gaisberg, Fred, 196
Geissmar, Dr., at Bayreuth festival, 62-63
dismissed by Nazis, 118
in London, 180, 183-184
protected by Furtwängler, 96
secretary to Furtwängler, 62
secretary to Sir Thomas Beecham, 152
Gestapo, 117-118, 126, 146
Gieseking, Walter, 117
Göbbels, Frau, 142, 204
Göbbels, Joseph, 86, 96, 99, 101, 121, 143-144
bans use of Jewish librettists' names, 103
controls Reichs Music Chamber, 133
exploits German Broadcasting Company, 133-134
feuds with Göring over theater, 133-134
reports on anti-Jewish decrees, 202
scheme to build rival Festspielhaus at Bayreuth fails, 103
Göring, Hermann, 117, 129-130, 135, 143-145, 193, 223
aided by Wagners, 13-14
controls Prussian state theaters, 133
creates Prussian State Council (intellectuals), 118
feuds with Göbbels over theater, 133-134
gives annual opera ball, 132-133
gives ultimatum to Lotte Lehmann, 134

Götterdämmerung, x, 33, 53, 111, 144, 151, 204
Gravina, Manfredi (cousin to Wagners), 22, 52
Gravina, Maria-Sofia (wife of Manfredi), 22, 52
Grundlagen des 19. Jahrhunderts, by Houston Stewart Chamberlain, 42
Günther, author of "Aryan" books, 158

Harvey, Lillian, 127
Heifetz, Jascha, 117
Heiligengrabe (school), 73-82
Hitler Youth Movement, 90-91
"purged" by Nazis, 113-114
Heine, Heinrich, name omitted from Nazi schoolbooks, 103
Hess, Frau Rudolf, 85, 87
Hess, Rudolf, 69
Himmler, Heinrich, warns Frau Wagner about Friedelind, 218-219
Hindemith, 118
Hindenburg, von, 111, 130
Hitler, Adolf, 7, 42, 73, 88-89, 92, 102-103, 107-109, 115, 122, 128, 186-188, 202-204
appointed chancellor, 80
campaigns for Presidency, 70
concealment at Wahnfried, 31
courts England, 142-143, 146-148
denounces old followers, 86
early visits to Wahnfried, xi, 3-8, 31
"Exhibition of Decadent Art," 175-176
grandiose plans for opera, 138-139, 143-144
hypnotic power, 43-44, 73, 101-102, 110-111, 145-146
hypochondria, 115
imprisoned at Landsberg-am-Lech, 16-17
Mein Kampf written in jail, 17
Munich Putsch, 13
Poland invaded, 216
preparations for war, 136
remodels Berlin, 174-175
remodels Chancellery, 120-124, 130
Rhineland entered, 135
ridicules Göbbels and Göring, 143
relations with Unity Mitford, 141-142, 205-206

Set in Linotype Bodoni
Format by A. W. Rushmore
Manufactured by The Haddon Craftsmen
Published by HARPER & BROTHERS
New York and London